D1733323

The Greek Community of New York City
Early Years to 1910

PUBLISHED UNDER THE AUSPICES OF
THE SPEROS B. VRYONIS CENTER FOR THE STUDY OF HELLENISM
Sacramento, California

This work is the eleventh volume in the series
Hellenism
Ancient, Mediæval, Modern

General Editors
Christos P. Ioannides, Stylianos Spyridakis, Speros Vryonis, Jr.

The Greek Community of New York City
Early Years to 1910

Michael Contopoulos

Foreword by
Constantine G. Hatzidimitriou

Aristide D. Caratzas, Publisher
New Rochelle, New York

The Greek Community of New York City: Early Years to 1910

Copyright © 1992 Marios A. Contopoulos and Catherine K. Contopoulos

All rights reserved. Except for brief excerpts used in reviews, no part of this book may
be reproduced in any form without the written permission of the publisher.

Aristide D. Caratzas, Publisher
Melissa Media Associates, Inc.
30 Church Street, P.O. Box 210
New Rochelle, N.Y. 10802

ISBN: 0-89241-518-5

Printed in the United States of America
Bound by Hoster Bindery, Ivyland, Pennsylvania

To My Beloved Family

Contents

Tables

Appendices

Foreword

Michael Contopoulos, the author, had died on May 21, 1971, and with this tragic loss, the Greek-American community of New York City was deprived of a talented scholar and pioneer in local ethnic history. His work *The Greek Community of New York City: Early Years to 1910* was originally submitted to New York University as a doctoral dissertation in February 1972. The Ph.D. degree was awarded posthumously. As a result, he did not have an opportunity to implement the suggestions of his dissertation committee or make the revisions that any author preparing a doctoral study for publication would make.

It is remarkable that Contopoulos' partially revised was retyped and submitted to the university after his death. The credit for the preservation of this important contribution to Greek-American studies must go to his wife, Maria, and his brother Marios. Despite the shock of their loved one's death they found the strength torealize his goal. It is a testament to the importance and the quality of the work that New York University accepted it and awarded him a posthumous degree.

I did not have the privilege of knowing Michael Contopoulos. Had he lived, he would have been well known to many scholars interested in the history of the Greeks of New York, and that his study would have been published long ago and taken its place as a standard work on the subject. It is curious that the dissertation is not mentioned in any of the recent bibliographies or surveys of Greek-American studies that have appeared. Thus, it is gratifying that this heretofore little known contribution is finally being made available to the public.

I first became aware of Contopoulos' work while investigating the early history of New York's Greek community in connection with a study of the diaries of Christodoulos M. L. Evangelides (1834-1837). Contopoulos' investigations had led him to the same material in the collection of the New-York Historical Society, and he included editions of some of Evangelides' letters the appendix to his dissertation. What makes Contopoulos' history of the Greek community of New York particularly valuable is that it is based upon a survey of a wide variety of primary sources. This material includes the Greek and American newspapers of that time, archival materials from the Holy Trinity Church in Manhattan, federal and New York State census and immigration surveys, newspaper and statistical data gathered from sources in Greece, U.S. Consular reports and contemporary merchant directories and immigrant guides. Furthermore, because of his family' standing in the immigrant community during the 1960's, he was able to interview immigrants who had come to the United States during the early part of the century. He also corresponded with retired members of New York's Greek religious and business establishments.

Michael Contopoulos chose to study the formative period of the Greek community of New York, which he identified as from 1830 to 1910. He did so because it was during this period that the community developed its basic immigrant institutions: i.e. its churches, fraternal associations and newspapers. The decade ending in 1910 also marked the high point of Greek immigration to the United States, by which time the number and social class of those who had arrived profoundly influenced the development of the city's Greek community. Contopoulos traces the formation of these immigrant institutions from the period when New York's Greek community consisted primarily of a few pioneering commercial representatives, who used the city as a base of operations in international network, and the occasional Greek sailor who decided to stay, to the period of mass immigration when New York's religious, fraternal associations and newspapers became national models that influenced Greek-American communities throughout the United States.

The work deals with all of the basic aspects of immigrant life work, family life, political action, crime, education, eating habits and recreational pursuits. Contopoulos pays particular attention to economic relations and the class structure of the developing immigrant community. His analysis shows that these social and economic relationships had a profound impact on the community institutions that were created. Although the early leadership of the community fell to the prominent Greek merchants who also acted as official representatives of the Greek government in New York City, this leadership did not remain unchallenged. He credits Solon Vlasto, the founder of the newspaper *Atlantis*, as being the most dynamic and influential of the community's new leaders. The large numbers of provincial and less affluent Greek immigrants who began to arrive at the end of the nineteenth century, found in Vlasto a representative who could identify with them and address their problems.

The international and American contexts are also included as part of Contopoulos' analysis. Utilizing diplomatic sources and local and foreign newspaper accounts from New York and Greece, he shows how political and economic events in Europe affected the Greek immigrant community of New York. Similarly, he uses statistical data and the local immigrant and American press to discuss the relations between the immigrant Greeks of New York and resident Americans. His analysis provides a mine of information concerning the treatment of Greek immigrant seamen, peddlers, professionals, laborers, factory workers, merchants, and small shopkeepers by the native American establishment and should serve as a basis for researchers interested in investigating these subjects in more detail.

Contopoulos' book is the first systematic and detailed history of New York City's Greek community for the period up until 1910. Until now researchers seeking information on the subject were limited either to contemporary general surveys of the Greeks of the United States, such as those by Burgess, Canoutas, Lacy and the later work of Malafouris (all of which Contopoulos used) or to the standard general history of the Greeks in the United States by Saloutos. Contopoulos is the first historian to have systematically "mined" the issues of the newspaper *Atlantis* and contemporary American press for supplementary information focused on the New York community not contained in these and other general accounts. Despite the fact that it is an "unfinished" dissertation, his history approaches the methodology and sophistication of Saloutos' classic study.

The only other published work specifically on the subject of the Greeks of New York is an article by Eva E. Sandis, "The Greek Population of New York."* Most of the information that Sandis presents concerning the community's establishment is drawn from Burgess and Saloutos. Contopoulos' dissertation is not even cited. Although there have been several popular articles on the community in English and Greek language newspapers over the years, no one has attempted anything like a comprehensive community history. With the publication of the present volume it remains for some other scholar to continue Contopoulos' work and bring the history of what might be considered America's most important Greek-American community up to the present. I have sketched the outlines of what such a community history could include in an article on the Greeks of New York for the *Encyclopedia of the City of New York* which will be published shortly by Yale University Press.

One category of primary source material that was not exploited in Contopoulos' study and that remains to be investigated is that of the documents contained in the various units of the New York City Municipal Archives. It is uncertain how much information concerning the Greek community they might contain, but until they are surveyed for data of this type they remain *terra incognita*. Recently, George Tselos, the archivist and historian, has launched a project to help make Greek immigrants and their organizations more aware of the need to preserve their archival materials and personal papers, and to conduct and record interviews. It is still possible that personal papers and documents from the late nineteenth and early twentieth century Greek community of New York might be found and used to supplement the present study. The preservation of community records from the post World War II period is crucial and must be systematically pursued.

Several dissertations and published studies have appeared since the early 1970's written by educators, sociologists, anthropologists and psychologists which either concentrate on New York's Greek-American community or deal with the community as part of a larger focus. References to these and other works on Greek-Americans can be found in the bibliographic guide by John G. Zenelis contained in

---

*In *The Greek American Community in Transition*, edited by Harry J. Psomiades and Alice Scourby, (Pella Publishing, New York, 1982).

the publication edited by Psomiades and Scourby cited above. In 1989, the distinguished sociologist, Charles C. Moskos, published the second edition of a general survey entitled *Greek Americans: Struggle and Success* which continued Saloutos' pioneering study beyond the 1950's. Although more modest in scope and methodology than the studies of Saloutos and Contopoulos, it contains much valuable information on the Greek Community of New York based on interviews, statistical data, newspapers and local printed sources. George Papaioannou's *The Odyssey of Hellenism in America* (Patriarchal Institute for Patristic Studies, Thessaloniki, 1985) contains some new information on the community's church affairs.

Dan Georgakas, a labor historian, has recently touched upon aspects of the Greek community of New York in his revisionist studies of Greek immigrant involvement in union and communist party activities. His debate with Moskos over issues relating to the methodology, direction and emphasis of previous research on the Greek immigrant experience also occasionally relates to aspects of the Greek community of New York. These debates and a series of articles devoted to the Greeks in America appeared in the Spring-Summer 1987 issue of the *Journal of the Hellenic Diaspora*. Two years later, a conference on Greek-American studies hosted by the University of Minnesota resulted in a rich harvest of new scholarship on various topics relating to Greek immigrant history. Many of these studies have now been published in the Spring-Summer-Fall-Winter 1989 issue of the *Journal of the Hellenic Diaspora* and a collection edited by Dan Georgakas and Charles C. Moskos entitled *New Directions in Greek American Studies*.* Nevertheless, although these studies contain articles on the histories of several other Greek urban communities, none focus upon the Greek community of New York. Perhaps the publication of Contopoulos' pioneering study will stimulate more research on this subject.

Contopoulos' history is being published almost exactly as it was submitted to New York University. It was decided to publish it in this form, whatever imperfections it may have, rather than delay publication until all of the references could be verified and the scholarship brought up to date. The benefit of making this valuable resource available to a wide audience outweighs any minor

*Pella Publishing, New York, 1991.

errors that remain in the text. The book's copious notes will lead researchers to many primary and secondary sources yet to be fully exploited.

Finally, one must comment upon the timeliness of the publication of the present volume. As Contopoulos pointed out, the mayor of New York City officially recognized the Greek community of the city for the first time in April 1893 when a Greek flag was flown above City Hall in commemoration of Greek Independence Day. Thus it is fitting that the publication of the first history of New York's Greek community will occur in time to commemorate the centennial of this event.

CONSTANTINE G. HATZIDIMITRIOU, PH.D.
ASTORIA, NEW YORK, JUNE 1992

Preface

The history of the evolution of the Greek immigrant community transcends local interest because it includes national and
international aspects of Eastern European, Near Eastern and
American history. The development of immigrant communities
demonstrates an important aspect of the urbanization and accul-
turation of diverse social groups in the United States. The
National aspirations and traditions of the Greeks provide a key to
the appreciation of their motives, actions and goals in their migration to America and settlement in New York. The New York community had a distant effect on Greek affairs in the Old World.
Moreover, Pan-hellenic nationalism, as manifested by the Great
Idea, influenced the New York community.

A study of the Greek immigrant community in New York City
can be divided into four periods: (1) from the independence of the
small Greek state in 1830 to 1910, (2) from 1910 to the proceedings of the Convention of Lausanne in 1923 and the enactment of
the Immigration Act of 1924, (3) from 1924 to the World War II
and, finally, (4) from the end of the war in 1945 to present times. I
have chosen to study the primary period of immigration and settlement in the city, 1830 to 1910. The period covers the development of the basic immigrant institutions: church, fraternal associations and newspapers. The Greek Orthodox churches in the state
were protected from the aggressive influence of the Russian
Orthodox hierarchy by 1909. The decade ending in 1910 saw the
greatest Greek immigration to the United States. The year 1910
also closed a period of political vacillation and instability in
Greece.

In the execution of this project, I am deeply obligated to the
guidance of Professors Bayrd Still and David M. Reimers. The

personnel of the Newspaper Department of the New York Public Library, of New York University Library and of the Manuscript Department of the New-York Historical Society have been highly cooperative, as have the professional staff, especially, Miss Eurydice Demetracopoulou, of the Gennadius Library of the American School of Classical Studies in Athens. No less cooperative in making available the useful and pertinent materials at their disposal were the late Stavros Skopetas, N.Verros and the reference staff of the Library of the Chamber of Deputies in Athens, Evangelos Photiades and the staff of the National University Library of Athens, E.P. Despotopoulos and C. Anastasopoulos of the Economic Research Department of the National Bank of Greece, directors of the G. & L. Ralli Investment and Trustee Company Limited of London and the trustees of the Greek Archdiocesan Cathedral of the Holy Trinity. I am indebted to the Very Reverend George J. Bakopoulos, Chancellor of the Greek Archdiocese of North and South America, Reverend Constantine Kazanas and Reverend George Papadeas, former Deans of the Greek Archidiocesan Cathedral of the Holy Trinity. Other persons who assisted me included the late Reverend Demetrios Callimachos, former editor of the Ethnikos Kyrix, the late James Karabatos, former member of the editorial staffs of the Atlantis and Ethnikos Kyrix. I should like to express a debt of gratitude to my mother, Catherine, for her constant encouragement. My brother, Marios, and my wife, Marie, have read portions of the manuscript and have given me the benefit of their criticism. I am eternally grateful to my late father, Nicholas, who instilled in me a passion for history. His reminiscences for the period from, 1907 to 1912 were enlightening.

MICHAEL CONTOPOULOS

1

Prolegomena

The common struggle against foreign domination and the drive for national unity were the basic political forces that motivated the Greek people from the promulgation of the London Protocol of February 3, 1830, which established a tiny independent state, to the Treaty of Lausanne of July 24, 1923, which terminated Greek national aspirations in Eastern Thrace and Asia Minor,[1] and these political and diplomatic developments had a bearing on the size and nature of the Greek community that developed in New York City in these years.

The new political realm created by the three protecting powers, Great Britain, France and Russia included only a fraction of the Greek population in 1830. The territory of the resurrected state was limited to the Peloponnesus, Attica and the Cyclades Islands. The protecting powers and the Ottoman Empire stressed that the post-revolutionary agreements established the permanent settlement of the Greek frontier.[2] After the brief administration of Count John Capodistrias, the protecting powers selected a young German prince as the first royal sovereign of the resurrected state, Frederick Otto von Wittelsbach, second son of King Ludwig I of Bavaria.[3]

The new state, with its artificial boundaries, excluded the numerous Greek-inhabited and historic territories such as Crete, Cyprus, Chios, Epirus, Thrace and Macedonia. The provinces of Asia Minor with its expanding population, Pontus, Ionia, Cappadocia and the large cities of Constantinople, Smyrna, Trebizond, Sinope, Proussa were still under the sway of the Turkish sultans.[4]

Despite the united opposition of the great powers to rectify any frontiers, the Greeks in Europe, Asia, Africa and the Americas participated in a national movement that worked for the emancipation of their Christian brethren. Although they lived in different countries, the Greeks shared a common tradition and religion and maintained identical national aspirations. The Greek communities in London, Manchester, Liverpool, Paris, Marseilles, Trieste, Vienna, Odessa, Bucharest, Alexandria, Chicago, New Orleans, Boston and New York supported this national movement with their wealth and blood in the subsequent wars of national liberation in 1897, 1912, 1913, 1916–18 and 1920–22.[5]

The Greek nationalist movement was known as the Great Idea. According to the historians, Steven Runciman and J.C. Voyatzidis, the concept of the Great Idea could be traced to the period of the Frankish conquest of Constantinople in 1204 and the succeeding period of the Latin overlordship in Greece and the Aegean region. Runciman indicated that the concept was the "idea of imperial destiny." It was the Greek Emperor Michael VIII Paleologus who first voiced this idea "in a speech that he made when he heard that his troops recaptured Constantinople from the Latins [on July 25, 1261]."[6] The Emperor Michael exhorted his fellow Orthodox Christian Greeks to liberate all of the occupied territories from Frankish rule and unite them under the Orthodox Christian crown of Constantinople.[7]

After the second fall of Constantinople, this time to the Ottoman Turks, on May 29, 1453, a contemporary Greek historian, Laonicos Chalcocondyles, prophesied that "some day a Greek king and his successors will establish a kingdom in which the sons of the reunited Hellenes will, in forming a nation, administer their affairs themselves." After the fall of Constantinople in 1453, the nationalist cause of the Great Idea was directed against the Ottoman Empire until 1923.[8]

The concept of the Great Idea, the mission of the Orthodox Church and prophecy of Laonicos Chalcocondyles lent themselves to the development of a doctrine of national liberation. The hopes of the Greek people, especially those in the remote villages and interior provinces, were kept alive by the *threnes* or laments on the fall of Constantinople. Not only did they lament the fall of their Christian empire, but the provincial Greeks acknowledged that the cause of the imperial debacle was its sinfulness:[9]

Three things spoiled Romania: Envy, covetness and vainglory. And this is the truth and no one should deny it.

The Greeks of Pontus, however, had a deep faith that "even if Romania had passed on, she will flower once more and bear fruit."[10] The Great Idea became a source of strength and hope to the downtrodden Greek nation.[11] A deep faith was developed in the eventual triumph of the Great Idea. Pious Orthodox Christian Greeks lived and prayed for the restoration of the Christian Roman ideal of a universal Orthodox Christian commonwealth centered in Constantinople.[12]

In addition to the *threnes*, popular ballads depicting the heroic exploits of the *klephts*, armed mountaineers who fought the Turks from the eighteenth century, and the *armatoli*, a Christian quasi-constabulary, became an integral part of the Greek tradition. The ballads, legends, songs and dances of these mountain warriors were loved and known by the Greeks everywhere. The editors of the *Atlantis*, between 1894 and 1910, published and sold books and pamphlets which romanticized these mountaineers.[13] By the nineteenth century the concept of the Great Idea became the "motive force in the politics of the new state."[14]

Furthermore, the legacy of the Ottoman sultans was influential in the growth of Greek ecclesiastical and secular institutions after the fall of Constantinople. The Turkish rulers reinforced the traditional Islamic theocratic concept that peoples should be segregated according to their religious beliefs. After the conquest of Constantinople, Sultan Mohammed II found himself the master of a polyglot empire with a large Orthodox Christian population composed of Greeks, Slavs and some Syrians.[15] The conquering sultan and the subsequent Ottoman sovereigns realized that the non-Moslem subjects could never be accepted as full citizens of an Islamic state. But as long as the Christian subjects were to remain in a state of subjugation, they were to receive toleration and protection from the Moslem rulers.[16]

With the emerging policy of religious communal autonomy, a noted Greek theologian, George Gennadius Scholarius was appointed as the Eucemenical Patriarch of Constantinople in 1453 by the Turkish sultan.[17] The new patriarch was granted important privileges and immunities to carry out his functions as an ecclesiastical and ethnarchic leader. Subsequent prerogatives were bestowed on other Ecumenical Patriarchs by succeeding sultans. The reservoir of edicts, rescripts, immunities and custom created a distinctive religious-cultural autonomy and quasi-theocratic basis of Greek society within the framework of the Islamic theocracy of the Ottoman monarchy.[18] This moderate practice was based on the history of Islamic Arab tolerance to Christian minorities in the Eastern Mediterranean.[19]

Many sultans adhered to this Islamic tradition of leniency toward the Orthodox Christian Church, but this toleration was often counterbalanced by periods of suppression and tyranny from the fifteenth to the twentieth centuries. The Turks considered Christians as an inferior class, to be scorned, humiliated and exploited.[20] Ghiselin de Busbecq, sixteenth-century emissary of the Habsburg sovereigns, observed that the "Turks think that their Temples are profaned, if a Christian does put his foot within..."[21] Centuries later, Ray Stannard Baker wrote that the average Turk regarded it "no sin to take what he can from the Christian, who is ever a dog [sic]."[22] Corruption, stagnation and rapaciousness increased the frustration and restlessness of the Orthodox Christian Greeks.[23]

Although the Ottoman sultans stationed military garrisons in the interior and appointed the provincial administrators, pashas and beys, in the Balkans, Asia Minor and Syria, the several subject peoples were organized into self-governing *millets* that were supervised by the respective ecclesiastical hierarchs.[24] Each *millet* controlled its own religious, educational, judicial and social affairs. The several *millets* maintained separate legal systems and tribunals relating to marriage, divorce, annulment, adoption and guardianship of minors. Wills and the rights of bequest and inheritance were included in the separate systems. Runciman states that "lay courts set up by the Patriarch dealt with all other civil cases between Orthodox litigants." The Turkish sultan reserved, however, primary jurisdiction over criminal cases and those in which "a Moslem was involved went to a Turkish court."[25] The Greek bishops became the guardians of the Orthodox peoples in the several provinces, while the Ecumenical Patriarch of Constantinople became the legal intermediary between the Orthodox Christians and the Ottoman sovereigns.[26] As indicated by Runciman, the right of the Orthodox Church "to administer the Christian community seems to have been taken for granted."[27]

The Orthodox Christian Greeks were members of the *Roum millet*, that is, the Roman nation.[28] In the religious pluralistic society of the Ottoman sultans, membership in the church community meant membership in the nation. The two elements were synonymous. Greeks who were not Orthodox Christians alienated themselves from the mainstream of Hellenism.[29]

As responsible members of the community, the Greeks organized and maintained church parishes, established schools and supported hospitals and other philanthropic institutions. The Greek communities in Constantinople, Smyrna, Trebizond, Chios and in other towns and cities established communal councils for the maintenance of lay institutions. For example, in the city of Smyrna, the Greeks had for the "management and support of their own institutions, such as their schools, hospitals, etc., formed themselves into a municipal body, called the *Graekiki Koinotis.*" This organization created a common fund in which "every Greek [was] obliged to contribute according to his means."[30] In addition to the activities of the Greeks within the Ottoman Turkish Empire, Greek merchants resident in foreign lands followed the same practices in community responsibility and participation. Churches and chapels were organized and supported by the merchants in Venice, Trieste, Vienna and later in London, Manchester, Liverpool and Paris.[31] The merchants also supported Greek schools in Venice, Bucharest and Jassy.[32] Following the same tradition in the nineteenth century, the Greek merchants and agents participated in the establishment of the first and second Greek Orthodox churches in the United States, the Greek parishes of the Holy Trinity in New Orleans (1864–65) and New York (1892).

One of the unanticipated results of the Ottoman conquest was the restoration of Greek mercantile activity and the decline of Italian commerce in the Eastern Mediterranean. The Turks destroyed the Italian trading monopoly in the Levant by granting their subject nationalities the privileges of sabotage. Foreign merchants and traders were excluded from domestic trade of the empire "as well as from the conduct of through trade while crossing their lands."[33] The principal benefeciaries were the Armenians, Jews, Syrians and the Greeks. The "Greeks, largely because they were the best sailors, were the dominant group."[34] The origins of the Balkan Orthodox Christian merchant class, which included Greeks, Greek-Albanians, Vlachs, Hellenized Vlachs and Slavs could be traced "back to the fourteenth and fifteenth centuries." Not until the eighteenth century did the Orthodox Christian merchant class become "sufficiently strong to capture the trade of

Hungary, South Russia and the eastern Mediterranean."[35]

In a short period of time after the Turkish conquest, "Greek merchant dynasties emerged at Constantinople." Eventually, when the Ottoman forces occupied Chios, many of the island's prominent families settled in Constantinople. The Greek Chiote merchants "showed a particular genius for business."[36] By the turn of the seventeenth century Greek merchants controlled a considerable portion of the trade and commerce of the "eastern half of the Balkan peninsula."[37]

Traian Stoianovich noted that distinguished Greek aristocratic families, the Azaioi, Batazidai, Chrysoloroi, and even the Athenian Chalcocondyles among them, monopolized a portion of the Black Sea commerce and "the fur trade of Russia."[38] The Greeks became the principal fur merchants and furriers in the Ottoman Empire. Angeliki Hadjimichali, a Greek historian, claimed that all the furriers were Greeks.[39] Some merchants, especially Michael, Constantine and Demetrius Cantacuzene and Demetrius Chalcocondyles, amassed large fortunes, which enabled them to enter banking and finance.[40]

It appeared that a "fur triangle" developed. The fur merchants purchased the furs from Russia and used the ports of Odessa and Constantinople. The pelts were then distributed among the Greek furriers in Constantinople, Salonika, Kastoria, Siatista, Kozane, Serres, Monastir, Larissa, Moschopolis, Ioannina and Philippopolis. Finally, traders and fur merchants sold the finished goods in Venice, Trieste, Vienna, Budapest, Leipzig, Dresden, Amsterdam, Warsaw and other centers in Austria, Hungary, Poland and the German states. The Greek furriers of Kastoria were very prominent and affluent in the seventeenth and eighteenth centuries.[41]

The Greek merchants and furriers were organized into guilds and economic brotherhoods or confraternities that defended not only their economic interests but provided social, charitable and medical services to their members and their families. Moreover, these economic brotherhoods participated in community affairs. They supported and organized churches, chapels, schools, hospitals and even provided scholarships for worthy students. The social functions of these organizations were maintained for centuries after the fall of Constantinople.[42] When the Greek immigrants settled in New York during the nineteenth century, they continued this practice and tradition into the twentieth century.

Toward the end of the nineteenth century, however, there was an economic decline in the Greek fur industry which affected most merchants, furriers and towns.[43] It was at this time that some Greek furriers from Kastoria, Siatista and other Macedonian towns emigrated to New York. They opened their small shops along Eighth Street in the late 1890s.

Within a relatively short period of time, after the Turkish conquest, the Jews and more so the Greeks became "the bankers and financiers of the Empire."[44] By 1700, the noble merchants of Chios were among the most thriving and influential of Greek merchants. A century later, these very same adroit Chiote merchant-adventurers and factors owned a considerable portion of the important mercantile establishments of Smyrna that "maintained correspondents or branches in Vienna, Trieste, Livorni, Genoa, Amsterdam and Paris, in Russia and in the ports of the Black Sea, and perhaps in London, Manchester and Liverpool."[45] In the nineteenth century the enterprising Chiote merchants expanded their commercial activities to the cotton and grain trade in the United States.

The mercantile aristocracy of Chios was the most prominent commercial group that established branches and agencies of the parent firms in New York from 1850 to 1910. The origins of this moneyed nobility could be traced to the Genoese occupation of the island from the fourteenth to the sixteenth centuries. The *Mahona* of Chios was a chartered company that was founded by Genoese merchants in the later Middle Ages. The purpose of the privileged corporation was to develop and control the trade of Chios and its surrounding region. When the Turks occupied the island, they granted the *Mahona* important privileges of autonomy and economic activity in 1567 and 1578.[46]

Virtually all of the Genoese families intermarried with the local Greek nobility and gentry and converted to Orthodox Christianity. Within several centuries the 37 noble families were fused into one cohesive class reinforced by intermarriage, Orthodox Christianity, Greek ethnic consciousness and mutual economic activities. The aristocratic families were Agelasto, Argenti, Avierno, Calouta, Calvocoressi, Carali, Casanova, Castelli, Chryssoveloni, Condostavlo (Contostavlo), Coressi, Damala, Frangiadi (Franghiadi, Franghia), Galati (Galatti), Grimaldi, Mavrocordato

(Maurocordato, Mavrogordato), Maximo (Massimo), Negreponte, Paspati (Paspates), Paterii, Petrocochino (Petrokokino), Prassachachi, Ralli, Rodocanachi, Roidi, Salvago, Scanavi, Scaramanga, Schilizzi, Sechiari, Sevastopoulo, Sgouta, Vlasto, Vouro (Vouros), Ziffo, Zizinia and Zygomalia.[47] At least 21 of the families sent members of their immediate families and firms to act as agents or factors in New York from about 1850 to 1910. Interlocking partnerships and joint ventures were established in New York with several cotton market towns in the South. The families that participated in the American cotton and grain trade were Agelasto, Argenti, Calvocoressi, Carali, Contostavlo, Franghiadi, Galatti, Maximo, Negreponte, Paspati, Petrocochino, Prassachachi, Ralli, Rodocanachi, Roidi, Scaramanga, Schilizzi, Sechiari, Sevastopoulo, Vlasto, Vouro and Zizinia. The remaining families intermarried with them.[48]

In contrast to the noble classes of Western Europe, from the fourteenth to the nineteenth centuries, the Greeks did not stigmatize their aristocracy who engaged in commerce and banking. The Greeks took pride in the growth of a moneyed nobility. The commercial aristocracy of Constantinople, Chios and some of the Aegean and Ionian islands and the middle class merchants of Smyrna, Salonika, Ioannina, Moschopolis and other towns and provinces of the Ottoman Empire were closely knit "by common aims and interests and by intermarriage, but open to newcomers." It was not uncommon for some very successful merchants, of humble origins, to marry into distinguished Byzantine families.[49]

In addition to social approval and intermarriage, the Greek merchants practiced three basic principles that proved successful "acting as middlemen themselves but avoiding the services of other middlemen, running their businesses as family affairs, and accepting the counsel and arbitration of a 'consul' or judge of their own nationality and religion."[50] Thus, the New York City Greeks, patrician merchants and provincial immigrants were heirs to an entrepreneurial tradition. They adhered to its tenets up to 1910 and beyond.

Wealthy aristocrats and merchants settled in the Phanar district of Constantinople, to be close to the center of power among the Orthodox Christian Greeks, the Ecumenical Patriarchate. These patrician families called themselves the *archontes* of the Greek nation. Ultimately, they realized their ambition to control the Church and the *Roum millet*. These families, known as Phanariotes, eventually gained dominance in the Ecumenical Patriarchate by controlling the high offices, which were transferred to a lay status.[51]

In addition to the expansion of their power within the administrative apparatus of the Ecumenical Patriarchate, the ambitious patricians found another avenue to power and wealth. The realities of imperial administration forced the Turks to recruit Orthodox Christian Greeks as administrators, fiscal officials, tax farmers and provincial functionaries. It seemed that there was a dearth of trained and trusted public servants among the Sultan's Moslem subjects.[52] According to Anthony Bryer, the diplomatic language of Mohammed II and "of his first successors was Greek; and their contacts with the Venetian Empire and the West were made through Greek agents, whose anti-Latin [sic] phobia was sufficient to ensure their loyalty." Bryer added that the Greek Phanariote control of Turkish diplomacy only "declined between 1814 and 1913, when the Empire was dismembered into its component *millets*."[53] By 1669 the Grand Vizier Achmet Koprulu appointed a Greek Chiote, Panagiotis Nicoussios Mamonas, to the vital post of Grand Dragoman of the Sublime Porte. This position was that of chief interpreter and acting chief of the Turkish ministry of foreign relations.[54] Another important holder of this office was Alexander Mavrogordato, a member of a distinguished Chiote noble family. His tenure was long. It lasted for 25 years. For his services to the state, in 1698 he became "Minister of the Secrets, Private Secretary to the Sultan, with the title of Prince and Illustrious Highness. Mavrogordato was also the chief Ottoman negotiator at the peace conference of Carlowitz in 1698–99. At the same conference, Mavrogordato was rewarded by the Habsburg Emperor with the title of Prince of the Holy Roman Empire.[55] Another imperial post of great importance was established; it was that of Dragoman of the Fleet, which controlled the Aegean. This vital office was held by Greeks until the Greek Revolution.[56]

Some members of the Phanariote patrician families became princes of the Trans-Danubian provinces of Wallachia and Moldavia.[57] From the Greek Revolution to the Balkan Wars, Greeks and some members of Phanariote families, Moussuros, Aristarchi, Callimachi, Mavrogheni, served as princely governors of Samos.[58] Runciman stated that up to the end of the Balkan Wars in 1913 some Greeks "still took service with the Sultan." Furthermore, Runciman noted that Turkish fiscal affairs were still administered by Orthodox Christian Greeks. There were Greeks in the Ottoman foreign service, "such as Musurus Pasha, for many years Ottoman Ambassador to the Court of St. James."[59]Equally important in rank during the nineteenth century was Alexander Karatheodory, principal negotiator at the Congress of Berlin in 1878, princely governor of Samos and later mediator to the troubled island of Crete.[60] After the Greek-Turkish War of 1897, however, the Turkish authorities began to limit the use of Orthodox Christians in imperial service. After the Young Turk revolution in 1908 "participation by the Greeks in Turkish administrative affairs declined and eventually ended.[61]

In addition to enhancing their personal and class interests, the patricians nurtured the concept of the Great Idea among the Greeks. Princes, patricians and peasants supported the common ideal of a resurrected Christian empire with Constantinople as its spiritual and temporal capital. The Phanariote rulers of Moldavia and Wallachia copied Byzantine court rituals and introduced Byzantine ceremonies, offices and traditions to their princely courts.

They built schools, encouraged education and promoted Greek learning in Bucharest, Jassy and Constantinople. The princes, Chiote merchant-aristocrats and wealthy merchants encouraged a cultural renaissance and promoted the introduction of new Western ideas to the Greek nation. Some of the most important leaders of the literary movement were Adamantios Korais (1748–1833), Constantine Rhigas Velestinlis (1760–99) and Dionysius Solomos (1798–1857). Furthermore, the literary movement cooperated with the nationalist activities of various secret societies and a few masonic lodges.[62]

In support of the national movement, three wealthy merchants, Nicholas Skouphos, Emmanuel Xanthos and Athanasius Tsakaloff organized a secret revolutionary society, *Philike Hetaireia*, at Odessa in 1814.[63] There were also other smaller secret groups such as the *Athena, Phoenix* and the *Hotel Grec*.[64] The *Philike Hetaireia* was the forerunner of the *Ethnike Hetaireia*, which was organized in the 1890s and played an important role in the Greek-Turkish War of 1897. Furthermore, it was suggested by several New York newspapers that the *Ethnike Hetaireia* was functioning among the Greek immigrants in New York during the Greek-Turkish War of 1897. The society allegedly raised funds and volunteers to fight for the nationalist cause in Crete and Thessaly.[65]

When armed revolution finally occurred, it was actually a Phanariote nobleman, Prince Alexander Ypsilanti, who first "unfurled the flag of Greek independence in Moldavia" and not in mainland Greece. The prince's unskillfully executed revolt of February 23, 1821 (O.S.) was a failure.[66] A few weeks later, a successful revolution was launched in the Peloponnesus on March 25, 1821, the Feast of the Annunciation.[67]

The bloody revolt lasted for more than seven years. With the conclusion of hostilities in 1828, only a very small fraction of the Greeks received their independence. Consequently, a Greek economic historian, Andreas M. Andreades, noted that the great powers had granted the Greeks only a form of "limited independence."[68] In addition to this view, a wealthy merchant, Demetrius Bikelas, expressed the nationalist judgment that it was "impossible for the Greeks to forget that by their own War of Independence they were the first to set an example before their fellow bondsmen and propound to all Europe the principle of nationalism."[69] With the vast majority of the Greeks still under Turkish rule, the struggle for national liberation and unification, i.e., the dogma of the Great Idea, continued until 1922.

One of the cruelest episodes of the Greek Revolution was the Turkish massacre of the Christian Greeks of Chios in 1822.[70] Mavrogordato claimed that 25,000 Christians were killed and 45,000 were sold into slavery.[71]

The revolution and the massacre accomplished five results of significance for the development of the Greek community in New York. First, it stimulated the proselytizing activities of the American Protestant missionaries in the Eastern Mediterranean. Under the auspices of the American Board of Commissioners for Foreign Missions, some Greek orphans and unprotected children were brought to the United States. The objective of the missionaries, however, was to train these young men as teachers and native missionaries for the conversion of the Orthodox Christian Greeks. Protestant missions and schools wera established in Malta, Argos, Nauplion, Spetsae, Hydra and on the island of Syros, the principal refugee center for victims from Chios.[72]

Second, some of the refugee children from Chios brought to the

United States were members of the aristocratic families of the island. For example, there were only 17 known immigrants from the embattled regions of Greece in the period from 1820 to 1829. In the same period, only 19 persons emigrated from Turkey-in-Europe. This group included Greeks and possibly some Armenians, Slavs or other nationalities.[73] Of the group of 36 immigrants and aliens, the American Board of Commissioners for Foreign Missions brought 12 youths to America: Anastasius Karavelles, Photius Kavasales, Nicholas Petrokokinos, Alexander G. Paspati, Stephen G. Galatti (Galati), Pantoleon G. Galatti, Gregory Perdicaris, Nicholas Z. Prassos, Constantine T. Ralli, Pandias T. Ralli, Evangelinos Sophocles and Nicholas Vlassopoulos.[74] Moreover, half of the Greek youth were members of the merchant aristocracy of Chios: Stephen G. Galatti, Pantoleon G. Galatti, Alexander G. Paspati, Nicholas Petrokokinos, Constantine T. Ralli and Pandias T. Ralli. Several decades later, their relatives established agencies, partnerships and independent firms, dealing in cotton and grain, in New York between 1850 and 1910.

Third, after the massacre of 1822, many members of the mercantile families of Chios scattered to the various cities of Europe: London, Liverpool, Manchester, Paris, Marseilles, Vienna, Trieste, Leghorn, Bucharest, Odessa, St. Petersburg and Constantinople. They found refuge with their relatives, friends and compatriots in those large commercial centers. Once settled in those Greek communities, the refugees and their children quickly reentered trade, commerce, shipping, insurance and merchant banking.

Fourth, one of the important results of the tragic massacre of 1822 was the reinforcement of stronger bonds among the friends and kinsmen of the victims. This trend was clearly reflected in the business relations and economic activities of the Chiote patrician merchants in Europe, Egypt, India and New York. They rapidly adjusted their commercial and blood alliances and developed an informal association of interlocking groups of family partnerships and affiliated firms. Fraternal cooperation was substituted for the ruthless competition of the nineteenth century. The Chiote merchants acted as factors, agents, commission merchants and brokers for each other in the various cities of the world. Temporary joint ventures were also established to serve specific objectives. Furthermore, they followed the three traditional principles of business operations: (1) use of family partnerships and associations, (2) avoidance of the services of middlemen, and (3) acceptance of the authority of an impartial arbitrator to settle disputes.

Finally, there was a steady growth of good will and genuine affection for the United States and Americans. In spite of the aggressive proselytizing of the Protestant missionaries, the Greeks believed that the Americans were their friends.[75] The Greek attachment to the United States was noted by John M. Francis, United States Minister to Athens, during his tour through the Peloponnesus and other parts of Greece in 1873. On a trip through the villages of the several provinces, Francis and his party witnessed the deep appreciation of American assistance during the Greek Revolution. He wrote to Hamilton Fish, Secretary of State:[76]

On every hand the expressions of gratitude to the American people for aid and sympathy in the hardships of their revolution were eloquent . . . and admiration for our institutions and for the grand progress of our country was expressed in simple language without stint . . . in several cases the men who ate American bread and wore American clothing in the Greek Revolution gave utterances to their thanks and their prayers for those whose charity had saved their lives and the cause.

There was respect and friendship for the United States among the Greeks from London to Constantinople and Athens and from St Petersburg to Alexandria and Marseilles. The Greeks never forgot American assistance to the nationalist cause during the Greek Revolution.

The period from 1828 to 1887 was an era of continued instability and frustration for the Greeks and the nationalist cause. The basic motive force was again the attempted realization of the Great Idea. In quest of the national goal, the Greeks and Greece became involved, directly and indirectly, in many crises in the Balkans. The first important political struggle was the Crimean War, 1854–56. The Greeks sided with their co-religionists, the Orthodox Christian Russians. King Otto attempted to seize Epirus and Thessaly during this conflict. The Anglo-French fleets, however, blockaded Greece and occupied the port of Piraeus from 1854 to 1857. King Otto's efforts ended in utter failure. Furthermore, the king's misjudgment of the Greek national temperament eventually contributed to his exile in 1862. The most important domestic cause for Otto von Wittelsbach's fall was his refusal to gratify popular demands for a democratic constitution and responsible parliamentary regime.[77]

In the search for a royal successor, the Greek electorate favored the selection of Prince Alfred, second son of Queen Victoria of Great Britain. The British government, however, favored the selection of Prince Christian William George Adolphus of the Royal Danish House of Holstein-Sonderburg Glucksburg. Moreover, they offered the Ionian Islands as a prize, if the Danish prince was approved. This gift was eagerly accepted by the Greek nationalists.[78]

In addition to a new royal dynasty and king, the Greeks received a democratic constitution, which was promulgated in November, 1864. The new instrument provided for a legislature elected by direct, secret and universal male suffrage. Responsible local government, constitutional safeguards and the basic human rights were also guaranteed by the new constitution. Thus, with the attainment of these constitutional and political goals, the Greeks of Greece no longer had any striving for political equality and legal rights. They were among the first peoples of modern Europe to achieve their basic legal and political rights. Although influenced by the ideals of the French Revolution and European liberal constitutionalism, the Greeks remained, however, ardent nationalists, and the majority of them continued as pious and devout Orthodox Christians.[79]

After the Crimean War and the fall of Otto von Wittelsbach, Greece became involved in numerous Balkan crises: the Bosnian insurrection of 1875, the Russo-Turkish War of 1877, the Treaty of San Stephano, 1878, the Congress of Berlin, 1878 and the Eastern Roumeli insurrection, 1885–88. It was actually the last crisis that first encouraged the emigration of the agrarian classes of provincial Greece to New York and the United States. It was the psychological shock and economic pressures arising from the initial military preparations and demobilization of the Greek troops that fostered the movement to America in the late 1880s.[80]

Furthermore, it became gradually apparent that another influence created conflicts within the Greek nation. It seemed that there was an increasing antagonism between the westernizing influence of the French Revolution and the Orthodox Christian tradition. The former ideas were more readily accepted by the educated princes, patricians and merchants, while the latter ideals were more tenaciously held by provincial Greeks, clergy, farmers and small tradesmen.[81] An English writer, Patrick Leigh Fermor, in his book on twentieth century Greece, *Roumeli: Travels in Northern Greece*, supports a theory which presupposes that "inside every Greek dwells two figures in opposition. Sometimes one is in the ascendant, sometimes the other, occasionally they are in concord." Fermor indicates the possibility of conflict between the Hellenic and Romaic traditions. The former represents the ancient Greek and secular heritage, while the latter represents the Christian Byzantine influence. Fermor describes this conflict as the Helleno-Romaic dilemma.[82] Traces of this ideological antagonism seemed to come to surface between the wealthy merchants and poor immigrants in New York during the Greek-Turkish War of 1897.

In spite of these apparent ideological and economic tensions, the Greeks shared a common aspiration that called for the restoration of a Christian Hellenic empire, extending from the Ionian to the Black Seas and from the Bosphorus to the Mediterranean. Therefore, the Greeks in New York City were directly and indirectly affected by the progress and setbacks of the nationalist movement of the Great Idea from 1850 to 1910 and beyond.[83]

The New York Greeks were still dedicated to the dogma of the Great Idea in 1910. Liberation and unification of their unredeemed Christian brethren were fundamental tenets of their faith. Prayers were offered for a resurrected Christian Hellenic empire, with Constantinople crowned as its capital. Ballads and lamentations or *threnes* dwelt on these hopes. By song, dance and word of mouth, they remembered the fall of Constantinople and believed in the prophecy of the restoration down to the twentieth century.[84] With passion and devotion, the New York immigrants shed their blood and treasure in four wars after 1910 to approach their ultimate aspiration.

In a letter to the editor of *The Nation*, Kenneth Sills, an American traveller to Greece during the Balkan Wars, stated that tens of thousands of Greek immigrants voluntarily returned to Greece to fight for their brethren's emancipation. Sills stated that the immigrants "were devoted to Greece... They were equally loyal to their home in the new country."

With admiration of their sacrifices, Sills asked:[85]

Is there any parallel in history of the return of such large numbers of men who speak gladly and proudly of their new home and dying for their native land?

Another American traveler also noted the vast numbers of immigrant volunteers from the United States. In spite of the somewhat shabby treatment received at the hands of the Greek authorities the returned immigrants were "animated by a truly ferocious Greek patriotism." They fought and died for the Great Idea.[86]

2

The Newcomers

From 1850 to 1910 the Greeks comprised only a fraction of one percent of the population of New York City, of New York State and of the United States. Accurate and complete statististical data on the Greek immigration to New York and the United States is not available for the period.[1] The Greeks formed a very small segment of the population. In many cases they were included in the census category of "Other Countries." Prior to 1913–1914, the majority of the Greeks lived in the Turkish Empire, Russia, Rumania, Egypt, Austria-Hungary, England and other countries. Therefore, New York Greeks born in these countries were included in the census data as foreign born from those states. Nevertheless, the majority of the Greeks in New York City came from the provinces of the small Greek kingdom. The number of persons born in Greece increased from 43 in 1870 to 8,038 in 1910.[2] The data in Table 1 indicate the minimum number of Greeks in New York City: Number of Persons Born in Greece, residing in the United States, in New York State, and in New York City: 1850–1910

According to Table 1, 15.38 percent of the foreign born from Greece were residing in New York State in 1870; 12.11 percent in 1880; 21.89 percent in 1890; 18.47 percent in 1900; and 9.96 percent in 1910. Furthermore, New York City included 11.03 percent of the total foreign-born Greeks in 1870; 8.89 percent in 1880; 13.94 percent in 1890; 15.37 percent in 1900; and 7.94 per cent in 1910. Finally, the majority of the foreign born from Greece living in New York State, resided in New York City, which contained 71.67 percent of this group of Greek immigrants and non-immigrant aliens in 1870; 73.40 percent in 1880; 63.68 percent in 1890; 83.22 percent in 1900; and 79.61 percent in 1910.

TABLE 1

NUMBER OF PERSONS BORN IN GREECE, RESIDING IN THE UNITED STATES,
IN NEW YORK STATE, AND IN NEW YORK CITY: 1850–1910

Census Years	United States	New York State	New York City
1850	86	NL	NL
1860	328	35	NL
1870	390	60	43
1880	776	94	69
1890	1,887	413	263
1900	8,515	1,573	1,309
1910	101,282	10,097	8,038

Notes:

(1) NL indicated that the Greeks were listed in the "Other Countries" category.

(2) The figures were adjusted for each census report to Greek boundary changes from 1850 to 1910.

(3) Data included only those persons born in the small Greek kingdom. It excluded Greeks from Turkey, Russia, Austria-Hungary, Egypt, Rumania, United Kingdom and other countries.

Sources: U.S. Census, *Seventh*, 1850, pp. xxxvii; *ibid.*, *Eighth*, 1860, pp. xxii, xxxi, 196, 346, 628–29; *ibid.*, *Ninth*, 1870, *Statistics of Population*, pp. 340, 342, 376, 390; *ibid.*, *Tenth*, 1880, pp. 494, 776, 540; *ibid.*, *Eleventh*, 1890, I, cxxxvi, 673; *ibid.*, *Twelfth*, 1900, *Population*, I, 733, 801; *ibid.*, *Thirteenth*, 1910, *Population*, I, 815, 824; *ibid.*, III, 213, 217ff.

In the New York State Census of 1855, Greeks from Greece, Cyprus and the Ottoman Empire were included in the general category of "Turkey and Greece." In addition to the Greeks, it is possible that some Armenians, Syrians, Arabs, Slavs and Jews may have been included. The state survey reported persons in this category, of which 40 resided in New York County; one in Kings County; and seven in other counties.[3] In the next state census of 1865, some 53 foreign born from Greece were listed, of which 24 lived in New York County, ten in Kings County and 19 in other counties. The distribution among the city's wards was as follows:

Ward IV (2), XI (2), XII (2), XIV (3), XV (2), XVI (2), XVII (1), XVIII (6), XIX (1), XXI (1), and XX (2).[4] Finally, in 1875 the state authorities reported 91 foreign born from Greece, of which 65 resided in New York County, ten in Kings County and 16 in the remaining counties.[5] The federal and state census returns indicated that the Greeks did not represent an important ethnic group until 1910.

Theodore Saloutos was correct when he stated that the "exact number of Greeks reaching the United States probably will never be known."[6] This statement was also valid for New York City. The basic problem was the determination of Greek nationality for the American authorities. The most logical definition was the one fully accepted by the Greeks during the period from 1850 to 1910: Greek nationality was synonymous with Greek Orthodox Christianity. In other words, all Greek Orthodox Christians were considered as Greeks who were in the ecclesiastical jurisdiction of the Ecumenical Patriarchate of Constantinople, Autocephalous Church of Greece and the Church of Cyprus. Greek ethnic origin and Greek ancestral language were secondary factors. The least important determinant was one's birth in Greece. This traditional definition was within the framework of the concept and practices of the *Roum millet* between 1453 and 1923. Reverend Thomas J. Lacey noted that the contemporary Greek "was born to his religion" and that no nation "presented greater religious homogeneity" among the Europeans than did the Greeks.[7]

The accepted traditional definition, however, was in conflict with the contemporary American belief that a person received his nationality and citizenship from the country in which he was born. Nevertheless, the U.S. Bureau of the Census realized the basic limitation of this American notion when it attempted to count and classify immigrants from the Russian, Austrian and German empires in 1910. The census authorities stated that "confusion would arise from identifying country of birth with race and nationality." It added that individuals born in Germany, for example, were "not all Germans, but [included] Poles, Hebrews and others, while there [were] many Germans who were born in other countries, particularly, Austria, Switzerland and Russia."[8]

In his study of Turkish-American relations, Leland Gordon supported the viewpoint of the Bureau of the Census. He estimated that the Greeks represented 27 percent of the immigration from the Ottoman Turkish Empire. Gordon believed that only five percent of the "total number departed were Turks."[9] The Greek immigration from Turkey was almost entirely concentrated in the decade from 1903 to 1913 when "political unrest in the empire was general.[10] The ethnic distribution of the Ottoman immigration to the United States for 1900 to 1923 was estimated by Gordon as follows: Turks, 5 percent; Greeks, 27 percent; Syrians and Arabs, 25 percent; Armenians, 18 percent; Slavs (Serbs, Montenegrins and Bulgars), 12 percent; Jews, 6 percent; and others, 7 percent.[11] The vast majority of these immigrants settled in the large northern urban centers, especially, in New York City. Consequently, any data based on these figures must include considerable numbers of Greeks, Armenians and Syrians.

According to the traditional definition of Greek nationality, the data on membership in the Greek Orthodox Church would serve as realistic indicators of the maximum number of Greeks in New York. Unfortunately, there are no comparable available statistics that coincide with the regular reports of the federal and state census decades from 1850 to 1910. The only federal census surveys that covered the several church organizations and their members were issued in 1890, 1906, 1916, 1926 and 1936. There were no Greek parishes established in 1890. Therefore, the federal census reported that there were no members of the Greek Orthodox Church in New York City. It was, however, reported in 1906 that New York City contained three parishes and 12,575 Greek Orthodox communicants.[12] A decade later, the federal census in 1916 reported the existence of four parishes and 22,680 communicants.[13] This data clearly shows that there were more Greeks in New York than the number specified by the statistics based on nativities. Some of these were, of course, American-born Greeks.

In the attempt to resolve the contradictions and apparent difficulties in counting the various ethnic groups, the Bureau of the Census made an extended inquiry into the mother tongue of the immigrants. The mother tongue or native language of the newcomers was defined as the "customary speech in the homes of the immigrants before immigration." The federal authorities noted that in certain circumstances, however, the census enumerators in their returns reported "in fact ethnic stock or ancestral language instead of the language of customary speech." Notwithstanding these errors, the census bureau concluded that in most cases "the returns for mother tongue" could be taken "as indicative of ethnic stock."[14]

The survey of the customary speech or mother tongue by the thirteenth census gave a more relevant and realistic overview of the number of Greeks in New York. In 1910 the federal census listed 8,039 foreign born who listed Greece as their country of birth. Moreover, 10,299 foreign born reported Greek as their mother tongue.[15]

In other words, there were possibly another 2,360 Greek speaking foreign born who could be included in the New York Greek community. The great majority of this group, 2,040, settled in Manhattan. These additional persons came from Turkey, Austria, Russia, England, Egypt and other countries.[16] Furthermore, Greece was the country of birth of 78.06 percent of the Greek speaking foreign born population in New York City. New York State and the United States contained 79.16 percent and 71.16 percent and 71.60, respectively, of the Greek speaking foreign born who reported Greece as their country of birth.

The inquiry concerning the Greek-speaking foreign stock revealed 11,623 persons. The foreign born and their native children numbered 10,299 and 1,324, respectively. The majority of the foreign stock resided in Manhattan. They numbered 9,539. In comparison with the national figures, New York State and New York City contained 11.25 percent and 8.91, respectively, of the Greek speaking foreign stock. Finally, New York City included 79.23 percent of the state's Greek speaking foreign stock.[17]

The mother tongue survey included, however, certain limitations. Among the New York immigrants there were some Greeks who came from Cappadocia, Asia Minor. After centuries of Seldjuk and Ottoman subjugation in the isolated districts of Anatolia, these Greeks lost their fluency in their ancestral Greek language. Some of them were called Karamanlis. Their Turkish dialect was written in Greek script. The liturgical language of their Greek Orthodox Christian churches, however, remained Greek. Some Karamanli Greeks also subscribed to a newspaper, *Anatoli*, published in Constantinople. The newspaper used the Karamanli Turkish dialect in Greek script. All the Karamanli Greeks regarded Greek as their ancestral language. Many indicated Greek as their mother language in the census of 1910. A few listed Turkish as their customary language. These linguistic variations also occurred among a few Armenians who also lived in similar isolated regions. Although their acknowledged ancestral language was Armenian, they spoke an Armeno-Turkish dialect that used the Armenian script. In Macedonia and Asia Minor, a handful of Jews followed a similar pattern. These Turco-Jews were known as Dunmehs. [18]

There was also a handful of Greek speaking foreign born who did not become an integral part of the New York Greek community. They were the Franco-Levantines from Smyrna, Syros, Tinos, Naxos, Constantinople and the Ionian Islands. These aliens and immigrants were the descendants of the crusaders, Venetians, Genoese and the merchants of the various chartered trading companies of England, France and the Italian states. Some were the lineal offspring of the Levant Company's English agents and factors.[19] Furthermore, the Franco-Levantines were mostly Roman Catholic and some Protestants. When these few persons came to New York, they joined the local Roman Catholic and Protestant parishes. It was not uncommon for them to intermarry with Americans of their own religious persuasion. Therefore, by religious affiliation and intermarriage, most Franco-Levantines alienated themselves from the New York Greek community in the same manner that they separated themselves from the Greek population in the Old World during this period from 1850 to 1910. Finally, there were no known Franco-Levantines who influenced and participated in the affairs of the New York Greek community.

The Karamanli Greeks and the Greek speaking Franco-Levantines illustrated the contradictions and limitations of ethnic determination based solely on mother tongue classification. There were more important factors than language that determined Greek nationality. The Karamanli were staunchly Greek in feeling and devoted to the cause of the Great Idea. Although the Franco-Levantines spoke fluent Greek, their sentiments, loyalties and citizenship were tightly bound to Great Britain, France and Italy. Both groups, however, were too negligible to modify any data and generalizations on the New York Greeks.

In addition to the number of Greeks in New York, the characteristics of sex, age and occupations were important in determining the nature of the community. By 1900 the number of foreign born from Greece was reported as 1,309, of which 930 were adult males over 21 years. The adult males represented 70.10 percent of the New York Greeks. The remaining 370 were young boys, youths and a handful of females of various ages.[20] A decade later, the federal census of 1910 reported an increase to 8,038, of which 5,314 were adult males over 21 years. The group represented 66.11 percent of the New York Greek community. The remaining 2,004 were boys and females. The data clearly illustrated that the New York Greeks formed a predominately adult male society from 1900 to 1910. Very few women, girls and families resided in the city during the decade.[21] The majority of the Greeks lived in Manhattan. Brooklyn contained the second largest concentration of Greeks. Moreover, the Greeks from the Ottoman Empire were a similar male-dominated immigrant group during this period.

Equally important was the occupational background of the immigrants and non-immigrant aliens. Because of the small number of Greeks in New York, there was no vocational data published between 1900 and 1910. The federal census authorities did not list the immigrants from Greece and the Turkish Empire by sex, age and selected occupations in 1900. These Greek immigrants were included in the classification of "Other Countries."[22] In 1910 the federal census classified occupations according to ethnic group: (1) Native White, (2) Negro, (3) Foreign Born White, (4) Indians, Chinese, Japanese and Others.[23] Although the census did not list the Greeks, a comparison of the relevant immigration data from 1899 to 1910 clearly showed that the vast majority of the Greeks were classified as unskilled, farm laborers or common day laborers. Therefore, it may be assumed that the majority or at least half of the New York Greeks were in these job categories when they first settled in the city.

In the study of Greek communities in New York and other localities in the United States, it is important to distinguish between a colony and a community. According to traditional Greek practices in New York, London, Trieste, Vienna, Constantinople, Boston, New Orleans, Chicago and other cities, a bona fide community existed when a Greek Orthodox church was formed and religious services were continuously maintained. By this definition the Greek community in New York was established with the creation of the Greek Orthodox parish, Holy Trinity Church, in 1892. Prior to the formation of the community or *koenotis*, there was an amorphous unorganized aggregation of Greeks known as a colony, settlement or *paroekia*. The former, *koenotis*, was structured with an administrative hierarchy, while the latter, *paroekia*, was unstructured without any formal community leadership for the group. Therefore, the Greeks in New York formed an unorganized colony or *paroekia* from 1850 to 1892. The only known and recognized symbol of authority was the Greek consul, Demetrius Botassi, for this early period.[25]

Whenever Greeks in New York or any other town wanted to establish a community or *koenotis*, they organized their compatriots of the district or town into a fraternity or association. This brotherhood was formed "with officers, executive committee and financial obligations." The primary objective was to establish and maintain a Greek Orthodox church in the district or city. Greeks who became enrolled and paid members of the community had the right to vote and hold parish offices. All church services and sacraments, however, were available to all Orthodox Christians in the district or town.[26]

There have been various unsubstantiated estimates of the Greek population in New York City. Many exaggerated claims were based on fragmentary evidence. One newspaper, *New-York Daily Tribune*, in May, 1896 claimed that the New York Greek community had grown rapidly to 4,000.[27] The federal census data, however, indicated that the number of New York City Greeks born in Greece increased from 263 in 1890 to 1,308 in 1900. The newspaper estimated an increase of more than 1,520 percent between 1890 and 1896. There was no documentary evidence to support this claim.

A year later, *The Sun*, in February, 1897, challenged the official federal census returns that placed the number of Greeks from Greece in the United States at less than 2,000 in 1890. The editors claimed that there were not "1800 Greeks but 18,000. They have increased by 1,000 percent in less than seven years." The newspaper added that there were "4800 in New York City..."[28] The federal census authorities indicated that the total foreign born from Greece were 8,515, 1,573 and 1,309 for the nation, state and New York City, respectively. The journalistic estimates showed an increase of more than 10,000 percent from 1890 to 1897. There was no known statistical evidence to support this claim. Moreover, the peak period of immigration to New York City and the United States was between 1900 and 1910. In addition to the foreign born from Greece, the Greeks from the Ottoman Empire came to New York City and the United States during the period from 1903 to 1913. The immigration to the United States from Greece and

Turkey-in-Europe between 1890 and 1899 was 12,732 and 3,543, respectively.

In his study of the Greek immigration, sociologist Henry Pratt Fairchild claimed that the New York Greeks numbered about 20,000 in 1910 to 1911.[29] The thirteenth census of 1910 listed 8,038 foreign born from Greece, 10,299 Greek speaking foreign born and 11,623 Greek speaking foreign stock. Reflecting the various boundary changes of Greece from 1913 to 1920, the fourteenth census of 1920 listed 21,455 foreign born from Greece and 25,014 Greek speaking foreign stock. The federal surveys of religious denominations reported 12,575 communicants of the Greek Orthodox (Hellenic) Church in 1906 and 22,680 in 1916.[30]

A conservative estimate of the New York Greek population in 1910 can be based on the number of Greek speaking foreign born, 10,299; foreign stock (including foreign born), 11,623; and the Greek Orthodox (Hellenic) communicants in 1906, some 12,575. As there was no reduction of Greek immigration from 1906 to 1911, it is assumed that there was a probable increase in the Greek community of New York. Therefore, the basic minimum of Greeks probably numbered more than 13,000 in 1910. The community may have contained a maximum of 5,000.

As stated above, the church membership data probably serves as the most relevant indicator in determining the number of Greeks. With the increase in the number of families after 1910, the indicator had a limiting factor. The Greek Orthodox Church usually counted only the head of household as a communicant and not each member of the family. Consequently, it reported the minimum number of church members.

Furthermore, the traditional principle of religious affiliation as the determinant of Greek nationality was recognized and reinforced by the Greek and Turkish governments in an international convention. After the collapse of the Greek forces in Asia Minor, Greece and Turkey agreed to the compulsory exchange of minorities by the convention of January 23, 1923. This agreement clearly established religious criteria for Greek nationality. The first article stipulated that the exchangeable minorities were "Turkish nationals of the Greek Orthodox religion established in Turkish territory and of Greek nationals of the Moslem religion established in Greek territory."[31] The Greek Orthodox Church and its members were considered as "an ethnic entity within the Turkish Empire."[32]

Furthermore, any Greeks who claimed to be members of the Protestant and Roman Catholic churches "were provisionally excluded from the exchange."[33] The Turks regarded the Orthodox Christian Greeks as the threat to their existence. There were only a handful of Greek converts.

New York City gradually developed a special position for the Greeks in America. From 1820 to 1859 most of the Greek immigrants and aliens from Greece and the Turkish Empire landed in Boston. A few may have landed in New York during this period. Very few, if any, known Greeks were recorded as entering the city between 1820 and 1846. It was reported that in 1844, Basil Constantim [sic], 30 years old, arrived on the vessel, "Great Western," on July 6, 1844. The alien listed Turkey as the country of his last permanent residence. Because of his Christian name, it is doubtful that he was of Turkish nationality. He was probably a Greek, or a Slav, Armenian or Arab Christian. Nothing is known of this alien in the later records and references concerning the Greeks in New York and the United States. None of the well-known families and individuals who became prominent in New York were noted in the passenger lists between 1820 and 1846.[34] Lacey claimed that a Greek arrived in 1848. He added that "ten years later there were two."[35]

With the rapid growth of the port of New York, the city became the principal port of entry for the Greek immigrants and non-immigrant aliens after 1860. From 1860 to 1890, most of the Greeks sailed to New York through English and German ports. After 1890 the Greek newcomers journeyed to the city from English, German, French, Italian and Greek ports. The first scheduled direct maritime services between New York and Patras, Piraeus, Smyrna and Constantinople were established in the twentieth century before World War I.[36]

New York City became the terminus of the oceanic transportation between the Eastern Mediterranean and the United States. Its maritime position encouraged the growth of kindred services and commercial enterprises that catered to the Greeks in New York and the United States. Many Greeks, merchants, immigrants and non-immigrant aliens, traveling to other parts of the country or Europe, usually remained in New York from one week to several months. These persons formed the temporary floating population that sometimes gave the erroneous impression that the New York community was larger than it really was during this period, especially after 1890.

The New York Greek colony gained greater importance with the arrival of the provincial and rural immigrants from Greece in the late 1880s. Prior to the entry of the rural newcomers, the foreign born from Greece in 1860 numbered only 328 for the United States, of which 93 lived in California, 65 in Arkansas and 35 in New York.[37] A decade later in 1870, the foreign born from Greece numbered 390, of which 97 resided in California, one in Arkansas and 60 in New York. According to the federal census, more Greeks lived in California in 1870 and 1880 than in New York.[38] The rural immigrants made New York the state with the largest number of Greeks after the 1880s.

The relative size of the New York Greek colony vis-à-vis other selected cities is illustrated by the distribution of foreign-born Greeks in 1870: New York, 43; New Orleans, 42; San Francisco, 27; Boston, 13; Chicago, 10; and Charleston, S.C., 0.[39] In the tenth census the distribution was as follows: New York, 69; San Francisco, 61,; New Orleans, 31; Chicago, 27; Boston, 23; and,.Charleston, S.C., 23.[40] By the 1890s New York City became the undisputed center of the Greek immigration. On occasion, New York's leadership was mildly challenged by the Greek communities in Boston and Chicago. Nevertheless, the New York Greeks remained the most numerous Greek urban population in the United States.

In conclusion, the permanent community in New York, with its structured organization, increased from several hundred in 1892 to a minimum of more than 13,000 in 1910. With the absence of complete documentary evidence, the exact number of New York Greeks in 1910 will probably never be known. They may have numbered from 13,000 to 15,000. The immigrant community was an overwhelmingly adult male society. There was a minimum of family life. The majority of the Greeks came from the provincial and rural regions of Greece and Asia Minor, especially after the late 1880s. The newcomers were part of the surplus rural population that had negligible technical and vocational skills suitable for an expanding American industrial economy.

Most immigrants left Greece because of the mounting pressures of inflation, urbanization and political disorganization between 1885 and 1910. The vast majority of the Orthodox Christian

TABLE 2
Population of Foreign Birth or Parentage from Greece and Turkey in New York City and Its Boroughs in 1900 and 1910

	TOTAL		FOREIGN BORN		NATIVE BORN		Foreign Born Pop. 1900
	Number	%	Number	%	Both Parents Foreign Born	One Parent Foreign Born	
New York City							
All Countries	3,747,844	100	1,927,703	100	1,445,465	374,673	1,260,918
Greece	8,925	0.2	8,038	0.4	661	226	1,309
Turkey-in-Asia	7,508	0.2	6,160	0.3	1,229	119	
Turkey-in-Europe	4,071	0.1	3,695	0.2	317	59	1,400
Bronx							
All Countries	334,081	100	148,935	100	140,661	44,485	61,258
Greece	336	0.1	260	0.2	54	22	14
Turkey-in-Asia	248	0.1	180	0.1	59	9	
Turkey-in-Europe	177	0.1	151	0.1	19	7	26
Brooklyn							
All Countries	1,234,939	100	571,356	100	515,214	148,369	353,750
Greece	1,223	0.1	1,017	X	136	70	172
Turkey-in-Asia	2,405	0.2	1,781	0.3	584	40	
Turkey-in-Europe	489	X	402	0.1	71	16	248

TABLE 2 (cont.)

	Number	%	Number	%	Both Parents Foreign Born	One Parent Foreign Born	Foreign Born Pop. 1910
Manhattan							
All Countries	1,922,227	100	1,104,019	100	678,846	139,362	782,714
Greece	7,199	0.4	6,637	0.6	450	112	1,100
Turkey-in-Asia	4,693	0.2	4,085	0.4	554	54	1,069
Turkey-in-Europe	3,345	0.2	3,090	0.3	222	33	
Queens							
All Countries	200,084	100	79,115	100	88,152	32,817	44,615
Greece	104	0.1	71	0.1	17	16	19
Turkey-in-Asia	140	0.1	97	0.1	30	13	45
Turkey-in-Europe	39	X	35	X	3	1	
Richmond							
All Countries	56,513	100	24,278	100	22,592	9,643	18,581
Greece	63	0.1	53	0.2	4	6	4
Turkey-in Asia	22	X	17	0.1	2	3	3
Turkey-in-Europe	21	X	17	0.1	2	2	12

Greeks left the Turkish Empire because of severe religious and political persecution by the sultans and the Young Turks between 1903 and 1913. Eventually, it was the New York experience and not their Old World background that developed the Greeks' occupational patterns and social attitudes in an urban setting. Nevertheless, the Greeks were still dominated by the traditions and teachings of the Greek Orthodox Church and the nationalist movement of the Great Idea.[41]

The Merchants

The Greek merchants with family ties to the nobility of Chios were the most influential force in the New York Greek colony from the 1850s to the 1890s. They provided the emerging Greek community with leadership and direction. The most influential leaders were Solon J. Vlasto, Demetrius Botassi, Theodore P. Ralli, Anthony P. Ralli, Pandelli A. Fachiri, Pandelli Y. Fachiri, Theodore Fachiri and Paul S. Galatti.[1]

Also several refugees from the Greek Revolution resided in New York. These persons were not personally very influential in the emerging Greek immigrant and mercantile community. Prominent New Yorkers such as Samuel Ward and Peter Vandervoot aided these war orphans from the Eastern Mediterranean. One of the most prominent young Greeks was John Cleivergos Zahos, orphaned son of an aristocratic Greek family of Constantinople. He was brought to the United States by Samuel Gridley Howe in 1836 and was educated at Kenyon College. During the Civil War, Zahos enlisted as a surgeon in the Union Army. Thereafter, he converted to Unitarianism. In 1867 he was ordained as a Unitarian minister. Zahos became the curator and professor of literature at Cooper Union in 1871. Mourned by his colleagues at his death in 1898, Zahos was described as "a man of lovable nature and genial and kindly temperament with a mind of the most classical Greek type."[2]

Another refugee, Christodules L.M. Evangeles, was brought to New York by Peter Vandervoort. His education at New York and Columbia Universities was financed by a prominent banker, Samuel Ward. Evangeles' association with the Ward family brought him into contact with the Vandervoort, Verplanck and other influential families. He was the inspiration for William

Cullen Bryant's poem, "The Greek Boy."[3] The young man wrote in his diary that he was the first born son of Evangeles of Agrapha. Although his parents baptized him Christodules, he was called "by his friends in America, Christy or Christie."The second name Lysaimachos "was given to him by one of his teachers in America." Later, Evangeles changed it to Leonidas because he preferred "the character of the latter." The young Greek indicated the letter M was added to his name by "his dearest friend, the Chancellor of the University in New York City," and the diarist expanded it to Miltiades. Impressed by the poetic qualities of his newly acquired name, Christodules, son of Evangeles of Agrapha, became Christodules Leonidas Miltiades Evangeles in New York.[4]

Although deeply devoted to American ideals and sincerely grateful for efforts of the Protestant missionaries, young Evangeles was a proud and patriotic Greek. On several occasions he visited his friend, Professor Nathanial Moore, in a Greek costume.[5] When Julia Ward sent him $2.00 for "the support of Anette [sic] a Greek girl at Athens," the young diarist became ecstatic and gleefully wrote, "Hurrah for Greece! Three Cheers..! Who would not be a Greek!"[6]

The educator returned to his fatherland in 1836. Once in Greece, Evangeles adopted the name of Evangelides. He established a school, the Greek Lyceum, in Hermoupolis, Syra, and sought the services of Americans for his teaching staff.[7] The aims of the school were based on Evangelides' American experience: the fusion of spiritual, moral and academic values, essential in the development of God-fearing and self-reliant individuals. He wrote to Verplanck:

> I taught them everything I thought was good. I always held up to them America and her institutions for them to aim at and aspire. I taught them to (understand) the Bible. And they translated your speeches and were delighted and instructed by them.

By the 1850s some 400 young Greeks attended the Greek Lyceum. They came from the scattered outposts of Hellenism. They traveled from Macedonia, Thessaly, Epirus and Thrace. They crossed the Aegean from Chios and Asia Minor. They sailed across the Mediterranean from Egypt. They came to learn. They returned to their homes with American idealism. Evangelides spread the idea that America was the land of opportunity and equality of status.

Although Evangelides returned to his native land, he maintained his contacts with his New York friends and Protestant missionaries.[9] He sent his son, Alexander C. Evangelides, to the United States to seek his fortune and improve his status in life. Alexander secured a clerical position with the New York Customs House in 1869 through the recommendation of William Cullen Bryant. A decade later, Alexander Evangelides obtained a post on the editorial staff of the *Brooklyn Daily Eagle*. In 1886 he was appointed assistant secretary to Brooklyn's mayor, Daniel D. Whitney. Evangelides simultaneously held the position of Secretary of the Brooklyn Civil Service Commission.[10]

A more famous Greek educated by Protestant missionaries was Michael Anagnostopoulos or Michael Anagnos. He was associated with the Perkins Institute in Boston. Anagnos married Julia Romana, daughter of Samuel Gridley Howe, in December, 1869. Although not a New York Greek, Michael Anagnos was an inspiration to the immigrant. He never disassociated himself from the rural immigrant community, which was growing steadily after the 1890s. He represented a symbol of success and accomplishment attained by merit and diligence.[11] Other young Greeks educated at American schools after the Greek Revolution included Stephen and Pantelis Galatti, Constantine and Pandia Ralli, Nicholas Petrokokinos, Alexander Paspatis, Evangelinos Apostolides Sophocles, Constantine Fondulakis-Rodocanachi, Gregory Perdicaris and George M. Colvocoresses.[12]

The Ralli brothers, Petrokokinos, Paspatis and others returned to Europe, while Constantine Fondulakis-Rodocanachi adopted the name of Constantine Newell and found employment with the firm of William B. Reynolds of Boston.[13] The latter's nephew, John Rodocanachi, emigrated to Boston from Smyrna and became a prominent cotton merchant. He actively participated in the thriving export trade with England.[14]

According to *Burke's Peerage*, a family of the name Ralli, settled in Constantinople before its conquest by the Turks in 1453. The family later moved to the island of Chios, and remained there until the massacre of the Christian population during the Greek Revolution. Stephen Ralli (1755–1827) established himself as a merchant in Marseilles, while another brother, John (1785–1859), emigrated to England and entered the cotton trade with his brother, Eustratios.[15] This was a very large family with many brothers, cousins, sons and nephews, who worked in the world wide family enterprise. They intermarried with the other prominent Greek families, such as Sechiari, Storni, Scaramanga and Mavrocordatos.[16]

The first known member of the Ralli family to settle in New York as a merchant was Constantine P. Ralli (1824–89). He was born in Vienna on August 3, 1824. C.P. Ralli married Xanthippe Franghiadi (1833–1905) in Manchester, England on January 2, 1851. Their son, Pandia Constantine, was born in that city on May 14, 1854. Ralli came to New York as the resident manager of the firm of Rodocanachi & Franghiadi whose offices were at 66 Beaver Street in 1855. His residence was at 60 Ninth Avenue. From 1855 to 1880 he was associated with several firms including Ralli & Fachiri and Ralli Brothers. In 1873 he was a member of the New York Gold Exchange. From 1880 to 1886 he was a member of the New York Produce Exchange. C.P. Ralli represented the firm of Ralli Brothers at the exchange. He returned to Greece and died on the island of Syros in 1889. His son, Pandia Constantine, remained and died in New York in 1911.

The firm of Ralli Brothers opened a New York branch office at 21 Beaver Street in 1846.[17] The firm's first resident manager was Leonidas Prassacachi, who also acted as the Greek consul in New York from 1852 to 1857.[18] In 1856 he was replaced by Demetrius N. Botassi as the Ralli Brothers' resident manager who held that post until 1867. Botassi was also appointed the Greek consul-general in 1858 and remained in that position until 1914. The Botassi brothers, John N. and Demetrius N., were prominent cotton exporters in New Orleans. They were also friends and associates with another wealthy Greek cotton merchant, Nicholas Marinou Benaki.[19] The Ralli, Botassi and Benaki families were friends. They were associates in joint ventures; acted as agents for their respective enterprises in various cities in the South; and, on occasions, worked for each other. Rigid employer-employee caste relations never existed among the wealthy Greek cotton entrepreneurs. Personal relations were fraternal and business associations were temporary.

The second most important firm was Fachiri & Co.[20] It was established in 1855. They were general importers and exporters, commission merchants and brokers. The firm and its successors dealt in grains, wheat, flour and cotton. They also started as importers of Greek currants but eventually concentrated on cotton and grains. The company had an agency in Patras and general headquarters in London during these years. The general partnership included Andrew Fachiri, Nicholas Fachiri and Nicholas Gunari. The former two principals were residents in London, while Nicholas Gunari was the resident partner in New York. The Fachiri company, like Ralli & Co. and other Greek firms in New York, continuously changed partners and created new firms and joint ventures.

According to the several New York City directories, the first known Greek merchant listed was Anastasius Nicholas in 1850. He was a broker with offices at 74 Wall Street. His residence was 9 Cortlandt Street. In the federal census of 1880, A. Nicholas was listed as a proprietor of mines and lived with his native-born wife and daughter at the International Hotel on Park Row.[21]

According to Saraphim G. Canoutas, the first known Greek merchant to live in New York was Leonidas N. Prassacachi (1828–58). He was the resident manager of Ralli & Co. (Canoutas claims that Prassacachi was the firm's representative from 1846 to 1856. If this was true, then the young man would have been a manager at the age of 18 years.) The New York City directories, however, indicate that L. N. Prassacachi and Ralli & Co. were first listed in 1851. The London-based company had offices at 11 S. William and 59 Stone Streets in that year. In a few months the firm moved to new quarters at 21 Beaver Street. Prassacachi was also the consul of Greece from 1851 to 1856. His residence was at 45 Ninth Avenue. The young man returned to Europe and died in Marseilles in 1858.

The most influential of the Greek patricians were two brothers, Theodore P. Ralli and Anthony P. Ralli. Theodore was born in London in 1849 and emigrated to New York in 1875. On September 29, 1882, he married Blanche de Lussan. At the age of thirty-five, he was elected in 1885 a member of the Board of Managers of the New York Cotton Exchange, a position that he held to the end of 1888. Theodore Ralli also served as a member of the exchange's finance committee for the years 1886–88 and 1891–97. The enterprising merchant was admitted to membership in the New York Produce Exchange during the same period. He was also a member of the Consolidated Stock Exchange. His wife was chief of Greek war relief activities during the Greek-Turkish

War of 1897. On August 23, 1899, he returned to London to assume the leadership of the worldwide family company, while Anthony P. Ralli and Paul S. Galatti remained to manage the New York branch of Ralli Brothers. Theodore Ralli died in London on January 2, 1906.[22]

Anthony P. Ralli (1852–1916), the brother of Theodore P. Ralli, married Despina Ziffo in London on August 2, 1884. Shortly after his marriage, Anthony P. Ralli came to New York and worked in the New York branch of Ralli Brothers.

The herculean energy of the brothers was directed not only for the enhancement of the family fortunes, but also for the establishment of the most important immigrant institution in New York in 1892, the Greek Orthodox Church of the Holy Trinity. Anthony P. Ralli directed the activities of the family concern until his death in New Canaan, Connecticut on August 12, 1916. The obituary in *The New York Times* emphasized that he "came from a distinguished Greek family," while the *Ethnikos Kyrix* eulogized Anthony Ralli as "a great benefactor" to the Greek church and immigrant community in New York. The parish's recognition of their services to the church is manifested by the inscription of Ralli Brothers as the first of the great benefactors on a marble plaque in the exonarthex of the Greek Archdiocesan Cathedral of the Holy Trinity, 319 East 74th Street.[23]

A member of another prominent Greek family, exporters of currants and raisins, Theodore Fachiri (1843–96), emigrated to New York from Patras. He entered the family business in New York and, with the rapid growth of New York's "cotton triangle," Fachiri extended his operations to exporting American cotton to England and Europe. He was a charter member of the New York Cotton Exchange in 1870. His zeal to advance the importance of the exchange and his tireless efforts to increase cotton exports were rewarded by his election to the Board of Managers from 1870 to 1872 and in 1875.[24] The Greek broker's importance to the commodity market was further evidenced by his selection to serve on the exchange's Finance Committee in 1875. He was also a member of the Liverpool Cotton Exchange. He was a contributor and a founder of the Greek Orthodox Holy Trinity Church in 1892. On his death in 1896, his firm was the "second largest exporter of cotton."[25]

Pandelli Y. Fachiri (1838–1903), Theodore's brother, a wealthy cotton and grain merchant, was born in Smyrna on September 18, 1838. After he married Hariclea Ralli in London on September 15, 1879, he came to New York and was associated wlth the firm of Ralli Brothers for forty years. He died in New York on February 3, 1903. He was a member of the New York Cotton, New York Produce and Consolidated Stock exchanges. The merchant was also a contributor and founder of the Holy Trinity Church.

The Greek titans traveled in the fashionable circles of New York. Theodore P. Ralli, Pandelli Y. Fachiri, Eustace Ralli, Paul S. Galatti and Pandia Calvocoressi were listed in New York's Social Register.[26] They held memberships in such exclusive New York clubs as the Riding and Manhattan Clubs. John E. Ralli and Miltiades Psiachi were members of the New York Club in 1867, while P.A. Fachiri was admitted in 1877. The other cotton magnates, Theodore P. Ralli and Pandelli Ypatios Fachiri, were accepted in 1883. The last prominent Greek entrepreneur to join the New York Club was E.A. Fachiri in 1893.[27]

Solon J. Vlasto was one of the lesser entrepreneurs. Scion of a distinguished Greek family of Chios, he emigrated to America in 1873. Ambitious, restless and intelligent, the young man at the age of 21 attempted to amass his fortune in the commercial community of New York. He found employment in a confectionery establishment in 1873. By 1876 he became involved in legal and financial difficulties with his confectionery business.[28] After 1881, Solon J. Vlasto joined the firm of Vlasto Brothers, ship brokers and grain merchants. The late 1880s found Vlasto leasing a flat in the fashionable Dakota Apartments on Central Park West. He pioneered the export of American petroleum products to the Near East.[29] His younger brother, Demetrius J. Vlasto, assisted him in the various business ventures. From 1881 to 1887, he was a member of the New York Produce Exchange. Once again, Vlasto became involved in business difficulties because of excessive speculation. He was unable to meet his financial obligations in various oil transactions. In 1887 Vlasto withdrew from the New York Produce Exchange.[30] Although an aggressive entrepreneur, Vlasto reached neither the commercial zenith nor the social prominence of the Ralli, Fachiri, Galatti and Calvocoressi families in New York. When antagonists questioned his business ability, Vlasto retorted with passion.[31] He wrote to the editor of *The Evening Post*:

As to my business standing, it will be sufficient to inform you that I am an importer of minerals; that I supply the paper-manufacturers of the country with nearly a million dollars worth of sulphur every year; that I am an exporter of petroleum, shipping hundreds of thousands of cases abroad; that I am one of the few importers of Mocha coffee here, and that I have large contracts with Messrs. Carnegie to whom I supply manganese for armor-plate.

However, his limited success in the commercial world was completely overshadowed by his meteoric rise as a controversial leader of the rural Greek immigrants. Solon J. Vlasto directly influenced the development of the Greek immigrant community in New York as well as in the United States. He was most influential during the period from 1894 to 1910.

In 1894 he established the oldest existing Greek-language newspaper in the United States, the *Atlantis*, With the rare gift of moving masses to action, Vlasto achieved his pinnacle of fame as a publicist. As publisher of the *Atlantis*, Vlasto continued his rivalry with Demetrius Botassi and the Greek cotton merchants from 1895 to 1900. Vlasto supported vehement anti-dynastic and strong republican sentiments in Greek politics up to the turn of the century. After 1908–09, the *Atlantis* began to change its Greek policies. By 1914–17, the newspaper became staunchly royalist. Vlasto achieved his greatest triumph in 1920 when he assisted in the return of exiled King Constantine of Greece. This royal ruler was the very same person that Solon J. Vlasto condemned as an incompetent military commander during the Greek-Turkish War in 1897.

The principal Greek commercial houses and known dates of establishment were:

Ralli & Co.	1851
Eustratius Petrokokinos	1854
Fachiri & Co.	1855
Rodocanachi & Franghiadi	1855
Peter P. Rodocanachi	1855
Coco G. Scaramanga	1855
George Pitzipios	1856
Roidi, Rodocanachi & Carali	1857
Negreponte & Agelasto	
(represented A.Ralli & Co. of London)	1861
Thomas Zizinia	1862
Scaramanga Brothers	1863

Benachi, Botassi & Co.	1865
Miltiades Psiachi	1865
Nicholas Psomades	1865
N.P. Psomades	1865
Etienne Ralli	1865
John Ralli	1865
Theodore A. Ralli	1865
Munzinger & Pitzipios	1865
Stamay Covas	1866
Calvocoressi & Rodocanachi	1868
Frangopoulo & Agelasto	1868
Pantoleon Fachiri (banker)	1868
Botassi & Co.	1870
P. Gunari & Co.	1870
John Kontostavlos	1871
Constantine Menelas	1871
Eutichidi Brothers	1871
P. Galatti & Co.	1872
Menelas & Mikas	1878
Ralli & Fachiri	1878
P.Z. Rodocanachi & Co.	1879
Ralli & Searle	1879
A.G. Nicolopoulo	1880
Vlasto Brothers	1881
P. & T. Fachiri & Co.	1883
de Vallière & Negreponte	1890
P.C. Ralli & Co.	1895
Ralli & Samuels	1895

After 1890 new firms were established for the manufacture of oriental cigarettes, such as Boultbee & Contopoulos, 1895.

As a matter of interest, it is noted that in his listing of principal taxpayers in 1856–57 William H. Boyd included the following Greeks and listed their assessed personal property or real estate: Constantine P. Ralli, personal property assessed at $10,000; Coco G. Scaramanga, personal property, $15,000; P.P. Rodocanachi, personal property, $10,000. The non-resident taxpayers were Andrew and Nicholas Fachiri, real estate, $3,000. Andrew and Nicholas Fachiri were resident in London at this time, while their New York firm, Fachiri & Co., was managed by Nicholas Gunari.[32]

At this time the most striking change in American overseas trade was the sudden development of cotton exports to England. Formerly, British woolens from Yorkshire headed the list of American imports in value, but the newer cotton textiles from Manchester and other communities in Lancashire rapidly surpassed them as the principal item of value.[33] English merchants in Liverpool, dealing in Lancashire cotton goods and overseas cotton, organized the Cotton Supply Association to provide staple to the mills from the United States and later, from Egypt and India.

The New York merchants developed the trade pattern of the "cotton triangle," which shipped American cotton exports to England and Europe through the port of New York, instead of shipping directly from New Orleans, Savannah and Charleston. The Greek merchants took advantage of the increased cotton exports and the pattern of the "cotton triangle." They established New York as their principal American center of commercial operations.

In 1855 *The New York Times* described the activities of the Greek cotton factors and merchants in the United States in a three-column feature article. These merchants established agencies in "Constantinople, Smyrna, Teheran, Odessa . . . Vienna, Marseilles, Trieste, Alexandria, Liverpool, St. Petersburg, New York, New Orleans . . . and many points of the globe." These Greek factors dealt in cotton, grain, silk, coffee, tea, spices, currants and other commodities. Many merchants, e.g., members of the Ralli, Calvocoressi and Argenti families, had emigrated to England and New York from the island of Chios after the Turkish massacre of the Christian populaticn during the Greek War of Independence.[34]

The exports of English goods to the Ottoman Empire had been exclusively granted to the British based Levant Company.[35] After the surrender of its royal charter in 1825, the same merchants opened offices and agencies in London, Liverpool and Manchester and traded with the Turkish Empire. The energy of these patricians, as well as their knowledge of the Near Eastern market, gave them a considerable advantage in "the distribution of Manchester cotton goods." Assited by their accumulated wealth and experience, some of the merchants entered the export trade with India, Egypt and other world markets. Their descendants were "in the foremost rank of British merchants."[36]

The New York Times writer stated that the rapid growth in

America of the great commercial firms of Ralli Brothers, Rodocanachi, Argenti, Baltazzi, Spartalli and Schilizzi was "one of the most brilliant episodes of the commercial annals of the nineteenth century." He accredited the primary cause for their ascendancy as the "power of cooperation." *The New York Times* article concluded that the Greek merchants were "as superior a class of business men as the commercial world has seen ... they [were] not surpassed by any race of merchants of [the] day."[37]

The major Greek firms were controlled by, or associated with, the Ralli, Rodocanachi and Fachiri families in New York and the southern cities. The firms were organized as individual proprietorships, general and limited partnerships, joint ventures and syndicates. The principles of cooperation and competition were paramount. Friends and relatives formed temporary business organizations. Not ruthless competition, but fraternal cooperation existed.

Prior to his appointment as the New York resident manager for Ralli Brothers, Demetrius Botassi opened a cotton exporting house at 45 Exchange Place in 1857. He joined the firms of Fachiri & Co., 6 Hanover Square, Rodocanachi & Franghiadi, 66 Beaver Street and Petros P. Rodocanachi, 45 Beaver Street. To these firms were soon added Roidi, Rodocanachi & Carali, Negreponte & Agelasto and Thomas Zizinia. These entrepreneurs exported American cotton to Liverpool and other European cities. On the return trips, the vessels carried British cotton goods, which the Greek firms distributed as commission merchants.[38]

To have closer contact with the pulse of the cotton trade, the entrepreneurs opened branch offices and agencies in New Orleans before the Civil War. The bulk of the cotton trade was carried through the companies of Benaki & Co., Ralli & Co., P.P. Negreponte, P. Fachiri & Co., Covas & Negreponte, Rodocanachi & Franghiadi and Negreponte & Agelasto. Their business activities were centered in New York.[39]

After the Civil War, the Greek mercantile concerns reorganized their activties in New York and the southern cities. Partnerships and joint ventures were realigned to meet the needs of the changing pattern of the world cotton trade. The Civil War and its consequences aroused interest in the production and exportation of Egyptian cotton. The New York and London companies expanded their activities in Alexandria, Egypt. Prior to 1860 the companies of Stephen Zizinia, Cassavetis Brothers, Tositza Brothers and Choremi, Mellor & Co. were established in Egypt. The latter firm was founded in 1856, but later was reorganized as Choremi, Benaki & Co. After 1860 the cotton factoring concerns of A.G. Nicolopoulo & Co., Rodocanachi & Co. and Ralli & Co. were entrenched in Alexandria.[40]

In New York more Greek firms were formed, such as Psiachi & Co. in 1865; Stamaty Covas, Calvocoressi & Rodocanachi, Benaki, Botassi & Co. in 1868; Frangopoulo & Agelasto in 1869 and Constantine Menelas in 1873.[41] The large entrepreneurs revamped their offices in New Orleans. The Ralli and Benaki interests in Louisiana were managed temporarily by a new firm, Ralli, Benaki & Co. Nicholas M. Benaki became the Greek consul in New Orleans and Demetrius N. Botassi, the Greek consul in New York, was listed as a cotton broker in the southern port. The intimate commercial relationships can be attested by the fact that Ralli & Co., Nicholas M. Benaki and Demetrius N. Botassi were listed separately in the business directories, as cotton brokers, but all maintained their New Orleans offices at 14 Union Street in 1867.[42]

Twelve Greek merchants were members of the New York Produce Exchange in 1873.[43] They included old familiar names with some new additions: Pantaleon Gunari, Leonidas M. Calvocoressi, Basilios and Nicholas Eutichidi, Pandoleon Fachiri, Paul S. Galatti, Christos D. Georgiades, Constantine Menelas, John C. Maximos, George N. Paspatis, Pandia Ralli and Thomas Zizinia. By 1875 the Greek membership in the New York Produce Exchange was reduced to only five merchants. In 1890 the only company to maintain participation in the exchange was Ralli Brothers, with two members, Pandelli Y. Fachiri and Theodore P. Ralli.[44] The principal reason for the decline in membership was the transfer of commercial interests to the New York Cotton Exchange, which was founded in 1870. Ralli Brothers was the only firm that consistently maintained its connections with the various exchanges and maintained a permanent organization.

It should be noted that the following Greek merchants were members of the Consolidated Stock Exchange from 1883 to 1910: P.A. Fachiri, P.Y. Fachiri, Constantine Menelas, George Pitzipios, Anthony P. Ralli, Theodore P. Ralli and Thomas Zizinia.

The Greek merchants had more influence in the New York

TABLE 3
GREEK MEMBERS OF THE BOARD OF MANAGERS OF THE NEW YORK COTTON EXCHANGE: 1870–1888

Members	Years
Theodore Fachiri	1870–72, 1875
John Negreponte	1873
Constantine Menelas	1874
P.A. Fachiri	1876–85
Leonidas M. Calvocoressi	1878
John M. Rodocanachi	1880
Theodore P. Ralli	1885–88

Cotton Exchange than in the other commodity exchanges. Theodore Fachiri was one of the 106 charter members of the exchange. A Greek merchant was always a member of the Board of Managers from 1870 to 1899.[45] The Greek members of the Board of Managers usually represented the interests of the Ralli and Fachiri commercial enterprises. Although the Greek members were not elected as officers of the exchange, they were members of important committees from 1870 to 1899. There were 12 members in 1872 and 11 in 1899. The Greek merchants were more numerous in the decade of the 1870s than any other period. There was also a Greek member on the exchange's Finance Committee from 1874 to 1898, except for the years 1875, 1878, 1880, 1889 and 1890.[46]

In 1888 the managers of the New York Cotton Exchange published a directory of members in the annual report which included: Basilios S. Eutichidi, P.A. Fachiri, P.Y. Fachiri, Theodore Fachiri, Paul S. Galatti, Constantine Menelas, Paul P. Negreponte, A.G. Nicolopoulo, Constantine Psomades, Anthony P. Ralli, Lucas E. Ralli, Theodore P. Ralli, John M. Rodocanachi and Thomas Zizinia. The principal brokerage houses were Ralli Brothers, 13 Old Slip; P. & T. Fachiri Co., 55 Beaver Street; and de Vallière & Negreponte, 17–19 William Street.[47] With the changing trade patterns, the number of Greek houses was reduced in 1915 to Alexander A. Ralli of Richardson & Ralli, 14 Chapel Street, Liverpool, England and Anthony P. Ralli of Ralli Brothers, 15 William Street, New York.[48]

TABLE 4
GREEK MEMBERS OF THE FINANCE COMMITTEE
OF THE NEW YORK COTTON EXCHANGE: 1874–1898

Members	Years
John Negreponte	1874
Theodore Fachiri	1876
P.A. Fachiri	1883, 1884
P.Y. Fachiri	1877, 1879,
	1881–84
Theodore P. Ralli	1886–88,
	1891–97
Paul S. Galatti	1898

The Greek cotton magnates rapidly extended their activities into the hinterland of the "Cotton Belt." They created a vast network of branch offices and purchasing agencies. They opened accounts with local American brokerage and warehousing companies in Charleston, Norfolk, Savannah, Augusta, Galveston, Columbus, Mobile and Memphis. To have more active control and supervision of their interests, the entrepreneurs selected some of their associates and friends to accept membership in the several local cotton exchanges. These participating exchange members would purchase cotton and represent the New York companies. The most prominent agents were Paul S. Galatti, Basilios S. Eutichidi, Constantine Menelas and Thomas Zizinia. They were active members of the Savannah Cotton Exchange between 1878 and 1892.[49]

Thomas Zizinia participated in the business of the Savannah Cotton Exchange from 1881 to 1889, and was elected a director of that exchange in 1884. Examples of flexibility and cooperation among the Greek cotton merchants were Galatti's representation of Zizinia in 1878 and 1879 and Zizinia's representation of Ralli Brothers from 1883 to 1885 and 1892. The Ralli firm was associated with B.S. Eutichidi in 1890, while P.T. Timayenis was admitted as an attorney for Zizinia in 1887. Timayenis was accepted as a full participating member of the exchange in 1889. Constantine Menelas was elected as a director of the exchange and chairman of the cotton classification committee in 1887 and 1889. The last important Greek representative was Paul Negreponte, who was admitted as an attorney in 1890.[50] In Tennessee, Ralli Brothers was represented by W. B. Fisk on the Memphis Cotton Exchange, while, in Galveston, Texas, the company was represented by Thomas Zizinia in the last decade of the nineteenth century.[51] According to the *Atlantis* in 1906, the Ralli interests established "some twenty agencies in the United Statas and exported from $40 to $50 million of cotton to Europe."[52]

The most important areas of residence and economic activity in the nineteenth century were Hanover Square and Madison Street districts in Lower Manhattan.[53] The former ranged from the Battery to Fulton Street and from Broadway to South Street. This was the principal area of economic activity up to 1890. The Greek merchants maintained offices on Exchange Place, Wall, Broad, Beaver, Pearl, Old Slip, William and Stone Streets. The New York Cotton and New York Produce Exchanges formed the axis of Greek commercial activity. The New York Cotton Exchange was housed in India House up to 1885. In that year it crossed the square and found quarters in a new building. The latter and adjoining district, Madison Street, ranged from Fulton Street to Pike Slip and from Chatham to South Streets. The principal streets of residence were Madison, Roosevelt and Catherine Streets. Hucksters, seamen and unskilled Greeks found their lodgings and homes in this area. After the late 1880s and 1890s this district became most closely identified with the New York Greek immigrant community up to 1910.

Some Greek merchants lived in Stapleton, Staten Island, Brooklyn and New Jersey. They commuted to the Hanover Square district by several ferries that operated during this period. The more affluent merchants, friends and associates followed the uptown residential development of the city. They usually rented lodgings and houses. Sometimes they purchased one-family residences. It was not uncommon for members of the same family to share quarters. Partners, relatives and close business associates usually lived within walking distance of each other.

In 1870 John M. Calvocoressi and Theodore J. Ralli shared quarters at 12 West 45th Street. Ambrose, Pantoleon and Theodore Fachiri lived together at 29 West 49h Street. Christos D. Georgiades resided at 204 East 21st Street; Constantine and Pantaleon Gunari shared quarters at 347 West 34th Street. Thomas Zizinia lived at 6 West 51st Street.

In the period 1878 to 1880, Constantine Menelas and Andrew Mikas shared quarters at 348 West 57th Street. The two men were principal partners of the firm of Menelas & Mikas, which had offices at 80 Beaver and 127 Beaver streets. In the tenth census, 1880, the manuscript population schedules indicated that Theodore Fachiri lived at 45 West 28th Street with his 25-year-old wife, Marigo, and two-year-old daughter, Despina. His 40-year-old brother Pandelli and 34-year-old Antonio also lived there. The household also included four English and Irish female servants.

Another example was Constantine P. Ralli who resided at 235 East 57th Street with his wife, Xanthippe, son, Pandia Constantine, 25 years old,and four daughters, Mary, Argyro, Julia and Xanthippe, 21, 13, 11 and 7 years old, respectively. Constantine Gunari, a cousin, lived with the family. A male servant was included in the household. A few avenues away, Christos D. Georgiades lived at 683 Lexington Avenue. The household included his New York-born wife, Victoria, 34 years old, son, Aristides C., 11 years old,and his 73-year-old French-born mother-in-law, Victoria. A few minutes away lived George D. Pitzipios at 18 East 50th Street with his 30-year-old, New York-born wife Adrienne, and son, Demetrius, 4 1/2 years old. The household included three female servants. Demetrius N. Botassi, 45 years old, lived at 172 Lexington Avenue, between East 30th and East 31st Streets. Several blocks away lived John M. Calvocoressi at 120 Madison Avenue, between East 29th and East 30th Streets.

As indicated in Chapter I, membership in the Greek Orthodox Church determined Greek nationality. The Greek Church, therefore, was the most important institution. A Greek-American immigrant community did not exist until a Greek Church was established. Thus, as has been pointed out, there was no formal Greek community in New York until the organization of the Holy Trinity parish in 1892. Prior to 1892, the Greeks in New York had family loyalty and a community of interests rather than a bona fide community. These interests were based on the following elements: family and marital relationships, a system of interlocking family partnerships and joint ventures, mutual commercial interests, strong Greek ethnic consciousness regardless of country of birth, common Orthodox Christian heritage and membership, shared experiences and a tradition of Turkish oppression.

In October, 1864, Demetrius N. Botassi, Greek consul asked an

Ukrainian missionary, Father Ahapius Honcharenko, to serve and minister to the spiritual needs of the Greek community in the New York area. In 1865, Father Honcharenko left New York and assumed the first pastorate of the first Greek Orthodox church in the United States, Holy Trinity Church in New Orleans.

From 1865 until 1870 the Greeks did not have the services of an Orthodox Christian priest in New York. In 1870 the North American Mission of the Russian Orthodox Church formed its first parish, Greek Russian Chapel, at 942 Second Avenue. The liturgical services were in Slavonic and English. The parish was open to all Greeks, Syrians, Rumanians and Slavs in the city. The first rector of the Greek Russian Chapel was the Reverend Nicholas Berring. From 1870 to 1892, whenever the New York Greeks needed the services of an Orthodox Christian priest, they used the services of the Russian clergy.

Although it was customary for most of the Greeks to marry Orthodox Christian women, it was not uncommon for some men to enter into mixed marriages, especially with Americans of the Protestant faith since very few Greek women came to the United States and New York, except for the wives and daughters of the Greek merchants. Usually, the Greek merchants, agents and factors were married in Europe. This practice cut down the need for Orthodox clergy to perform marriages. Moreover, the New York Greek merchants, agents and cotton factors often traveled to New Orleans, where they could take advantage of Greek Orthodox religious facilities. For example, Anthony P. Ralli's son, Pandia Anthony, was born in New Orleans in 1885. New Orleans had the only Greek Orthodox Church in the United States until 1892.

John Ralli, a resident merchant, had made proposals for the establishment of a Greek Orthodox Church in 1865. His efforts were unsuccessful at the time because of the lack of such clergy in New York. It was a common practice to perform the several sacraments, e.g., baptism, marriage, holy unction and funeral, at the individual homes during the period, 1870 to 1910.

No known fraternal society was formed until the Brotherhood of Athena was established in the 1890s by Solon J. Vlasto. No immigrant newspaper was formed in New York until the *Atlantis* was established by Solon J. Vlasto in 1894.

As mentioned before, the mercantile class associated with each other on a social and family basis. The Greek seamen lived for short periods of time in the Madison Street district. Some huck-sters intermarried with non-Greek women and did not have too much contact with their compatriots during these early years.

The only known amusements of the New York Greeks, includ-ing merchants, sailors and hucksters, were card playing backgam-mon and chess.

The eventual decline of the Greek commercial families was due to a number of significant causes. By the 1880s many large American industrial corporations established their own branches, marketing organizations, sales and promotional agencies. The cor-porations did not want to be dependent on the services of the com-mission merchants, agents and independent factors. This trend affected both the Greek and non-Greek merchants in New York City. It was the result of the emerging industrialism that swept Europe and the United States.

After the Civil War, there was a greater development and use of the limited liability corporation with its decided advantages of per-manence, anonymity and greater financial resources. The Greek firms continued, however, to use the individual proprietorship and general and limited partnerships as the principal business associa-tion. Their joint ventures were temporary associations.

According to Lucas Ralli, in a letter dated September 23, 1964, the firm of Ralli Brothers "relinquished their American cotton business" because it had "become unprofitable and unduly specula-tive." This occurred in 1903. The firm of Ralli Brothers, however, maintained membership in the New York Cotton and New York Produce Exchanges until 1961–62.

American grain exports declined because of the development of competition from Argentina, Australia, Canada, Rumania and Russia during the period from 1870 to 1910. American cotton exports to Europe declined because of the development of new sources of supply in Egypt, India, Brazil, China, Mexico, Peru, Russia and the Sudan during the period of 1870 to 1910. Moreover, after the 1870s some Greek commercial families partici-pated in the cultivation and exportation of cotton from Egypt, India and the Sudan. These cotton merchants and planters includ-ed the families of Ralli, Benachi, Choremi, Sakellarides, Zervou-dachi, Galatti, Zizinia and Calvocoressi. Furthermore, there was a change in the nature of the Greek immigrant community in New York during the decade of the 1880s. The number of persons born in Greece increased from 69 in 1880 to 263 in 1890. The majority of the newcomers had provincial-agrarian origins. The newly-arrived Greeks introduced the rural element which became the most important aspect of the social fabric of the Greek community after 1887.

The contributions of the patricians to the formative immigrant community were beneficial. Although the cotton magnates and Solon J. Valsto clashed on national and community questions and competed for leadership, they preserved the tenets of Orthodox Christianity and nurtured the principles of private property, individual initiative, social responsibility and self-reliance. For example, the active educational propaganda of the *Atlantis* reinforced the individualist tenets of the Greek immigrant ideology. Always led by an educated and economic Greek elite whose social values were very similar to those of the American middle class, the New York immigrants had little desire to identify themselves with the ideologies of Karl Marx, Sigmund Freud and Eugene V. Debs.

The prosperous merchants provided the consular services for the immigrants. They encouraged the expansion of Greek exports to the United States. They contributed their wealth, influence and energy in establishing the first, second and fourth Greek Orthodox Churches in the United States. Basil Zustis wrote that John Ralli of Ralli Brothers organized an unsuccessful drive to form a Greek Orthodox Church in August, 1865, in New York.[54] John Ralli's second attempt was fruitful when Nicholas M. Benaki, Demetrius and John Botassi contributed the foundation funds and plot for the establishment of the first Greek Orthodox Church in New Orleans.[55] The Ralli, Fachiri, Calvocoressi and Vlasto families were the spearheads for the organization of the Church of the Holy Trinity in 1892 and the Church of the Annunciation in 1893, in New York.[56] The Greek entrepreneurs paved the way for the rural immigrants from provincial Greece. They established New York as the way station for the incoming immigrants on their way to the several states and cities in the South, Middle West and West.

4

The Provincial Influx

The late 1880s witnessed the beginning of the influx of the rural classes of Greece. These newcomers eventually formed the basis of the permanent Greek community in New York by the turn of the century. The majority of the Greeks emigrated from the agrarian provinces of the Peloponnesus. Immigrants from the emerging urban centers of Athens, Piraeus and Patras formed an insignificant element in the movement. Within a few years, the number of provincial and rural immigrants surpassed the Greek merchant class.[1] During the same period, the Greeks from the Ottoman Empire began to arrive in small numbers until the first decade of the twentieth century when religious persecution against the Christian population and the Orthodox Church was resumed with great intensity by the Young Turks.[2] The depredations started with the Turkish Constitution of 1908, while mass deportations were initiated in 1914.[3] United States authorities registered the entry of 12,732 immigrants from the Greek kingdom and 3,543 persons from the Ottoman Empire between 1890 and 1899. The latter group included Greeks, Slavs, Arabs, Albanians, Armenians and Jews.[4]

From the time of the Balkan crisis of 1886 political instability dominated Greek life.[5] At the beginning of the provincial exodus no apparent reason seemed to exist for the departure of Greece's agrarian classes. The economy of the Peloponnesus provided jobs for the vast majority of the people. The supply of agricultural labor rarely exceeded the demand. The United States minister believed that the expansion of education, especially among the rural and laboring classes, made the Greeks dissatisfied with their status. Education inspired them to seek higher goals in life and

TABLE 5		
IMMIGRATION TO THE UNITED STATES FROM THE KINGDOM OF GREECE AND TURKEY-IN-EUROPE: 1890–1899		
Year	Greece	Turkey -in Europe
1890	524	206
1891	1,105	261
1892	660	1,331
1893	1,072	625
1894	1,356	298
1895	597	245
1896	2,175	169
1897	571	152
1898	2,339	176
1899	2,333	80
1890–99	12,732	3,543

achieve some practical objectives.[6] Aristomenos Theodorides also believed the school stirred the forces of change. The restless youth wanted something more in life than what their fathers had in the villages. They wanted to be a part of the dynamic world of the nineteenth century. They wanted rapid improvement of their lot.[7]

The population of the renascent state increased from 1,457,894 in 1870 to 2,631,952 in 1907, with a persistent surplus of males.[8] Urbanization took its toll from the countryside, as Nicholas Pieropouios observed "a push to the cities."[9] There was a gradual reduction of agricultural and livestock pursuits and a proportionate increase in urban, commercial and industrial activities.[10] Villages were transformed into towns and cities. In less than forty years the urban population soared, Athens by 365 percent, Piraeus by 677 percent, Kalamae by 223 percent and Patras by 100 percent. The energetic and enterprising youth wanted "to live in Athens . . . or if possible, to emigrate to the United States."[11] The emerging urbanization, however, did not provide adequate opportunities for the ambitious. Pieropoulos described the ever-growing class of permanently unemployed in the towns and cities as the "unburied dead of Greece." By the first decade of the twentieth century, Repoulis observed that Greece became a land in which there were "jobs without workers and workers without jobs." In 1907, some 646,224 persons did not have any employment out of a total male population of 1,324,942.[12]

The disproportionate increase of the liberal professions encouraged sharp competition for clients, fees, patients and poliical appointments. The centralization of political power in Athens stimulated the growth of bureaucracy for the unemployed professionals. In 1879, Greece claimed one lawyer for every 990 persons and one physician for 2,312, while, in 1907, the authorities recorded one attorney for 828 and one physician for 880 inhabitants. The Greek minister of the interior compared this condition with that of Germany, which listed one lawyer for 6,444.[13] Social mobility aggravated the trend toward urban unemployment. The vast majority of the physicians, lawyers, pharmacists, engineers and teachers were of peasant origin. Once educated, most professionals turned their backs on the native village forever.

In the last decade of the nineteenth century, Greece was in the midst of social turmoil. Excessive taxation, spiraling inflation, unstable currency and frustrated national unification created a volatile atmosphere in the country. The catalyst that encouraged emigration was the decline of the Greek currant export markets in France and Russia. The commercial collapse in the 1890s was one of the important factors that encouraged the Greeks to emigrate to New York and the United States.[14]

The causes of the Greek emigration to the United States have been the theme of speculation for many writers. Some prominent experts, from Andreas M. Andreades to Henry Pratt Fairchild, Seraphim Canoutas, Babes Malafouris and Theodore Saloutos tend to accept the basic economic interpretation. The most influential inducement for the extensive emigration was the hope for rapid financial reward and returning to the fatherland with a small fortune.[15] "The quest for opportunities rather than the desire to escape military service or class discrimination" was the primary motive for the emigration, writes Theodore Saloutos. The author adds, however, that in the 1890s "the unmistakable fact is that some emigrated to avoid military duty."[16]

Percy Martin reported that farm wages in rural Greece ranged from 20 to 50 cents per day before the great transoceanic migration. When the emigration reached fever pitch after the turn of the century, the countryside was stripped of its able-bodied youth. The drastic labor shortage forced wage rates upwards to almost $1.00 per day. The expanding American economy, however, offered more than $2.00 per day for unskilled labor or twice the amount granted by Greek employers.[17] "Three dollars a day was regarded as a blesslng" by most Greeks.[18]

The prospect of earning more money in the New World made some the victims of labor contractors and padrones by an effective and persuasive method of the "letters from America." The correspondence, spontaneous or artificially stimulated, formed a continuous chain to the villages. It was the magnet that lured the immigrants' friends, sons and relatives to the cities and towns of North America.[19] It was common for the immigrant to write to his family and friends that "little children earn vast amounts of money and can quickly return to the fatherland."[20] Salopoulos portrayed them as the "false letters from America."[21]

In giving testimony at a hearing of the Sub-Commission on Manufactures and General Business on January 10, 1899, in Washington, D.C., Herman Stump, former Commissioner-General of Immigration, stated that the padrone system was revived among the incoming Assyrians, Arabs, Turks, Greeks and Armenians.[22] The United States Industrial Commission reported that Greek immigration presented "resemblances to the Italian padrone system." The immigrants were believed to be under the control of "central organization," which sent them out as peddlers.[23] At the New York hearing of the sub-commission on July 24, 1899, Edward F. McSweeney, Assistant Commissioner of Immigration at the Port of New York, testified that he had knowledge of the existence of the padrone system among the Greeks. The official stressed that "when the immigrants of that class come all provided with American gold and having about an equal amount of money, there must be something more than chance accountable for it."[24]

The editors of the *Atlantis* interpreted the causes of the widespread emigration as political and psychological. Inferior political leadership, vacillation and inability to maintain a stable political system were considered as paramount.[25] Heavy taxation, inflation and deficit finance were the ultimate results of political maladministration. The Greeks strove to escape from the "persecution of the petty party leaders who collected the taxes,"[26] and drained the land of any opportunity for personal self-improvement.

"Why do you come here?" the *Atlantis* reporter asked a New York immigrant.[27]

"To breath the air of freedom, to be free from the petty bureaucrat of the country," replied the street peddler. He added, "I want to work without giving all my blood to the public treasury . . . and to live under democratic laws."

"Here there are no kings, princes, sword-girdled men. . . . Here the poor and rich have the same rights . . . and each man may develop according to his own worthiness," stressed the young Greek.

In passing, the vendor volunteered to the reporter:

"I sell fruits in the streets. I save and send money to my orphaned sister . . . she is a graduate of the Arsakeion College . . . she is planning to [teach in the Greek] interior."

"Prosperity in America," wrote Konstantinos Maniakes, "is not the exclusive privilege of certain classes. Every diligent man, helped by the state, is able to acquire, easily, what is necessary for the support and comfort of himself and family. . . ."[28] In 1906, the Immigration Commission added that the economic factor was the determining cause of all emigration. The American authorities, however, stressed that there was little abject poverty in Greece. The land was fertile and not overpopulated in the sense that its economic resources were not sufficient for adequate support of the population. The American diplomats and consuls expressed the view that "emigration was actuated only by a desire for financial betterment." The commission was informed that "there was no difficulty for any Greek earning a living on the scale to which his parents have been accustomed, but that this no longer satisfied him and no opportunity was afforded him at home for his economic advancement."[29] Ambition was to be satisfied in the United States.

Michael Dendia described the emigration as an "onrushing river" that swept the countryside of its youth.[30] A Greek parliamentary committee reported that the Greek found it "easy to decide" to emigrate to foreign lands.[31] The Greek immigrant hoped to achieve economic and social regeneration in America.[32] The Prefect of Arcadia reported to the Minister of Interior on

September 22, 1912, that the "emigration sowed progressive ideas and reawakened the spiritual concept of the individual" and simultaneously it gave the impetus to desire amenities "unknown before to the villagers."[33]

Though economic factors seemed to predominate in motivating the migration, political, social and psychological factors were always present. A half century later, Phanos Michalopoulos interpreted the origins of the movement in a broader scope:[34]

> Certainly there were economic factors, but interwoven with these, others also existed. It was the despair and the hopelessness from the political and economic condition of the country. Economic decay, political division, social striving, lack of communications, plundering, absconding and the general wretchedness of the land provoked the unrestrainable impulse to emigrate.

Although Greece had a large pool of unskilled labor to serve the needs of a possible expanding industrialization, John A. Levandis claimed that the Greeks disliked factory occupations:[35]

> . . . the peasant farmer on whom industry relied for labor was averse to industrial employment. Whenever he was forced by circumstance to abandon his rural community, he sought his living and fortune in distant lands that offered uncertain but dazzling rewards.

The emigration impulse reached fever pitch in the years of 1906 and 1907. The Peloponnesus, heartland of modern Greece, was hardest hit by the provincial exodus. Thousands of young men depopulated the Greek countryside and flocked to the ports of Piraeus and Patras to seek passage to New York.[36] John B. Jackson, United States minister to Athens, stated that at first "it appeared that there had been no special reason existing for the extensive exodus of males." The American diplomat conjectured that possibly the increase in education among the rural classes might have made "them dissatisfied with their lot and inspired ambitions to realize some practical and materialistic objective."[37]

"Immigration fever was contagious" throughout the rural districts of the Morea. Many young males continued to emigrate to America without regard to the consequences. Emigration to the United States, stressed the *Atlantis*, was not a panacea for all the problems of the Greek people.[38] Thousands of healthy and energetic males depopulated their villages and practically ruined the economy of their respective regions.[39] The attitude of the editors of the *Atlantis* indicated apprehension. They were concerned with the welfare and happiness of the Greek newcomers. Conditions in America were like "a terrible pit" that swallowed, blended and fused the thousands of Greeks who for various reasons began to "forget their fatherland and faith," wrote the *Atlantis* editors. The newcomers, the newspaper continued, began to "identify themselves with the ways of the foreigners." The editors hoped that the immigrants would not forget their Greek heritage. In other words the *Atlantis* believed that a good Greek was also a good American. In addition, the newspaper believed that a bad Greek made a bad American.[40]

Prior to 1904 the vast majority of Greek immigrants traveled to English, French, German and Italian ports to secure passage to New York. In 1904 the Austro-American Line opened a New York-Mediterranean scheduled service. Gradually through the years the Austro-American Line expanded its service, operating ships from Adriatic and Italian ports and the Greek port of Patras. The Austrian shipping company, operating from Trieste, initiated the first organized efforts to exploit the Greek emigration from Patras to New York. This concern was well organized to capture a considerable portion of the early immigrant passenger movement because it already carried a large segment of the Greek currant trade to the United States. By 1906, the Austro-American Line carried both Greek and Italian emigrants to New York.[41] The company offered passage from Patras to New York for the sum of $31. The steamship company maintained agencies in New York, Naples, Piraeus and Patras. By 1908 the Austro-American Line dispatched 42 sailings from Patras of which 29 were destined for New York with immigrants.[42]

In view of the absence of direct Greek maritime service to New York, a group of Greek shipowners and capitalists organized a steamship company with regular Greek-Mediterranean service. Unfortunately, internal strife severed the new company into rival factions by 1905. The competing groups organized two steamship companies by 1908. One was the Moraitis Line, later reorganized as the Hellenic Transportation Co.[43] The first scheduled Greek vessel, *S.S. Moraitis*, arrived in New York on January 27, 1908.[44] The immigrant carrier made calls at Smyrna, Kalamata, Patras and Algiers before reaching New York. The rival shipping company, Navigation Company of Greece, Ltd., known also as the Greek

Line, opened its offices in New York at 95 Broad and 57 Pearl Streets in 1909. Its first scheduled vessel, *S.S. Themistocles*, arrived in New York on February 17, 1909 with 218 passengers.[45]

The two Greek companies and the Austrian company served not only the Greek immigrants but also the commercial interests of the United States by providing a direct maritime connection with Greece and the Levant. The Greek maritime companies provided 15-day service to New York. Prior to the formation of these steamship lines, it took from 20 to 40 days for Greeks to arrive in New York from Genoa, Marseilles, Le Havre and other European ports.[46] Nevertheless, Fairchild claimed that many Greeks continued to travel to New York by "way of Naples, or even Cherbourg and Havre."[47] With the increase in the Greek immigration numerous shipping firms planned some direct sailings to the Mediterranean during the peak periods. The steamship companies included Cunard, Fabre, White Star, Hamburg-American, Prince, Levant and other lines.[48]

The importance of the direct maritime service was expressed by Ernest L. Harris, United States consul in Smyrna. He wrote:[49]

One of the handicaps to the expansion of American trade with the Levant is the heavy freight dues and the amount of damage caused to goods, owing to merchandise having to be transshipped at Liverpool, Hamburg or Naples. . . . This has been partially remedied, a Greek company having started a direct contact between New York and the Levant.

Edward H. Ozmun, United States consul-general in Constantinople, also stated that the newly established Greek maritime service between New York, Naples, Piraeus and Smyrna would encourage American trade in the Eastern Mediterranean.[50] George Horton, United States consul-general in Athens, said that the sustained immigrant passenger service made the transoceanic operations to New York profitable and feasible.[51]

The major factors that encouraged emigration were rural underemployment; inflation which eroded the purchasing power of the provincial classes; usury and excessive personal indebtedness; high customs duties and taxation, which tended to increase prices at the expense of the agrarian occupations. The principal political factors were popular disillusionment with the national political leadership in peace and war. An American writer, S.T. Cooke believed that it was "really through the troubles between Greece and Turkey that the Greeks began by degrees to emigrate to America."[52] The spirit of adventure was ever present. The inability of the governing circles to face the realities of the changing economic and social world fostered the depopulation of the small Greek state. The Greek establishment's inadequacy in guiding constructively the dominant forces that engulfed Greece after the turn of the century encouraged emigration to the New World. The interlocking forces that accelerated the movement were urbanization, industrialization, education and Panhellenic nationalism as expressed by The Great Idea.[53]

5

Immigrant Society

The living and housing conditions among many of the New
York Greeks left much to be desired. Their lodgings were
overcrowded and the most inexpensive.[1] A considerable number
toiled endlessly like "galley slaves" to save and remit money to
their families in Greece and Asia Minor. The immigrants did not
live in concentrated ethnic quarters or ghettos as did other groups,
such as the Irish, Italians, Germans or Chinese. They were scattered throughout the boroughs, especially Manhattan and
Brooklyn. The majority of the New York Greeks resided in
Manhattan. There were higher concentrations of Greeks in three
general districts: Madison Street and the Lower East Side,[2] (2)
Sixth Avenue in the West 30s, and (3) Second and Third Avenues
in the East 20s and East 30s.

Unsanitary and overcrowded conditions existed in the "old and
undesirable" tenements in the Madison Street quarter. It was not
unusual for one or two immigrants to lease a large cold-water flat
in one of the old tenements. As primary tenants, they would sub
lease rooms, rent out beds and spaces in the various dingy rooms.
Some immigrants shared windowless rooms, which afforded very
little fresh air and no direct ventilation. In the summers, they were
stench traps that sapped the strength of more than one of the
unfortunate inmates. Sometimes the immigrant renters and
lodgers had limited cooking privileges in the shared kitchens. The
toilets, confined to water closets, were in the dark narrow hallways
and usually served six or more flats. Some apartments had bath-
tubs in the kitchens. Most immigrants washed in the kitchen sinks
and took their baths in the local municipal bath houses. The high
population density in overcrowded quarters was unhealthy, physi-
cally and emotionally. The stale aroma of kerosene, coal dust,

water closets and unkempt tenements was overpowering. The sour odor of cabbage, onions and garlic was trapped in the hallways and stairwells. The debilitating physical environment of the Lower East Side was a far cry from the underpopulated and sunny lands of Greece and Asia Minor. The smokey chimneys, elevated railroad tracks and the street gas lamps replaced the majestic cypress, fragrant pine and silver-grey olive.[3]

The Sixth Avenue district was more "Americanized" because there was greater intermingling with native Americans. The area of the East 30s was more residential in character. On Third Avenue it was not uncommon for several Greeks, such as Nicholas A. Contopoulos and Basil Zustis, to rent a flat in which each had his own room. Living conditions in these neighborhoods were adequate, cleaner and better than those of the Madison Street district. In general the Greeks lived and mingled with the Irish, Italians, Russians, Armenians, Chinese, Jews and Roumanians.[4]

Although the newcomers in New York were relatively well paid for unskilled and semi-skilled vocations, many Greeks sacrificed well balanced meals and some basic comforts in their mania to accumulate savings. Many were willing to survive on meager meals of lentil soup, boiled cabbage and whole wheat bread. J.P. Xenides stated that they were "careless of their diet and neglected their health, living on scanty food." The same writer claimed that the immigrants adhered to an "oriental proverb" that illustrated their attitude and practice: "one cannot save by working, but by not eating. Every penny unspent is a gain."[5] In other words, the highly underpaid oriental worker, such as the Turk, Kurd, Arab or Persian, was only able to save money by depriving himself of his basic necessity—food. To some Greeks, it merely meant "eat less and save more."

In 1896 there were numerous Greek eating establishments on and around Madison Street. The restaurants were "'plainly furnished; deal tables and cheap chairs" were the simple appointments. "But for 25 cents a Greek or anyone else can get a large amount of nourishing food." Roast lamb, chicken and rice, meat and vegetable stews were the favorite items. A New Yorker wrote that the Greeks did "not fancy potatoes, and none are to be found in a Greek restaurant." The statement was made in 1896. In time, eating habits gradually changed through the process of Americanization. Gradually, potatoes became an important staple in the New York Greek diet after 1900.[6] More than a decade later, Fairchild reported that at the better Greek restaurants along Sixth Avenue "a first rate meal, consisting of soup, roast lamb, potatoes, salad, Greek pudding and bread may be secured for thirty-five or forty cents." The prices in the most popular and modest eating places in the Madison Street quarter "were more reasonable."[7]

The Greek cuisine, a part of the Byzantine-Balkan-Levantine tradition, was introduced to New York during the heavy immigration from the Eastern Mediterranean. It was similar to the cooking of the Armenians, Serbs, Lebanese and Montenegrins. One of the basic differences between the Greek and Turkish cuisines is that the former used wines in pastries, marinades, braised meats, stews, gravies and sauces. Quartered and pared apples dunked in simple tulip-shape glasses of semi-sweet wine was highly esteemed by the New York Greeks. Moreover, pork, such as barbecued suckling pig, roast loin of pork and orange-flavored sausage was popular with the Greek immigrants. On the other hand, Turkish cuisine was heavily spiced with pepper, cumin, nutmeg, cinnamon and other condiments.

Spring lamb, natural rice, pearl barley, cracked wheat, lemons, dried pulses, mushrooms, eggs, nuts, cheese, chicken and fish formed the basis of Greek cookery. Yoghurt and olive oil took the place of milk, butter and cream. They were supplemented by eggplants, tomatoes, zucchini, peppers, okra, artichokes and quince. Braised meats, steamed vegetables, stews and ground meat dishes were extensively used. Grapevine and cabbage leaves, besides other vegetables, were stuffed with ground meat, rice, currants, wine and pine nut fillings.

The most popular meats of the Greeks were skewered lamb with rice and cracked wheat pilaf, roast leg of lamb with roast potatoes or rice, beef stew *stiffado* with onions and wine, lamb stew with okra, stuffed green peppers, sauteed eggplants with a garlic sauce made from ground walnuts and baked macaroni, Athenian style, *pastitsio*. Their favorite soup was chicken *avgolemeno*, a chicken-rice broth with whipped eggs and lemon juice. The soup was usually topped with chopped fresh dill.

The desserts were very sweet and limited in variety. The ingredients included currants, marzipan, oranges, honey, nuts, corn starch, dried fruits and pastry leaves, *phyllo*, which are very similar to strudel leaves. The flavorings widely used were mastic gum from Chios, mahlep from Syria, rosewater and orange-blossom water, grated orange peel, candied citron peel and cinnamon.

Some of the popular desserts and pastries were baclava, rose-petal jam, quince preserves, baked sweet custard, similar to the Spanish flan. A Greek pastry made with *phyllo* was Copenhagen. This rich dessert was made in honor of Prince William George of Denmark when he ascended the Greek throne as King George I in 1863. The Copenhagen was made with numerous layers of phyllo. The filling was a very rich almond marzipan. This type of pastry is not duplicated by the cuisines of the Turks, Arabs, Armenians, Lebanese and South Slavs. Traditional Greek cooking never used lard, bacon fat or inferior vegetable oils. Rarely, if ever, were flour, potato starch or corn starch used to thicken stews, soups, gravies and sauces. The quality level of Greek cuisine was based on a few basic rules: the highest cuisine meant (1) leaner meat, (2) thinner slices of meat, vegetables and lettuce, (3) use of limited amounts of pure olive oil and later the use of sweet butter, (4) restricted use of herbs and spices, and (5) use of fresh produce. The lowest level of Greek cooking would be the converse of these rules. Nevertheless, as years passed by, the process of Americanization gradually intro-duced the use of flour, corn starch, milk, butter, as it did the pota-toes, into the Greek cuisine of New York.[8]

The Greeks, in general, did not have any traditional Christmas cakes as did the Americans, English, French, Italians, Germans and other Western Europeans.[9] Some Greeks did, however, bake a regional bread, *Christopsomo*. This was not the general rule. The Greeks prepared a sweet yeast cake, St. Basil's Cake or *basilopeta*, to be served on the Feast of St. Basil on January 1. It was customary to include a gold coin in the yeast cake. At midnight on December 31, St. Basil's Cake was cut and each person present received a slice of cake. The fortunate recipient of the slice of cake which con-tained the gold coin was regarded as having good fortune for the coming year. Moreover, among the Greeks the practice of gift-giv-ing was not on Christmas but on the Feast Day of St. Basil. This custom was similar to the Scots who exchanged gifts on New Year's Day but different from the Americans, English and French. In the following generations, the immigrants and their children adopted the American custom of gift-giving on Christmas.

The Greeks drank "beer with their suppers in lieu of the lighter wines they were always accustomed to at home." They drank the local New York beer because it was available and inexpensive. Popular brand products from Greece, such as Achaia Clauss wines, Botsaris brandy and Metaxa liqueur were later imported in substantial quantities to meet the immigrant demand. The Greek immigrants introduced to New York a unique wine product, *retsina*, a resin-flavored light white wine. This wine did not readily appeal to the American palate.[10] Drunkenness was rarely known among the Greek newcomers. By custom, the Greeks sat and drank their wine and beer. They did not stand and drink at a bar in a saloon or tavern. Furthermore, the Greeks usually ate olives, feta cheese, small hot peppers, bread and anchovies with their alcoholic beverages. Drinking without eating was unthinkable and considered vulgar.[11]

Not only poor diet and voluntary frugality but also the absence of a normal family life caused strains on the immigrant's physical and emotional health. Family companionship, tidy quarters and substantial meals were lacking. Unofficial estimates reported that in an immigrant community of 20,000, there were only between 150 and 170 families in 1907; 150 and 170 in 1909; 250 and 300 in 1910; and, 700 and 800 in 1912. There were some mixed marriages in the Greek community. Unofficial estimates indicated that there were between 80 and 100 such unions in 1912. Although about 40 to 50 percent of the adult males were married, very few brought their families to New York during this decade.[12]

The New York Greek community, typical of most, if not all, Greek settlements in the United States, was male oriented. It was very similar to the early colonies founded by the Armenians, Serbs, Montenegrins and Roumanians. The immigrants missed the affection and compassion of their wives, children and parents. Some left their families when their children were nursing infants in their mothers' arms. When these families were reunited years later in Europe or New York, many of the children had grown to adolescence and a few to young adulthood. In many ways, the immigrants were strangers to their wives, children and families. In their minds, the Greeks believed, as did the Roumanians, Serbs and Armenians, that they would sacrifice only a few years in New York and return home with enough savings to establish themselves in the fatherland with neither personal indebtedness nor mortgaged real property. Unfortunately, they were not always successful in achieving their original goals of temporary emigration.[13]

The Greek community took care of the needs of its own members. The several fraternal associations, ladies aid societies and the two parishes cared for the sick and infirm. The most prominent medical facilities that served the New York Greeks were at French Hospital.[14] "As in Chicago, so in New York," wrote Fairchild, the Greek immigrants were "a negligible factor in the work of charitable organizations of the city." The Charities Organization Society stated that they had "extremely few cases of Greeks." In addition, the New York State Board of Charities reported only six cases of Greeks between January 1, 1906 and August 15, 1907. There is very little conclusive and documentary evidence to indicate that the New York Greeks sought any public assistance. Only emergency medical treatment and out-patient clinical services were probably used by the Greeks. Such medical and health services were usually provided at French Hospital. The Greek community usually took care of its own welfare problems.

The recreational interests of the Greek immigrants were limited. They did not participate in competitive sports and mass gymnastics to the extent that the Poles, Slovaks, Serbs and Western Europeans did. They loved picnics and group outings. Many New York Greeks attended such events three to four times a year.[15] Visiting friends and relatives and attending parties formed the basis of their social contacts. The traditional coffee houses and restaurants located in Madison, Roosevelt and Catherine Streets became the focal point of their daily relaxation. In the early years of the 1890s the Greek eating places in the Lower East Side provided the provincial newcomers with the use of the Arabian water pipe, i.e., *nargile*, and Turkish and Egyptian oriental cigarettes. A Greek recounted that "only pure tobacco was used" in the water pipe. The special tobacco was grown in Persia. It was thoroughly washed and all the juice was squeezed out by hand. The devotee of the water pipe claimed that all "the nicotine [was] deposited in the water, a delightful and innocuous smoke [was] the result."[16] In time the water pipe lost its appeal and it was replaced by oriental cigarettes.

Chess, backgammmon, dominoes and cards were their favorite games. Discussing Greek politics, the Greek national movement, business and local community affairs was their passion. Unfortunately, card playing and gambling were their greatest vices.[17]

There were certain occasions that encouraged ethnic consciousness and group action. The important events were the visits of Prince George of Greece in 1891 and the Greek warship, *Miaoulis*, in 1900. The immigrants' devotion to their fatherland was evidenced by the numerous celebrations of Greek Independence, usually held in City Hall Park. The first known commemoration was held in 1893 under the leadership of Solon J. Vlasto.

The visits of the prince and the warship stimulated tremendous pride, self-respect and group consciousness among the New York Greeks. In addition, Prince George is considered as the individual who encouraged the immigrants to organize a fraternal association and establish a Greek Church in the city. The period from 1890 to 1910 was the formative period in which the immigrant institutions were organized: fraternal societies, church and press.

The New York Greeks were ignored by the Roman Catholic hierarchy; but they were, however, cordially accepted by the Anglican or Episcopal communion, as fellow Christians and the descendants of classical Hellenism. The leading philhellene was an Episcopal clergyman, Reverend T.J. Lacey.[18] There was no apparent and organized anti-Greek sentiment in nineteenth-century New York. At the turn of the century there was also no organized resistance to the New York Greeks as a specific group, even though a sociologist like Henry Pratt Fairchild was not sympathetic to the Greek immigrants.[19] Though somewhat negative, Prescott Farnsworth Hall was not an overt opponent to the Greek immigrants,[20] and an avowed enemy of the New Immigration like Madison Grant was tolerant of the Greeks and sympathetic toward the mission of the Hellenic Byzantine Empire.[21] In other words, the New York Greeks did not experience any large nativist resistance and prejudice from 1850 to 1910.

The unofficial visit of Prince George of Greece to New York in 1891 excited the New York press and inspired the Greek immigrants. Although the young prince was traveling incognito from San Francisco, the New York press fully covered his transcontinental journey and activities. When Prince George arrived in Chicago, it was reported that he was wildly cheered at the railroad station by the "Greek Benevolent Association of that city."[22] To the immigrants, the prince was the living symbol of their fatherland.[23]

Accompanied by Commander Lomen of the Imperial Russian Navy, Prince George arrived at Grand Central Station at 8:50 P.M.

on June 30, 1891. He was met by Demetrius Botassi, Greek consul-general, at the head of a delegation of many Greek immigrants who joyously welcomed the prince to New York. The reaction of the New York press was equally enthusiastic. "All Hail the Royal Prince," were headlines in *The World* that greeted the young man. The *New York Herald* welcomed the prince with front page headlines in Greek, "Welcome Your Highness, Prince George." The visitor was said to be of "physical proportions that made him look like a Grecian God." Another newspaper caption referred to Prince George as a "Spartan Athlete in Swell's Suit." The arrival of the royal visitor created a cordial atmosphere in the terminal. One of the prince's compatriots, "the keeper of a Greek restaurant at Pearl Street," the *New York Herald* reported, "appeared . . . in his native costume and distributed handbills," describing the delicious Greek national dishes to be had at his restaurant for a "modest renumeration."[24] The *New York Herald* reporter claimed that when the prince descended from the train, he assisted two young ladies from the railway coach. One girl was reported to have said to her sister:[25]

"Papa can't buy that, rich as he is."
Her sister replied: "No deary, papa quarters and packs pork..."

The popularity of the young prince of Greece even caused a flurry in the advertising copy in *The Evening Post*. A hat advertisement captured the genuine enthusiasm of the day:[26]

Prince George of Greece has now arrived.
  And it is all the talk.
That Greek meets Greek when friends contrive
  To meet him in New York.
No doubt they'll show him all the sights,
  Parks, statues and all that.
And that in where a Prince delights
  A genuine Knox hat.

The welcoming Greek delegation was "representative of the Greek colony and included persons in all callings." The most prominent members of the Greek commercial community, the wealthy cotton merchants of New York, were present. They included Anthony P. Ralli, Theodore P. Ralli, John C. Maximos, Constantine Menelas and Demetrius Vlasto. Other prominent community leaders represented were D.C. Carra, N. Catrevas, J. Louisile and J. Charcary. After the initial greetings, Demetrius

Botassi, the Greek consul-general, and Alexander E. Gregor, Russian chargé d'affaires, escorted the prince to his quarters at the Brevoort House.[27]

That evening Prince George dined, unofficially, at Delmonico's. Later in the evening, the prince attended the Madison Square Theatre and viewed the "amusing antics of Richard Mansfield who played Prince Karl." An item in a newspaper claimed that the most gratifying incident for Prince George was the "playing of the Greek national anthem by Gilmore's band as he entered the theatre." It was added that the young man remained standing "uncovered throughout and a brace of tears rolled down his tanned cheeks as he thought of home and all her endearments."[28]

In his unofficial stay in New York, Prince George visited the Brooklyn Navy Yard and Central Park. The wealthy Greek cotton merchants invited the prince to be their personal guest at the New York Cotton Exchange.[29] An amusing incident occurred on July 2, which caught the imagination of the New York press and citizenry, when the prince visited the United States Navy installation at Willet's Point. The Greek prince, wishing to see the sights of the city, "drove to the Ninth Street Station on the Third Avenue 'L' road and rode to the Ninety-Second Street Station." The royal party then walked to the Astoria Ferry, where they were met by Captain Bergland, United States Army Engineers, who welcomed them on the government launch.[30] On the way to the torpedo station, according to the news story, the American officer asked Prince George what type of refreshments he desired:[31]

Prince: "I will have some beer."
Bergland: "Anheuser-Busch or Schlitz' Milwaukee?"
Prince: "No, I'll just take beer... Beer is all alike isn't it; only in different kinds of bottles?"

The prince, not comprehending the significance of the captain's simple question, captivated the press with his gracious and unaffected charm.

On July 3 Prince George visited Thomas Alva Edison at Menlo Park. He was interested in the scientific endeavors of the American inventor. The press reported that the young prince was startled when he heard his voice reproduced by Edison.[32]

That evening the wealthy cotton merchants, led by T.P. Ralli and P. Fachiri, invited Prince George to what the press called a "Greek Colony Dinner" at Delmonico's, to which only 24 selected guests were invited. The exclusive list contained only the wealthy Greek cotton merchants and prominent members of the New York Cotton, Savannah Cotton and New Orleans Cotton Exchanges. Some of the more important persons present at Delmonico's were Theodore P. Ralli, Anthony P. Ralli, Paul S. Galatti, Constantine Menelas, Constantine Psomades and Paul Negreponte. Immigrants of humble and provincial origins and limited wealth were specifically excluded by the hosts.[33]

After the dinner, Prince George prepared to board the *S.S. Servia* at midnight to return to Europe. He was surrounded by 300 cheering Greeks. Some were also lined up in front of the vessel, carrying and waving both Greek and American flags. The expatriates had come to bid farewell to one of the living links to their beloved fatherland. Excitement, joy and sadness filled the night air.[34]

The pier-side farewell was robust, earthy and emotional, while the one at Delmonico's was sophisticated, reserved and cordial. The contrast between the two events was striking. The reaction to the exclusive dinner at Delmonico's was immediate, intense and bitter. Discontent was so widespread among the Greeks that the press stated the vast majority of the immigrant colony thought that "the dinner should have been a subscription affair" open to any Greek who desired to attend.[35]

The social cleavage between the two groups never fully healed. Already in 1891 the poor and unskilled immigrants outnumbered the educated and wealthy merchants. There was very little social contact between the two classes except in church. The wealthy cotton merchants did not employ any Greek immigrants. They only hired their blood relatives and very close friends. Moreover, there was usually some tie of blood and marital relationship even among the most intimate of friends, especially the Ralli, Fachiri, Galatti and Calvocoressi. One of the Greeks whose name was not included on the exclusive guest list, Solon J. Vlasto, became the leader of the emerging majority of provincial immigrants.

The public celebrations of Greek independence fostered group activity and encouraged the participation of the provincial immigrants. In accordance with Greek tradition, the national holiday was always celebrated with religious services. In fact, the Greek Revolution began on the Orthodox Christian Feast of the Annunciation on March 25, 1821. The first known public commemoration service was sponsored by Solon J. Vlasto in April, 1893. The press reported in a headline, "Greek Flag Floats over New York City Hall."[36] Mayor Thomas Gilroy allowed the flag to fly over City Hall in response to a request by Vlasto. Mayor Gilroy's first reply to the Greek leader was that he would have been very happy to comply with the request but that City Hall did not have the time to procure a Greek flag at such short notice. The indomitable and resourceful Vlasto, however, found a flag and it was flown over City Hall.[37] Religious services were also held in the "Orthodox Church which was attended by the Greek society, Athena, in a body."[38] The press reported that "this will be a great day for the Greeks in New York."[39] In a letter to the mayor, Solon J. Vlasto wrote that "on the Acropolis at Athens, above the noble ruins of the Parthenon, every Fourth of July, the Stars and Stripes float as a remembrance of the debt of Greece to America.[40]

Again in 1894, the New York press reported a celebration commemorating the Greek Revolution. On this occasion the most important religious and official ceremonies were held at the Holy Trinity Church, 340 West 53rd Street. The divine liturgy was celebrated by Reverend P. Pherentinos. Demetrius Botassi, Greek consul-general, was the official representative of the Greek Crown.[41] There was another celebration sponsored by the Athena Brotherhood and Solon J. Vlasto at the Annunciation Church, "the recently established Greek Church in the basement of the Baptist Memorial Church, Washington Square South." Reverend Callinikos Dilveis officiated at the church. In addition to the religious service, a patriotic address was delivered by the president of the Athena Brotherhood, Solon J. Vlasto.[42] In the succeeding year another commemoration service was reported in the press. The important services were held in the Holy Trinity Church. Nevertheless, the *Atlantis'* publisher chided the Greek consul-general, Demetrius Botassi, for not attending the services held on March 26, 1895 at the Annunciation Church.[43] These events began to show that strains and stresses existed among the New York Greeks. The several simple celebrations of Greek Independence indicated that there was an undercurrent of personal antagonism and misunderstanding in the relations of the newcomers with the wealthy patrician merchants. There was, however, no shred of evidence to show the existence or even influence of Marxist class warfare or contemporary political radicalism. Most of the evidence points to conflicts of personalities, such as Vlasto, Ralli and Botassi, and personal interests.

The Brotherhood of Athena, under the leadership of Solon J. Vlasto, held another celebration on July 7, 1895, which jointly commemorated the Greek and American revolutions at City Hall Park.[44] In a feature article on the Fourth of July, the *Atlantis* correlated the Greek and American national struggles as similar movements for freedom. The American Revolution was praised in its struggle "against British despotism in the New World." In addition the *Atlantis* called it a struggle against England and "its German mercenary troops." The American Revolution set the example for the Greeks, claimed the *Atlantis* editors, for the rebirth of the fatherland."[45] The feature story also referred to the "continued enslavement of the provinces of Macedonia, Crete and Epirus" under the hegemony of the Turkish Empire. Another public celebration of Greek independence was reported in 1897 by the New York press.[46]

Another example of activity that encouraged ethnic identity was the drive among New York Greeks in 1894 for the relief of earthquake victims in Greece. This cooperative community effort also provided Solon J. Vlasto with the opportunity to act as the leading spokesman and leader of the New York Greeks. He actively participated in this humanitarian effort.

The earthquakes in Greece in 1894 evoked a wide sympathetic response among many native New Yorkers. The New York press carried stories and appeals for relief for the victims.[47] In a letter to the editor of *The New York Times*, S.J. Vlasto appealed for aid. He stated that the "editors of the Greek newspaper have opened a subscription list, and they appealed to good-hearted Americans and Philhellenes for donations." Vlasto added that "Americans have always been the most generous to the Greeks." The publisher believed that the appeal in one of Greece's most critical periods would not be "in vain."[48] A similar letter was sent to the editor of the *New York Herald*.[49] The Greek consul-general, Demetrius Botassi, reported a generous response from numerous native Americans in the earthquake relief drive.[50] The New York community, especially the Protestants, was generous in its response to the sufferings of the earthquake victims. The city's warm reaction reinforced the immigrant's attachment to his adopted country. Furthermore, Solon J. Vlasto received adequate publicity in the

New York press to assure his position as a responsible leader secure in New York.

Another event that encouraged group loyalty was the official visit of a Greek warship, *Miaoulis*, on September 27, 1900. This was the first time that a Greek naval vessel had visited the city. The Greek community was excited and proud of the historic visit.[51] The Greek naval visit was an act of good will in appreciation of America's support of Christian Hellenism in the nineteenth century. As a memento of the visit, the New York Greeks presented a silver loving cup to the commander, Captain Paul Koundouriotis, the officers and the crew of the *Miaoulis*.[52] The arrival of the vessel was wildly received by the Greeks and the "Greek colony of the city . . . took a holiday in honor of the historic event." The Greek neighborhood was virtually deserted. Following a marching band, the welcoming committee lined "Washington Street and Battery Place . . . carrying small Greek flags, marched in platoons to Pier A, North River."[53] With headlines, "New World Greets Greek of Old," the New York press welcomed the Greek warship to New York.[54]

Special religious services commemorating the historic occasion were held at the Greek Church of the Holy Trinity.[55] Plans were made to have the Greek naval commandant visit the Brooklyn Navy Yard and to meet with the mayor of the city.[56] The good will tour restored the pride of the New York Greeks after the catastrophic reverses suffered by Greece in the war against Turkey in 1897. The visit of the Greek naval vessel stimulated greater enthusiasm in the national movement for the liberation of the Greeks of the Ottoman Empire. Within a few years nationalist sentiment, pride and self-confidence were restored among the New York Greeks and the other Greek immigrants in the United States. In 1908 a campaign was initiated to solicit funds among the Greek immigrants for the purchase of warships for the Royal Hellenic Navy.[57] In the pages of the *Atlantis* were published the names of the contributors. The Greek newspaper encouraged the goals of this fund-raising campaign on behalf of the Great Idea.

With the exception of the numerous violations of the municipal ordinances covering street peddlers, a few gambling offenses and several charges of disorderly conduct, the New York Greeks were a peace-loving and law-abiding community. The New York Greeks were shocked by a series of articles published in December, 1898 to February, 1899 in *The New York Times* that reported the arrival of an alleged Greek brigand who was later murdered in the district.[58] In addition, the *Atlantis* reported that the first Greek to be condemned to death in the United States was John Zygouras for the murder of S. Farandos in 1899.[59] The trial was very important to the New York Greek community because of possible aspersions against the Greek immigrants, community and customs. The Greeks also felt the possible loss of good will among the native New Yorkers. The editors of the *Atlantis* claimed that the murder was neither deliberate nor premeditated. It was the tragic ending of two young men who were "expecting to find gold in the streets of America."[60] In reality, the young newcomers found despair, frustration and melancholia. Another disquieting event that upset the New York Greeks was another homicide that occurred in October, 1899, when, in one of the Greek boarding houses on Oliver Street, a man, known as a bankrupt and a drunkard, killed a companion known as "Charlie Greek." Such violence committed on non-Greek territory was regarded by the New York Greeks as a personal attack on the good name of the entire Greek people.[61]

Three Greek homicides committed in the Greek district within a period of several months shattered the composure and self-respect of the New York Greeks. The immigrants had always been overly sensitive to American public opinion. Any unpleasant publicity, unhealthy situation and alleged illegal act implicating Greeks was always regarded as a possible smear against the Greek community and nation. Therefore, the New York Greeks preferred to keep such unpleasant and unfortunate events from public view and discussion. They desired to air their differences and limitations among themselves. Homicide, however, could never be hidden from public scrutiny. Hence, shame filled the Greek community.[62]

In spite of some minor grievances, poor living conditions and personal frustration, the Greek immigrants neither lost their stamina nor their faith in the American dream. They underwent conditions identical to those experienced by the Irish, Italians, Germans, Jews and Scandinavians of the period. The Greek immigrant community was kneaded and formed in the dynamic environment of New York. The Greek Orthodox Church, immigrant press, fraternal associations, ethnic tradition and the economic experience in the city transformed the New York Greeks from an agrarian-provincial group with a conservative Christian outlook to an industrial-urban society with a more secular orientation.

6

Economic Foundations

Most Greeks came to New York to make money. They were in pursuit of the good life, to rapidly accumulate savings and to enjoy the social amenities of the contemporary, materialist world. When the Greek immigrants disembarked in New York, they were met by relatives, friends, travel agents and padrones at South Ferry. The latter handled the affairs of some Greeks destined for Midwestern cities. A fair number went to construct the railways in the far West and North Central states. Of the remaining Greeks, some sought employment as flower sellers and pushcart peddlers in New York. Others found job opportunities in the confectionery, fur, shoeshining, restaurant and hotel businesses, and in oriental cigarette manufacturing establishments. The immigrants who had neither relatives nor friends made inquiries at the numerous, nameless, little eating places in the Lower Manhattan Greek district. These little restaurants acted as unofficial clearing houses of employment opportunities. In this way, the newcomers found job leads, addresses and directions from their compatriots. They accepted openings as workers, busboys and cook's assistants in the laundries, dining rooms and kitchens of prominent hotels, such as the Belmont, Brevoort, Chelsea, Plaza, Prince George, Bretton Hall and Seville.[1] A New York newspaper added that many of the immigrants were seamen and were the "most ingenious of sailor-men at finding a job at shore."[2] The immigrants toiled endlessly. Pushing their small carts, the itinerant vendors plied the streets, selling chestnuts, flowers, peanuts and fruit. Illusions were conjured up in the minds of the newcomers that even grocery boys had their pockets filled with dollars.[3] The *Atlantis* glorified the United States as a "New Jerusalem." The newspaper eulogized America for recognizing initiative, individuality and self-respect.

To the *Atlantis*, America favored the "self-made man."[4]

On February 2, 1882, John Gennadius, Greek minister to the United States, arrived in New York with the mission of securing better and closer relations between Greece and this country." His principal objective was to encourage the reduction of American tariffs on Greek currants. After 1888 the Greek government explored new areas of market and commercial expansion to offset their tragic political losses in the Balkans.[5] Little was accomplished by Gennadius.

By 1895, the Greek government's efforts proved fruitless because of the rapid expansion of the California raisin industry.[6] The currant question rekindled a factional rivalry between Solon J. Vlasto, publisher of the *Atlantis*, and Demetrius Botassi, Greek consul-general.[7] In a series of feature articles and editorials, the *Atlantis* placed the blame for the failure on inferior merchandising of the Greek exporters and the indifference of the Greek government. [8]

Greek commercial interests, however, organized the Hellenic Currant Company to develop the currant export market. Its American headquarters and principal agency was established in New York in 1902. The company's staff was carefully selected to meet the needs of the American consumer. The firm was to collaborate in its sales effort with the National Bank of Greece. One of the outcomes of the commercial endeavor was to encourage indirectly Greek emigration to New York and the United States.[9] Its export activities were not too successful in competing with the California producers.

An insidious technique that induced some emigration to New York was the infamous padrone system patterned on the Italian model, which had flourished a decade earlier.[10] The Greek padrone was a contractor who facilitated the entry of youths and placed them under a form of indenture. The padrone usually paid for the passage and secured jobs for the immigrants in shoeshine shops. These young men and boys were forced to work long hours and repay the passage loans at usurious rates. They were obliged to surrender their gratuities and to pay for their lodgings. The *Atlantis* contemptuously referred to the padrone as the scourge of the Greek nation and "slave traders."[11] The exploitation of the youth was exercised by their own Greek compatriots. The padrone's accomplice would inform their unfortunate victims that

"Greeks of small means . . . can easily make fortunes in America," and offer to advance them passage money secured by mortgages on their real property "at 50 to 70 per cent interest." Sometimes the padrones provided the immigrants with adequate money to comply with the requirements of the United States immigration laws. As soon as the newly arrived left the Barge Office, the padrones quickly recovered the funds. Another ruse used by the padrones was to pose as relatives of the newcomers.[12]

Elia Eazan in his novel, *America, America*, depicted the terrible conditions under which these youths suffered. Nevertheless, many boys were willing to undergo the ruthless exploitation by the Greek padrones because they needed the money to send to their parents in Greece. The other important reason was to save enough money to bring their families from Greece and Asia Minor to New York and the United States. In the closing pages of his novel, Kazan captures the temperament of the youthful bootblacks in New York, through the words of the hero, Stavros Topouzoglou:[13]

> Come on you!
> Let's go!
> People waiting!
> People waiting!

On February 6, 1898, the New York press reported the deportation of Christos Laganos who had emigrated in violation of the American contract labor law. The immigration authorities stated that Laganos "was one of the many persons forwarded [*sic*] by the mayor of Castagna, in Greece, to Petro Pantasselos and Chalivos," who the officials stated were heads of "a pushcart band at Nos. 95, 97, 99 Cherry Street."[14]

The chief registry clerk in the New York Barge Office, said that in more than two years 100 persons were sent by Mayor Theophilopoulos of Castagna, Greece. These unfortunate victims were "vouched for by persons who claimed to be their relatives, and thus evaded the law." The immigration official in New York informed the press that the padrone plot was discovered before Laganos' arrival in New York. The Barge Office received a letter that exposed the scheme. Under interrogation, Laganos admitted that "Theophilopoulos had brought about his departure for this country." The victim confessed that he did not know either of the leaders of the "pushcart band." When the chief registry clerk investigated the Cherry Street premises, he found 40 persons under the charge of Pantasselos and Chalivos.[15]

According to the federal officials, the movement to import and exploit Greek boys as bootblacks started about 1895. The Greeks replaced the Italians and the American Negroes who formerly held the jobs.[16] The Immigration Commission investigators reported that the padrone system in New York was promoted by the Yokaris brothers. "Most of the boys originally employed as bootblacks in the United States," indicated a federal report, "came from the province of Arcadia, district of Tripoli, for the reason that all padrones operating shine places here came from that section of Greece."[17] The padrones earned from $100 to $200 per year from their youthful victims.[18] Practically all of the shoe polishing activities in Chicago were done by the Greeks. Kansas City, St. Louis and other midwestern cities had extensive padrone enterprises.[19]

The padrone system, however, was not as successful in New York as it was in the smaller towns and cities of the United States. The vigorous activities of the publisher of the *Atlantis* and the Greek consul-general dampened the fervor of the padrones. These leaders were assisted in their efforts by the parish councils of the churches of the Holy Trinity and Annunciation and the most important fraternal organizations in New York, Brotherhood of Athena and Panhellenic Union. [20]

Still another deterrent to the expansion of the system was New York's great labor market, which provided many jobs for the unskilled. Moreover, the growth of a self-supporting Greek community provided the victims with an escape into economic independence. The urban vastness, with its sprawling boroughs, made it difficult for the padrones to harass the immigrants.[21] The influence of the New York padrones was lessened further when the newcomers learned English at the evening schools at Henry, Hester, Christie and East 42 Streets. Philhellenes, such as Professor Carroll N. Brown, classics professor at City College, taught many eager Greeks in these classes.[22]

In addition to those working through the padrone system, others became peddlers. They worked for their relatives and friends. The peddlers sold flowers, fruits and nuts. Limited English fluency and inadequate observance of the city license ordinances were among the major problems faced by the immigrants. Conflicts with the municipal authorities over the latter problem were aggravated by allegations of police extortion toward the end of the century A Greek manufacturer, Telemachos T. Timayenis, asserted to the New York press that the police were "persecuting Greek flower peddlers." Timayenis claimed that the arrested peddlers were taken to the Tombs Police Court where they were unjustly treated because they could not speak a word in English "in their own defense." Moreover, he court interpreter could neither speak nor understand Greek.[23]

"It is a great outrage the way these poor people are treated," remarked Timayenis to the reporter. The businessman added that he purchased "some flowers from one of these peddlers. . . and requested him to deliver them" to him. The peddler was immediately arrested for selling without a municipal license. Upon posting bail for his compatriot, Timayenis attempted to explain the situation to the judge at the Tombs. The judge, however, refused to pay any attention to Timayenis' appeals. "The charge was stated and the interpreter at once answered 'guilty' for the accused."[24]

Timayenis claimed that the unfortunate man was fined five dollars. Another group of Greek peddlers underwent the same procedure and they were also fined. Infuriated at the mistreatment, Timayenis added:[25]

I can furnish dozens of instances where the police have demanded money from these Greeks to allow them to prosecute their business. . . There are. . . Greeks in this city who can hardly speak a word of English, and there is not an attempt to give them an opportunity to be heard in their own defense when they are arrested, but they are adjudged guilty and fined.

In another situation reported by the *Atlantis*, 50 Greek pushcart peddlers were arrested by the authorities in July 1895, because of improper licensing.[26] Within a week, a more prominent flower seller, Gerasimos Priamos, was also arrested on similar charges at Grand Central Station.[27]

With the coming of the twentieth century, the lot of the Greek street peddler did not improve. The peddler in lower Manhattan, especially at Fulton and William streets and the Bowery, faced another problem with the authorities—alleged police corruption in the execution of the municipal ordinances concerning pushcart peddling. In headlines, the *Atlantis* reported the alleged "persecution of Greek fruit peddlers."[28] The newspaper intimated that the problem of adequate police protection for the immigrant peddler was an unresolved problem. The *Atlantis* asserted that Alexander Howery, the only Greek on the municipal force, was one of the persons accused of intimidating Greek fruit peddlers.[29] Charges were leveled against the police by an immigrant peddler, Charalambos Kolotouros, which implicated Howery and a police captain in an extortion ring.[30]

The Greek peddler said that about 50 pushcart men met under the Brooklyn Bridge and paid the police officer $6.00 each. Kolotouros appeared in court "with one eye closed, his face cut and his clothing almost torn from his body." The detained man claimed to have been assaulted by Patrolman John McGrath on the "Bridge of Sighs" en route from the Tombs to the court room. The charges placed against him were violation of the corporation ordinances at William and Fulton Streets.[31]

The *Atlantis* reported that Kolotouros was fined $2.00 and that, in general, the Greek peddler was fearful of reprisals from the police.[32] Moreover, the *New-York Daily Tribune* in a feature story entitled, "Greek Peddlers' Woes," indicated that the Tammany policemen were said "to have been robbing the peddlers under a regular and organized system of extortion." The newspaper estimated the existence of several thousand peddlers whose ranks multiplied between 1897 and 1900.[33]

It was reported that some police officials considered that Alexander Howery was vindicated by a letter received from Park Row merchants, praising the policeman for the manner "in which he enforced the pushcart ordinance."[34] Nevertheless, Howery was fined by the police chief for seeking "bribes from the Park Row peddlers."[35] The following summer saw a recurrence of the same trouble with the arrest of two Greek fruit peddlers in Coney Island. They accused a policeman of demanding payment of $1.50 per week for protection against arrest.[36] The harassment of the peddlers in New York reached even the Athens press.[37] In addition, the Republican-oriented and reform-minded *Atlantis* sharply criticized the Democratic party for its relations with alleged police graft. In spite of its anti-Tammany stand, the Greek newspaper did not encourage any anti-Irish sentiments. Its attitude toward other ethnic minorities was commendable.[38]

Some other Greeks were to make substantial contributions in the American cigarette industry. The Greeks who entered this business were primarily immigrants with provincial origins, either as merchants or rural laborers. A few of the Greek cigarette manufacturers had some previous experience in Greece, Asia Minor and

Egypt. The majority, however, gained their experience in the small New York cigarette factories and shops.[39] The Greek cotton merchants lived in a closed society, while the remaining Greeks formed an open society that provided for upward mobility. However, more Greek immigrants progressed from the laborer to the businessman in the restaurant, fur, florist and confectionery fields than in the cigarette industry. Cigarettes were imported in considerable quantities from the West Indies, Russia and the Ottoman Empire before they were produced on a large scale in this country.[40] The habit of cigarette smoking and manufacturing flourished in the Turkish Empire in the middle of the nineteenth century and was later developed in Greece, Russia and Austria-Hungary.[41] The Greeks became "experts in the art of blending" cigarettes.[42] The first tobacco merchant listed in a directory was Demetrius Nicolopoulos who in 1889 conducted his business at 132 Pearl Street.[43] The cigarette manufacturing centers in 1900 were New York, Richmond, Durham and Rochester.[44] These cities produced 94 percent of all cigarettes. New York manufactured most of the oriental type.

In 1910 the Greeks represented the sixth largest group of foreign-born workers in the industry. The ethnic distribution included: Cubans, 3,547; Spanish, 2,011, Italians (South), 1,927; Germans, 607; Magyars, 534 and Greeks, 345. Most Cubans, Spanish and Italians were employed in the Tampa cigar factories; whereas, the Greeks and other foreign-born immigrants worked in the New York cigarette establishments. The earnings of the Greeks and Italians averaged about $1.14 per day, while those of the Irish and Polish were $2.06 and $1.64, respectively.[45] The federal authorities in 1905 reported that "a large part of the increase during the past few years" had been because of the increased consumption of oriental cigarettes. The initial consumers were Greeks, Lebanese, Armenians and other immigrants from Eastern Europe and the Levant.[46]

A merchant in New York, Soterios Anargyros, began to import Oriental cigarettes manufactured in Egypt in 1889 under the label of Egyptian Deities. In 1891, Anargyros started manufacturing this brand in New York and built a lucrative business by the end of the nineteenth century.[47] Originally, his firm was located at 192 Water Street.[48] The following year, another merchant, Telemachos T. Timayenis, opened an establishment at 25 Vanderwater Street and another important concern, Boultbee & Contopoulos, conducted business at 73 Pearl Street.[49] Notaras Brothers manufactured cigarettes at 9 William Street. The latter firm later moved to 1215 Broadway.[50]

To these firms were added those of Pappas & Cappatos, 1181 Broadway; Constantine Poulides, 84 Beaver Street; Demetrius Kazis, 183 Broadway; A. Zoniades & Co., 128 Pearl Street; George Morphides, 22 Beaver Street; Christodoulakis Larendos, 30 Cortlandt Street; and the Anglo-Egyptian Cigarette Co., 2 and 4 Stone Street.[51]

Efthimiou claimed that ten cigarette factories existed in the city between 1895 and 1896, of which the most important enterprises were operated by Contopoulos, Volvi, Varoni, Poulides and the Condaxopoulos Brothers.[52] Xenides included B.D. Dungundzis, Standard Commercial Tobacco Company and the Pialoglou Brothers.[53] Malafouris indicated that in 1910 New York contained 30 cigarette and tobacco establishments. The firm of Stephano Brothers was well entrenched in Philadelphia.[54] Notaras' Egyptian cigarettes were a popular brand at the turn of the century.[55] The firm of Z. Vassilades successfully sold the Egyptian Rainbow brand in New York.[56] The majority of the Greek establishments were engaged in hand methods in small shops. Most of the firms combined a retail outlet with their small manufacturing plant. Initially, the small Greek companies were successful because "the small scale of the industry . . . gave little advantage to machine production."[57]

The Greek cigarette manufacturers and employees faced competition from the tobacco trust and other rival interests for the control of the oriental cigarette trade. On July 22, 1899, the *Atlantis* reported that the Greek employees had created a mutual benefit society to protect their interests. Their attempts were short-lived in the face of severe competition from the American Tobacco Company.[58]

On December 31, 1899, the American Tobacco Company purchased the Monopol Tobacco Works in New York for $250,000.[59] Later, the purchase of the firm of S. Anargyros dealt a death blow to the expanding Greek cigarette industry in New York. The corporate giant purchased the Greek firm for $450,000 in 1900 and reorganized it as a subsidiary. The Commissioner of Corporations gave the reason for separate corporate identities because "the name of S. Anargyros, used in connection with certain brands of Turkish cigarettes, is a very valuable asset because of the reputation which the concern obtained before its absorption by the American Tobacco Company." The commissioner added that "not a little of the popularity of these brands would have been sacrificed had the name of the American Tobacco Company been substituted for that of S. Anargyros."[60]

The corporate giant regarded the acquisition of the business assets of S. Anargyros as vital to its desired market expansion. The commissioner indicated that the acquisition of "this well established business in the manufacture of cigarettes from foreign tobacco greatly strengthened the position which the American Tobacco Company had obtained in that branch of the cigarette business by purchasing the Monopol Tobacco Works in the previous years."

The Greek immigrant's enterprise was incorporated as S. Anargyros, Inc. on March 28, 1900. The amount of stock issued was $450,000, which was taken by the American Tobacco Company at par. "By October, 1906 it stood in the books of the American Tobacco Company at a book value of $1,575,000 or three and half times in par value."[61]

With the acquisition of the Anargyros firm, the American Tobacco Company's output of cigarettes made from Turkish tobacco expanded quickly. The production of the S. Anargyros company alone had "increased from 13 millions in 1900 to 571 millions in 1906." The commissioner emphasized that independent manufacturers, however, "principally Turks, Egyptians and Greeks, probably still make near 50 percent of the country's output of Turkish cigargttes."[62] The United States government indicated that the "most important subsidiary company engaged in the manufacture of cigarettes [was] S. Anargyros. . . ."[63] The firm's major brands were Turkish Trophies, Moguls and Egyptian Deities.[64]

During most of the period before 1910 the bulk of the Turkish cigarettes were handmade. The independent manufacturers of the so-called Turkish brands were prominent because "they occupied a very important position during the early part of the period." The oriental cigarettes, "previous to the acquisitions made by the American Tobacco Company, were almost entirely in the hands of the small companies controlled by Greeks and Turks [*sic*]." The government report indicated that some of the independent companies "had become more or less prominent, and judging from the liberal prices paid them by the combination when it absorbed them [they] must have been very profitable."[65]

The federal report continued, in pointing out that by 1906 some of the large independent companies "ranked not far below the concerns controlled by the Combination both in size and profitableness." A few of the powerful independent firms were M. Melachrino & Co., E.A. Condax & Co. and Nestor Gianaclis & Co.[66] After 1906 the profits of the independent companies progressively declined and the costs increased. In October 1912 the Tobacco Products Corporation was formed with the amalgamation of the Surburg Co., M. Melachrino & Co. and Border Tobacco Company. The firm of Stephano Brothers of Philadelphia surrendered 50 percent of its common stock plus a block of preferred shares. The corporate consolidations in the second decade of the century and the rising popularity of the blended American-type cigarette saw the demise of the independent Greek cigarette manufacturer in New York.[67]

Walter E. Weyl wrote a fictional account of the rise of an educated Greek immigrant in New York from a dishwasher to wealthy oriental cigarette manufacturer. Weyl's fictional hero, Pericles Antonopulo, supposedly came to New York after the disastrous Greek-Turkish War of 1897.[68] After landing in New York, Antonopulo "became a dishwasher in the Yale Club and began his struggle for a foothold" in New York.[69] After great personal sacrifice, Pericles Antonopulo saved some money from his meager wages. With his small savings Antonopulo was "persuaded to open a little cigarette establishment in the cellar of a downtown tenement." Through luck and hard work the hero prospered. Antonopulo eventually married "the daughter of a retired merchant of Alexandria, Egypt." In addition, his "six year old son was in a private school on Central Park West." In Weyl's narrative Antonopulo's firm was eventually purchased by the American Tobacco Company.[70]

Unlike the meteoric rise and fall of the cigarette manufacturers, scores of lesser businessmen formed a more permanent nucleus. They catered to the immediate needs of the immigrants. They dealt in imported products, olives, coffee, sesame, rice, cheese and olive oil. Greek-type coffee shops and restaurants were opened on Madison and Roosevelt Streets and on Third, Sixth and Seventh

Avenues. Lodging houses increased in the downtown Greek quarter and Chelsea.

Nicholas Catrevas was a general merchant at 130 Fulton Street.[71] The firm of Lekas and Drivas, established in 1892, became the foundation of a large food products enterprise. Its headquarters were situated at No.17 Roosevelt Street.[72] John P. Christodules & Brothers had fruit and vegetable shops at 82 Barclay and 211 Washington Streets.[73] Nicholas Dotoratos maintained a fruit store at 192 East 125 Street toward the end of the century.[74]

In the 1890s, merchants such as Solon J. Vlasto acted as agents for the Bank of Athens and the National Bank of Greece.[75] In 1906 the firm of Psiachi Brothers, 104 Wall Street, advertised in the local Greek press as agents for several banks that would transfer remittances to Greece.[76] The hardworking newcomers sent money to their families. These funds became a substantial element in the national economy of Greece. Immigrant monies reduced the usurious rates from 20 and 15 percent to 10 and 5 percent within a few years. John B. Jackson said that "some of the poorest villages became the richest.[77] Local New York banking facilities were adequate for the New York Greeks. Steamship agents also transferred funds. The Ionian Bank Ltd. of Greece advertised in the *Atlantis* and listed its New York correspondents as Chase National Bank, Hanover National Bank and the firm of Brown Brothers. The latter private banking firm maintained branch offices in Boston and Philadelphia.[78]

In the period 1890 to 1910, all financial transactions between Greece and the United States seem to have been effected through London.[79] It was actually more than a decade later that the Greek banks created branches in New York. The Bank of Athens established a subsidiary under the name of Bank of Athens Trust Company in 1922. The National Bank of Greece established an agency in 1925, which remained in operation until 1933. In the meantime, the "National Bank of Greece founded the Hellenic Bank Trust Co. in 1929 in cooperation with Greek-American and American capitalists." Both banks maintained separate identities until they merged on February 27, 1953 to form the Atlantic Bank of New York. "The principal consideration that caused the National Bank of Greece and the Bank of Athens to open subsidiaries in New York was . . . the intention to collect monies of

Greek immigrants . . . and to provide . . . banking services in their financial operations. . . ."[80]

Furthermore, the period 1900 to 1910 saw a steady decline in the influence of the merchant banking and cotton factoring firm of Ralli Brothers. "In 1903 they relinquished their American Cotton [sic] business which became unprofitable and unduly speculative."[81] Theodore Ralli returned to London in August 1899. His brother, Anthony P. Ralli, who remained in New York, died in August 1916. With the departure of the prominent leaders from the New York scene and the restriction of their economic interests, the Greek patrician families gradually lost their economic status in the New York immigrant community. The last important link with the aristocratic past was Leonidas J. Calvocoressi who maintained his ties with the Holy Trinity parish until his death on April 18, 1952.[82]

The roots of Greek participation in the flower retailing, fur manufacturing and restaurant business were planted in the period 1890 to 1910. These economic activities became prominent centers of employment and investment during and after World War I. Furthermore, it was not an uncommon sight, then and now, to witness a former employee open his own business either as an individual proprietor or family partnership. Henry Pratt Fairchild wrote, "Give a Greek a start in business and he will do the rest."[83] The merchandizing of flowers, furs and food provided New York's Greek immigrants with the opportunity for social mobility and economic independence.

According to Malafouris, the first known Greek florist in New York was Constantine Bambis, a seafarer, who arrived on a sailing vessel in 1852. In the story, long forgotten by the living immigrants, Bambis visited the outskirts of the city around 42nd Street and Fifth Avenue. Walking along the tree-lined paths, the young seamen picked some flowers, enjoyed the pleasant surroundings of the more sylvan environment. Returning to the Bowery, Bambis stopped at a corner with flowers in hand and waited to cross the street. The legend continued that a lady, mistaking him for a flower seller, took the bouquet and gave the young man a dollar. The idea suddenly flashed in his mind to become a florist.[84] Burgess claimed that the first permanent florist was George Giatras who opened a shop on Columbus Avenue in 1885.[85]

With the influx of the immigrants after 1887, many found

employment in selling flowers, first for wholesalers and later as independent contractors. Work, thrift and frugality lifted the flower peddlers from the streets on to the sidewalks and finally into well appointed shops throughout the city. By 1890 the most prominent flower dealers were George Giatras; George Konto, 148 East l4th Street; Gerasimos Priamos at Grand Central Station; George Polykranis, 663 Columbus Avenue; George Bombolin with establishments at 1664 Second Avenue and 115 Lexington Avenue; Nicholas Christatos at 611 Madison Avenue.

At the time that many immigrants were becoming flower dealers and peddlers, a handful of Greek furriers from the Macedonian district of Kastoria emigrated to New York. In the late 1890s, the firm of Giacos Brothers opened their shop and worked on mink pieces and ermine tails. They were soon joined by another firm, Papatina Brothers, which maintained workshops on McDougal and West 8th Streets in Greenwich Village. The latter company employed some 50 Kastorian Greeks in the first decade of the century. The weekly wages ranged from $10 to $20 during the period. The immigrants worked a 48-hour week during the seasonal period from July to December. In the off-seasons, the laid-off fur workers found openings as busboys and waiters until the fur season resumed operations in the summer.

After 1910, furriers from other Macedonian communes, such as Siatista, found employment in the expanding fur industry. Most of the workshops were located on West 8th Street and Sixth Avenue and on East 5th Street and Second Avenue. The Greek craftsmen gradually thrived. By 1912 the city contained 44 Greek fur shops, which employed Greek immigrants.[86]

Although the restaurant business was not the first important immigrant enterprise, it later became the most important endeavor with far-reaching and permanent results. It was the economic activity that created the Greek stereotype in later generations. In her novel on the early Greek immigration, Roxane Cotsakis attempted to describe the immigrant's interest in the restaurant business: "where a few Greeks are . . . they make coffee. . . . Someone starts a coffee house . . . it's natural."[87] Canoutas claims that the first known Greek restaurant keeper was Spyros Bazanos who operated the restaurant, Peloponnesus, at 7 Roosevelt Street in the 1880s. The eating place catered to the visiting Greek seafarers.[88] In the late 1890s numerous immigrants secured jobs in the restaurants, hotels, ice cream and confectionery stalls at New York's seaside resorts. Such employment was so widespread that the *Atlantis* gleefully wrote that Coney Island had become "a Greek colony."[89]

They learned the business, however, as busboys, waiters and cooks in the New York hotels and restaurants, which dotted Park, Madison, Fifth and Sixth Avenues from Madison Square up to Grand Central Station and beyond.[90] Wages and working conditions were good. Earnings were lower and the hours longer in the Greek-owned restaurants and coffee shops. Fairchild estimated that the waiters received an annual income from $500 to $1,500.[91] A few years later in 1918, it was estimated that Greek waiters earned from $1,000 to $3,600 in the better restaurants and hotels.[92]

Working in this economic endeavor, the humble immigrants ascended each rung of the ladder of success with thrift, self-sacrifice and perseverance. The lowest rung was that of dishwasher. From that level they climbed up the hierarchy to the ranks of busboy, waiter, captain, head waiter, and finally, manager or independent proprietor. They also elevated their status in the kitchen from dishwasher and potato peeler to scullery worker, assistant cook and chef. "So many [used] hotels and restaurant service as a stepping stone to something higher."[93] Some waiters were even graduates of the University of Athens. These professional men worked in this vocation until they became established in the city. Followiug in their footsteps, other waiters attended evening colleges.[94]

By 1913, Greek-owned restaurants had increased substantially in number. The only first class restaurant, owned by Greeks, was the Hotel Athens near Grand Central Station at 30 East 42nd Street.[95] The better places were located on Sixth Avenue between West 23rd and West 42nd Streets. These restaurants were patronized by the more affluent Greek immigrants.[96] There were over 300 third-class eating places along Seventh Avenue.[97]

After World War I the restaurant business was so widespread that statistics on the number, distribution, employment, income and investment of restaurants and waiters are rare and unavailable. The establishments ranged from frankfurter pushcarts and hamburger stands to fine restaurants. With limited capital, acquired skills and intense ambition, the New York immigrants could eke out a livelihood with frugality. With a few chairs, tables, counter, a

coffee urn and pots, they dispensed coffee, sold bean soup, potatoes and rolls to their compatriots and New Yorkers. After learning
the business in New York, some immigrants moved to Newark,
Charleston, Akron and other cities.

Closely related to the restaurant business were the ice cream
parlor and confectionery activities. Greek participation in this
industry was initiated by Eleutherios Pylalas. He first emigrated to
Springfield, Massachusetts, after the Civil War.[98] Another Greek,
Panagiotes Hatzitiris, came to the United States in 1869 and
developed a confectionery business, which produced gum drop
candies, e.g., Turkish Delight, Greek Prince and MM Drops. After
retiring from active business, Hatzitiris returned to his native
Smyrna. His business interests, however, were carried on by the
Haggis Greek-American Confectionery Co.[99]

The New York Greeks entered the field with enthusiasm. They
opened candy kitchens, ice cream parlors and confectionery retail
outlets. They hired their brothers, relatives, friends and compatriots. By 1907 some 61 confectioners were listed in the *Greek-
American Guide*.[100] Fairchild estimated that approximately 1,250
immigrants were engaged in this activity.[101] In 1913 the number
was increased to 150 confectionery shops.[102] One of the most
prominent confectioners was John Counes. He maintained two
shops at 2825 Third Avenue and 532 Willis Street.[103] The rise
from the lower echelons in the confectionery and ice cream parlor
stores to the status of proprietor was very similar to the mobility of
waiters to restaurant keepers.

In the period 1890 to 1910, there was considerable growth of
Greek enterprises in New York and Brooklyn. The reliable *Greek-
American Guide* for 1907 listed 480 firms in New York and 49 in
Brooklyn. A survey of the various firms indicated that 351 establishments or 73.5 percent of the total catered to the general public
and only 129 or 26.48 percent dealt wih the needs of the Greek
immigrants. In the former category there were confectioners, 61
(12.24); bootblacks, 15 (3.12); cigarette and tobacco manufacturers, 22 (2.50); furriers and fur dealers, 17 (3.54); fruit dealers, 12
(2.50); fruit retailers, 16 (3.33); florists, 97 (20.21); merchants and
general importers, 4 (0.083); and, restaurants, 107 (22.29). The
enterprises catering to immigrant needs were listed as grocers, 21
(4.38); Greek coffee shops, 30 (6.25); Greek pastry shops, 8 (1.67);
and, ticket agencies,7 (1.46).[104]

Among the 20,000 Greek immigrants in New York, in 1910 to 1911, Fairchild estimated the following occupation distribution: hotels and restaurants, 3,500; florists, 650; fruit dealers and peddlers, 2,000; and, bootblacks, 500. The balance of the newcomers were engaged in various trades and "independent business." There were "few Greek factory workers in New York outside of a small number employed in the cigarette factories."

In 1910 to 1911, the annual earnings for selected immigrant occupations were as follows: boy bootblacks, $500-$800; common peddlers, $600-$1,000; and waiters $500-$1,500.[105] The earnings of the New York immigrants were more or less in line with the level of American unionized workers. In striking contrast in Greece, the annual wages for common laborers, coachmen and office clerks were $120, $300 and $480, respectively.[106]

In contrast to the New York Jewish community, which had a high proportion of skilled workers among its incoming immigrants, the Greeks reported very high ratios of unskilled laborers: 1900 (60.03); 1907 (87.21) and 1910 (85.95).[107] Nevertheless, the Greeks were neither attracted to mass factory employment nor to trade unionism. Fairchild contended that the Greeks did not join the various labor unions because "they prefer their own organizations, and partly because they are not wanted by the union."[108] The immigrants sought those occupations where the greater effort and sacrifice brought larger rewards in terms of profits, mobility and independence, such as restaurants, florist, fur, fruit, ice cream and confectionery shops, bootblack and shoe repair establishments. The New York Greeks seemed to prefer to engage in their own businesses rather than work for others, except in service pursuits.

The Involvement of New York Greeks in the Greek-Turkish War of 1897

The response of New York Greeks to the conflict between Greece and Turkey over the status of Crete illustrates the extent to which New York Greeks retained their loyalty to the homeland and continued to be involved in its problems; but the incident also reflects the existence of some rising tension within the Greek community. In 1897, Greece fought the Turkish Empire for the liberation of Crete. Greeks in Europe supported this cause in a spirit of intense nationalism. George Averoff, a Greek millionaire who resided in Europe, contributed 40,000 uniforms for the use of the Greek Army. In addition, the Greek community of Marseiiles donated 250,000 francs to the struggle for liberation of Crete. With the same nationalistic fervor, the poor Greek immigrants in the United States and New York volunteered to fight the Turks on the battlefields for the emancipation of their subjugated compatriots. The immigrants even used their meager savings to pay for their passage back to Greece. The New York Greeks were an integral part of the worldwide Greek nationalist movement.[1]

The nationalist cause was led, organized and financed in 1897 by the National Society, Ethnike Hetaireia. The nationalist organization established a network, which covered the major Greek communities in Asia Minor, Great Britain, Egypt, Sudan, Austria-Hungary, France and the United States. It collected funds and dispensed nationalist propaganda on four continents. The principal aims were to strengthen the military system of Greece, which would be able to overwhelm the numerically superior forces of the Ottoman Empire, and to strenghthen its position within the Greek government, which would execute its purposes. In 1897, the Greek monarchy, succumbing to the pressure of the nationalists, intervened in Crete to protect the Christian islanders. Turkey declared war on Greece in April 1897, and moved its German-trained army toward Thessaly.

W. Kinard Rose, war correspondent for the Reuter's agency, remarked that Greek merchants, financiers and bankers from "all parts of the world, inspired by a patriotism which has something noble in it," had built grand mansions in Athens.[2] As a gesture of national identity, the wealthy classes resided in these homes for a limited period in the year. Many of these affluent and influential Greeks had secretly contributed to the nationalist movement. Clive Bigham, the war correspondent of The Times of London, reported that the National Society "had the reputation for wealth and influence . . . and its good will was so vital to the King's Government that it was allowed to have forces of its own in the field."[3] Zotos added that "fierce, uneducated peasants and distinguished aristocrats joined forces in the common effort to fight the oppressor."[4]

Like their compatriots in Europe, the Greeks of New York were excited with the possibility of the emancipation of Crete and its unification with the mainland realm. Exhilaration was bursting the seams of the small immigrant community.[5] The Greek newspaper, Atlantis, started a fund-raising campaign to aid the rebels and their families.[6] Most of the Greek immigrants in New York were "ready to contribute every cent of their savings and their lives," wrote the New-York Dailv Tribune.The newspaper quoted Solon J. Vlasto, who said that "if there be war with Turkey, it will be carried into Macedonia and Asia Minor. Every Greek in the world, wherever he be, stands ready to help."[7]

The sentiments of the majority of the New York press were with the Greek cause of liberation for compatriots in the Ottoman Empire. The only leading newspaper that attempted to maintain impartiality and neutrality in editorial policy concerning the Greek-Turkish conflict was The New York Times.[8] The editors of The World stated that the "Greek occupation of Crete is in no proper sense an invasion. It is rather the action of Greeks going to the assistance of kinsmen struggling to free themselves from the grossest oppression."[9] Another newspaper, the New-York Dailv Tribune, showed sincere sympathy for the Greek cause and emphatically registered its approval of the resolution passed by the United States Senate, which expressed its encouragement of the cause of national liberation.[10] In reviewing the situation in an editorial, "Crete, Greece and the Eastern Question," the editors of The Sun believed that the military action was the "practical triumph of the Cretan insurgents." They added that the problem of the Eastern Question "may at least be solved by the Christian subject population themselves."[11]

Greek intervention in Crete was also supported by the New York Herald. The editors wrote, "So far Greece has held the sympathy of the great world simply because of the splendid boldness of her adventure." The newspaper sharply criticized the great powers for their economic rivalries in the Near East.[12] The Brooklyn Daily Eagle expressed its support of the nationalist movement in Crete and Greece. It felt, however, that energetic diplomatic efforts should have been more fruitful in preventing bloodshed between Greeks and Turks.[13]

With the outbreak of hostilities and Greece's military intervention in Crete, the Greek foreign minister, Alexander G. Skouze, instructed Demetrius Botassi to call up all the Greek army reservists in the United States. The Greek consul-general stated that the situation was precarious and that he was even "instructed to call out the reserves that belong to the class as far back as 1866." Botassi reported, "poor fellows, they are only ready to go if they can afford the journey. The government has no appropriations for the transportation of reserves."[14]

The summoning of the Greek reservists met with positive results. A New York newspaper indicated that it was "likely to be largely obeyed." The newspaper reported that several men, Antony C. Demtovich, 246 West 26th Street, and R.S. Tharin, residing at 256 West 20th Street, were recruiting a regiment to send to Greece. Tharin claimed to have enlisted some 400 volunteers.[15]

The New York Greeks rallied to their leaders for guidance in the hour of national crisis. Solon J. Vlasto announced in the Atlantis a great rally for the support of Cretans and the Great Idea to be held on March 5, 1897. The Greek newspaper published letters from prominent New Yorkers supporting the cause of the Christian insurgents. In a letter, dated February 22, 1897, the Reverend Charles H. Parkhurst wrote Vlasto that "Europe supports Turkey" but that Americans had sympathy for Greece's cause. J.E. Hedges, personal secretary to New York City's Mayor Strong, wrote in a letter of February 23, 1897 that Strong would be unable to attend the rally but that the mayor supported its aims.[16]

A proclamation of undivided support for the Greek national cause was drafted by a committee of New York Greeks on February 23. The statement strongly reiterated the unanimous support expressed by the Greeks in the United States and their willingness to aid Greece in any manner in its struggle against Turkey. An official of the meeting, Alexander Evangelides, sent copies of the proclamation to the Ethnike Hetaireia and the several political parties of Greece.[17]

This meeting, held on March 10, at Webster Hall, reflected differences of opinion on the issue between the supports of S.J. Vlasto, publisher of the Atlantis, and the elite merchant elements of the New York Greek community who supported the consulgeneral, Demetrius Botassi. The Webster Hall meeting was managed by Vlasto's friends, Constantine Bouras, George Bouras, Alcibiades Serahis, Socrates Xanthakes, editor of the Atlantis, and S. Antoniades, a wealthy Greek merchant from Egypt.[18] The Times described the meeting, saying that a group of "about 750 men with swarthy skins, gleaming teeth and eyes that glowed like live coals, crowded the hall to the doors."[19] About 500 persons were present.

A major issue of the meeting was the question of who would pay for transporting the reservists to Greece. The assemblage condemned Botassi for his unwillingness to support this, and accused him of opposing the return of the Army reservists. They claimed that he was unworthy of representing the national interest in the United States. He was condemned also for failing to publish the names of the persons who had contributed funds for the national cause. Thirty hecklers, shouting in unison, "Consul-General Hireling," had to be expelled by the police.[20] On this matter, the Reverend A. Papageorgopoulos, rector of the Holy Trinity Church, issued a statement that up to March 10 some $1,616.26 had been received, of which $1,000 had been directly sent to King George I.[21]

The meeting adopted a resolution condemning Botassi for alleged neglect of duties. Cables were sent to King George and Premier Deliyiannis. It was announced at the meeting that S.J. Vlasto had contacted the Papayiannis Steamship Company in London for a vessel to transport the reservists and volunteers to Greece.[22]

The most exciting scene "came at the end of the meeting," when P. Furieos mounted the platform and "began an excited harangue in defense of Mr. Botassi." George Maro, another participant, was also speaking in another part of the hall. "Both men were pulled down and hustled out. . . . They waited in the street for Vlasto to leave the meeting. Finally, Vlasto appeared surrounded by his friends, "and no violence was attempted." A considerable amount of "rough words were exchanged, but no blows were struck."[23]

Reactions to the meeting were published by The Evening Post. Demetrius Botassi claimed to have said that the money collected by the immigrants would be spent on refugee relief and not on transportation of volunteers. Botassi had refused to print the information on the donations in the Atlantis because "the little sheet is so scurrilous" that he did not desire to deal with it.[24] The meeting was regarded as a trick by the Greek official.[25] Reverend Papageorgopoulos claimed that Vlasto was spiteful because he "was not recognized in business dealings, politics, or society by the Consul and other respectable Greeks." The clergyman added that the audience was made up mainly of "peddlers and ignorant Greeks" who were not aware of the ramifications of the diplomatic and economic aspects of the crisis.[26] On March 12 the Atlantis published the Webster Hall resolution condemning Botassi.[27]

Demetrius Botassi regarded the acrimonious criticisms leveled at him at the Webster Hall meeting as smear attacks by vindictive and uninformed persons. It was reported in the New York press that the attacks on the consular official were "engineered by Solon J. Vlasto, a sworn enemy" of the Greek official whom he had been condemning in the Atlantis. It was implied that "Vlasto profited from the dissatisfaction which [was] felt among some of the Greeks here at the Consul's refusal to pay for the transportation" of reservists to Greece. The official stated that there were no funds available for these expenses.[28] Vlasto, however, denied all charges made about him by Botassi. He denied any connection with the Webster Hall meeting. The publisher also indicated that he would seek legal redress from the consular official.[29] He nevertheless countered with a scathing attack on the Greek consul-general in the form of a letter sent to the editor of the Evening Post.[30]

Demetrius Botassi called another mass meeting to counteract the effects of the Webster Hall gathering. The new rally was to be presided over by Seth Low. In addition, Abraham S. Hewitt,

Theodore Roosevelt and other important New Yorkers were expected to speak on behalf of the Greek national cause.[31] The war relief committee included the following members: Reverend A. Papageorgopoulos; Demetrius Botassi; Charles E. Sprague, President, Union Dime Savings Bank; Mrs. Paul S. Galatti, Mrs. T. P. Ralli, Mrs. Anthony Ralli, Mrs. Pandia Ralli and Mrs. Thomas Zizinia, wives of the wealthy Greek cotton merchants of the New York Cotton Exchange.[32]

The supporters of Botassi and the Royal Government met at Chickering Hall on March 12, 1897 as a counter-demonstration to the previous rally, which attacked the political establishment of Greece and, indirectly, the leadership elite of the Greek community in New York. The backers of Vlasto were not present at this meeting, and according to the New York Sun Botassi "gained a distinct triumph over his enemies."[33] The interpreter of the rally was the well known educator from Perkins Institute, Michael Anagnos. "Enthusiasm ran high at the meeting of sympathizers with Crete held under the auspices of Consul-General Botassi and Seth Low."[34]

It was reported that the purpose of the meeting was:[35]

to call the attention of the American People to the condition of the Cretan refugee . . . America should say to Greece: You have our sympathy, our applause, our prayers.

Seth Low, presiding officer of the meeting, declared that James T. Woodward, president of the Hanovver National bank, had agreed to become the treasurer of the Cretan Relief Fund. The secretary of the gathering read a list of the vice presidents: Mayor Strong, Theodore Roosevelt, Abraham S. Hewitt, former mayor, Charles A. Dana, William C. Whitney, George J. Gould, Alexander E. Orr, William E. Dodge, General di Cisnola and J. Pierpont Morgan.[36] Letters from prominent American leaders, including Elihu Root, were read from the platform commending the Greeks' stand on Crete.

Anagnos was reported by the press to have sharply criticized Vlasto for indulging in criticism of the Greek consular official and attempting to create a divsion among the Greeks of New York.[37] Seth Low called for more energy in raising funds for the Cretan refugees. According to the Tribune "More than a thousand cheered wildly at every mention of Mr. Botassi's name.[38]

With the impending war with Turkey, the Greek government

had called up the reservists.[39] Many New York immigrants eagerly sought to enlist in their armed forces. They were willing to pay their own fares to Greece. In mid-March, ten members of the Greek Army reserve sailed on the S.S. Gascogne of the French Line to enlist in the army. D.J. Botassi secured reduced rates for the men in steerage. He also had the promise of the same rates for any future parties of Greeks sailing for Le Havre. Thus, in a somewhat unusual procedure, the reservists paid their own transportation to fight for the fatherland.[40] The Atlantis stressed the moral obligations of the immigrants to assist their fatherland and to help liberate their fellow Christian brothers from Turkish rule.[41] Another small contingent of Greeks left on the S.S. La Champagne of the French Line for Europe. The group marched in the evening of March 26 from 23 Roosevelt Street to the piers. The men came from various cities in the South and West. The majority used up all their savings to make the trip.[42] "The Greek quarter, in and about Roosevelt Street was a scene of great activity. . . . About 150 Greeks were to start for their native land to aid their struggling fellow countrymen. . . ."

The group received a benediction and a prayer offered by Reverend A. Papageorgopoulos at the Parthenon Restaurant, 23 Roosevelt Street. A prominent Greek immigrant, James Paterson, and C.D. Phassoularides made addresses. A procession was formed, consisting of about 500 men, which escorted the contingent. Some carried their own arms and were under the nominal leadership of Peter Socrates, The group included a detachment of twenty Greeks from Philadelphia headed by Michael Lombert.[43]

Early in April, a group of 50 Greeks departed on the S.S. La Touraine of the French Line. The group left from 25 Roosevelt Street. One of the spectators became so enthusiastic that he wanted to return to Greece. He boarded and hid aboard the vessel. The unhappy man was found by the crew and sent off the ship. John D. Farmakis, a confectioner, who "already paid the passage for some 25 of the returning Greeks, bought a ticket for his bewailing countryman."[44] It was reported that there were seventeen stowaways on the S.S. La Touraine, of which six were "found and dragged ashore."[45] Another incident was reported by the press to have started just as the gangplank was about to be pulled off the ship. A Greek immigrant who was "to have sailed was hurriedly saying his farewells to his friends and colleagues on the pier and was holding his ticket in his hand. Another Greek, a stranger to him, "saw his opportunity for enlisting under King George's banner, grabbed the carelessly held ticket and rushed up the already moving gangplank." The stranger sailed with the belongings of the rightful owner of the steamship ticket, while the latter was left behind looking at the departing vessel heading towards the Narrows. According to the Daily Tribune, these incidents revealed the "great desire of Greeks in this country to get back to their fatherland to fight against the Turks."[46]

The reports of the activities of the New York Greeks had been widely circulated and many immigrants from southern and western states flocked to the city expecting financial assistance for their return trip.[47] The minimum steerage rate of the French Line was $31.85 from New York to Piraeus. The special steamer proposition did not meet favor with the New Yorkers because they were able to get better terms on other lines. The Fabre Line offered transportation to Naples. The firm of C.B. Richards & Co., representing the Atlantic Transportation Company, offered $27 per person. It was announced, however, that the Greeks who had sufficient funds preferred to pay the extra $4.00 in fare and take faster boats and "reach the scene of action more quickly."[48]

Another contingent of about 450 Greek volunteers left New York in late April on the S.S. La Champagne. Following the established precedence, reservists marched from the Parthenon Restaurant, 23 Roosevelt Street, to the piers. There were about 250 Greeks from New York and about 150 from Chicago.[49] Another group of Greek reservists departed a week later on the S.S. Paris of the American Line.[50] More volunteers left New York on the S.S. Gascogne on May 1. The group congregated at the Parthenon Restaurant on Roosevelt Street at 8:00 A.M. and marched in procession to the vessel and all along "the route the little army was generally cheered."[51]

In a feature article, The New York Times wrote about the nationalist preoccupation of a New York Greek immigrant named Demetrius. People called him "Jack" for short in the restaurant. The immigrant conducted "a flower stand at a busy corner in upper Broadway. His wife [attended] to the flower business . . . , and Jack [devoted] himself to the cause of Greek freedom." The article claimed that the Greek was a "handsome fellow, and [was] arrayed in the white skirt and blouse of his native land, instead of the habiliments of Baxter Street." It also stated that Jack would make just the "kind of Greek that cultivated people like to read about."[52]

It added that "in an instant Jack was on a chair with a copy of the Atlantis. . . ." The New York newspaper claimed that the alleged telegrams which appeared on the front page of the Greek newspaper "were nothing but translations of New York newspapers."[53] "A philosopher among their number," continued the feature article, who had "disregarded his pushcart for two days," decided to return to work and encouraged others to follow his example.

In referring to the activities of the National Society it was emphasized that its agents collected funds in New York and received cables for the acquisition of dynamite cartridges for the Greek Army:[54]

The Greek nationalist organization works with the utmost secrecy. The Irish nationalists, in their palmiest days, did not succeed better in concealing from the right hand what the left hand was doing. The fact that the headquarters of the organization is at Alexandria, Egypt assists them. . . . No one knows exactly how much money this power organization has behind it. But the fact that George Gouses, president of the Anglo-Egyptian Bank, has been able to pay out $4,000,000 in two or three months without crippling the resources of the organization gives a fair idea of its strength. Agents . . . have for years been collecting money from Greeks all over the world. . . . The Greeks have implicit confidence in the men that compose it. . . .

The Ethnike Hetaireia was influential in the councils of the immigrants. It was the most respected organization because it supported the national goals with adequate funds and widespread propaganda.

On April 21, 1897 another mass rally was held at Webster Hall.[55] The gathering met to discuss its common efforts to assist the national fund-raising campaign. An unidentified person in the rear of the hall shouted:[56]

There is not $100 in the whole crowd. Why do not the rich Greeks of New York raise the money to send us home.

Reverend Papageorgopoulos reprimanded the disruptive elements for disturbing the meeting. He stated that if they had to quarrel and fight among themselves then they should return to Greece where all able-bodied men were needed to fight the enemy. "We are too poor to go home," shouted back the obstructionists.

"Call upon the rich. Why should we ask Americans for help when the rich Greeks will not aid us."[57] These references to the "rich Greeks of New York" were allusions to the wealthy patrician cotton merchants of New York. It was at this point when the audience was emotionally tense that Charalambos Monkakos walked to the chairman's table and put down his $5.00 bill, stating in a loud voice:[58]

Money talks. This is the last five dollars I have and there it goes to help Greece. How many more are there here to do this same thing?

A relative, Petros Monkakos, walked up the aisle and followed suit by placing another bill on the table. Three more provincial immigrants followed and placed money on the table. The gathered audience was stunned and rose up in an uproar. In a short period of time a sum of $100 was placed in the hands of the Reverend A. Papageorgopoulos. The persons who came to disrupt the meeting left the hall quickly. "The men who came to scoff didn't come to pray [sic] ."[59]

At the meeting a wealthy Cretan entrepreneur, Nicholas J. Coundouris, announced that he was offered from Philadelphia interests a vessel that would be chartered to the returning 1,000 Greek reservists, providing that 500 immigrants would pledge $20 each or in any other manner raise the $10,000 chartering charges. The announcement thrilled the audience and scores rushed to pledge some money for the venture.

In the audience, however, there was some scepticism over the proposal. "Sell your pushcarts," somebody shouted,". . . You cannot accomplish anything in a movement like this without some sacrifice." The immigrants remained until after midnight accepting funds in minor sums. A motion was carried by the group expressing their sincerest gratitude to the genuine interest and sympathy manifested by most New York newspapers.[60]

Most New York Greeks were thoroughly preoccupied with the prosecution of the war in Europe. They believed every Greek, rich or poor, powerful or weak, should support the fatherland in the national struggle against Turkish hegemony. They resented Greek immigrants who left their country in time of national peril and sacrifice. Three immigrants arrived on the S.S. Obdam in April. One of the group, a returning immigrant, immediately departed for Chicago. Unfortunately, the other two immigrants met a bitter reception in New York. On leaving the ship, they were taken with their belongings to No. 7 Chatham Square. There they met their infuriated compatriots and were "treated to a liberal fusillade of fruits and vegetables." The reception was so lively and emotional that the "two erring ones" were anxious to seek another location. The unhappy newcomers sought refuge at the headquarters of the Greek community, 23 Rooseveelt Street. Once again the two unworthy ones became the protagonists of another comic tragedy. They again felt the "practical expression of ill-feeling in the form of fruits and vegetables." Alone in a foreign land, denounced by their compatriots as traitors and cowards, the two frightened immigrants rapidly retreated. They finally found sanctuary and solace at Ellis Island.[61]

Not only was the majority of the New York press sympathetic with the Greek cause of Cretan emancipation, but a considerable number of prominent Protestant clergymen and laymen were also active in voicing their sentiments and contributed time and money in defending Christian Hellenism. Implicit in these actions is the New York community's sympathetic feelings toward the Greek immigrants in New York City. A survey of the New York press in the last decade of the nineteenth century shows a strong element of compassion and friendship toward the Greek newcomers. There was very little apparent hostility toward the Greeks in the 1890s. The Episcopal Church always extended its hand in a sincere manner of brotherhood. The native-born population of the city did not regard the small immigrant society as a threat to the social structure of nineteenth-century America. There were very few adverse letters to the editors, editorial comments and protests against the New York Greeks.

The Greek national cause and New York Greeks were so respected that, on April 24, 1897, the New York State Legislature passed a resolution by "unanimous consent" expressing its support:[62]

Resolved. That the legislature of the State of New York hereby expresses its sympathy with the Christian Greeks in its efforts to resist the oppression of Moslem hordes, and hereby calls upon the United States to lend its friendly interference in behalf of the Greek Nation.

An incident that occurred in a local gunsmith's shop was reported in the press. Three Greeks went shopping at Robert's Gunstore at West 23rd Street. "We're from Boston," they explained to the salesman, "and we are going back on the La Champagne tomorrow to fight the Turks." As one of the Greeks was preparing to pay for the weapons, a well-groomed middle-aged lady stepped forward. "On your way to Greece, are you?" The three young men answered that they were returning to fight. "I am interested in your country . . . ," she continued, "I've read much in the World about your country and its brave men. I want to help. I am going to pay for your arms." The benefactress was Mrs. Robert Hoe, wife of a manufacturer of printing presses.[63] In addition, Mrs. Hoe emphasized that the weapons "would be used in a noble cause."[64]

There was a widespread appeal for Greece by the Protestant clergy of New York. The ministers were asked to read a message from a group of women's societies. The communication was signed by Frances Willard, Women's Christian Temperance Union; Mrs. Donald McLean, State Regent, Daughter of the American Revolution; Mrs. Mary Towne Burt, President of the New York State Chapter, W.C.T.U.; Mrs. F. Schwedler Barnes, Chairman, Mothers' Congress of the State of New York; Countess di Brazzi, Italian Red Cross and Mrs. Spencer Trask.[65] Reverend John D. Peters made a strong appeal for justice for Greece on Sunday, April 25, 1897, at St. Michael's Protestant Episcopal Church, Amsterdam Avenue and 99th Street. The rector stated that "God helps the heroic and patriotic little country in the desperately unequal struggle which she is now waging to free from tyranny her enslaved countrymen in Crete, Epirus and Macedonia." The clergyman stressed that as Christians they owed Greece their "sympathy, . . . help and . . . prayers." He added that Americans were compelled to give their aid "to every oppressed nationality seeking to cast off the fetters of slavery."[66]

In another church, Calvary Baptist Church at West 57th Street, Reverend Dr. Robert S. MacArthur talked on "Christian Cretans and Turkish Intolerance." He ended his address with prayers for the Greek Army and closed with the words, "Our sympathies go out with genuine earnestness to the brave and Christian Greeks engaged in a desperate struggle against such tremendous odds."[67] Another distinguished American, Clara Barton, president of the American Red Cross, made a strong appeal for funds to assist the Greek refugees.[68] In a letter to the editor of The New York Times, Alice A. J. Dill emphasized that the United States as a "great free Nation . . ." should "protest in the name of justice, humanity and religion against any part of [Greece and Crete] being ever again subjected to Moslem rule."69 A well-known club of the 1890s, The Thirteen Club, scheduled a dinner on May 13 to "express sympathy with the cause of Greece." The club invited a group of "Greek patriots" to attend as special guests for the evening.70

An outgrowth of the March 12 Chickering Hall meeting in support of Botassi was the formation of a Cretan Relief Fund Committee.71 The organizers were Reverend Papageorgopoulos and Demetrius Botassi. The wives of the leading Greek cotton merchants were active on this committee. The committee elected Mrs. P. Y. Fachiri as president and Mrs. T. P. Ralli as vice president. The donations were to be deposited in a special account with the Knickerbocker Trust Co.72 The funds were to aid the wounded troops and homeless refugees.73 Protestant clergymen, the Reverend Dr. H. Newton and the Reverend Dr. Henry Van Dyke, collected donations from their parish of the Brick Church on Fifth Avenue.74 Mrs. Theodore Ralli informed the New York press that a socially prominent woman of New York contributed $1,000 as a donation for Cretan relief. The woman who wanted to be anonymous, said Mrs. Ralli, was a very modest person who belonged to the upper echelons of New York society. The donor, added Mrs. Ralli, was a thorough American. Her husband [was] also prominent and wealthy."75 A considerable amount of money was sent to Greece by the Cretan Relief Fund.76

In an editorial, the New-York Daily Tribune encouraged Americans to contribute to the Cretan Relief Fund.77 The members of the New York Chamber of Commerce collected $3,000 for the Cretan Relief Fund.78 Moreover, Mrs. Theodore Ralli reported that she had received $1,935 in the past several days. Among the contributors were the firm of Brooks Brothers, which donated $50; B. Altman & Co., $10; and a "reader of the Tribune," who gave $100.79 In May, Frances E Willard, president of the Women's Christian Temperance Union, announced that she had received from Crown Princess Sophie, Duchess of Sparta, an expression of the sincerest gratitude to the American people for their generosity and sympathy.80 Attesting to the magnitude of the Greek relief problem, George Horton, United States Consul in Athens, reported that as a result of the Turkish occupation of Thessaly more than 100,000 Greek refugees were scattered throughout Greece.81

Solon J. Vlasto was instrumental in organizing another committee, American National Fund in Aid of the Greek Red Cross. The publisher was the general secretary. A Greek section was formed by the American Red Cross local chapters at a meeting held on April 25, 1897 at the Waldorf Hotel. Mrs. Donald McLean was named president and Miss Frances Willard as first vice-president. The American Ladies Committee included Countess Cora di Brazzi, Mrs. Ogden Dremus and Mrs. Clarence Postley.[82] The Men's Advisory Committee included Roswell P. Flower, Frederic R. Coudert, Henry E. Howland, Asbel P. Fitch and Robert Maclay.[83] The Reverend Dr. Henry E. Cobb, West End Collegiate Church, contributed funds to the American National Fund.[84] In May, Countess Cora di Brazzi was elected as the president of the American National Fund to Aid the Greek Red Cross. Vlasto continued as general secretary.[85]

With Greece facing a complete military disaster at the hands of the German-trained Turkish Army in Thessaly, the New York Greeks prayed for a miraculous victory or compassionate armistice.[86] In a front-page editorial, entitled "National Calamity," the Atlantis published a scathing attack on the Greek royal family and the inept political leadership of Greece. The editors of the Atlantis blamed both the dynasty and the politicians for the military and political debacles that Greece suffered. It was outspoken in its denunciation and intimated that the end of the Glucksburg dynasty was near.[87] The majority of the Greek population in New York held Crown Prince Constantine, Duke of Sparta, responsible for the military difficulties. The royal family was in complete disfavor.[88]

The New York Greeks, however, held out for a possible victory and many were reported ready to return to fight. S.J. Vlasto was ostensibly optimistic about the possible outcome of the conflict. At another meeting at Webster Hall, in mid-April, it was reported that some 400 to 600 immigrants were ready to return to Greece.[89]

On April 30, 1897, in another front-page editorial entitled, "And a Traitor," the Atlantis published one of the strongest attacks on King George I and the royal family. The editorial alluded to the king's position in the crisis.[90] The New York press reported that the rage of the Greek people was chiefly directed against the royal family.[91] Vlasto was reported to have said that "Republican sentiment is very strong in Greece and I confidently expect that the end of the dynasty has come."[92] The New-York Daily Tribune praised the valor of the Greek soldiers but condemned the politicians, senior officers, General Staff and the Royal Court circle "who through ignorance, cowardice or treason presented the troops from winning victories which were actually within their grasp and turned triumph into almost hopeless defeat." "Victory was in reach," the editors wrote, "and it was deliberately sacrificed . . . intentionally or by ineptitude?"[93]

As the spokesman of the anti-royalist sentiment in the Western Hemisphere, the Atlantis continued to launch bitter attacks against the Glucksburg dynasty.[94] A year earlier the newspaper had condemned King George I as an indifferent monarch who was preoccupied with his own personal self-aggrandizement. In an editorial entitled, "Royal Activity," the newspaper claimed that the royal sovereign was more interested in grain futures speculation on the Chicago Board of Trade than in national liberation. The price of wheat was more important than the sufferings of the Greeks. The Atlantis editorial commented: "For the nation, for Crete, for Macedonia, for the inner feelings of the Greek yearning, for the army, for the navy, nothing is provided . . . the answer is, 'how is the market?' . . . the price of wheat. . . ?"[95]

After the military disaster the newspaper represented the king and his family as obstacles to the national ideals of the Great Idea. The royal family was represented as a tool of the Concert of Europe. According to the Atlantis, the only solution to the problems of the Greek question was the elevation of Demetrius Ralli as the prime minister of the Greek state. The young leader was regarded by the Atlantis as the potential savior of the nation.[96] The rise of Demetrius Ralli to power, after the Greek military defeat, was welcomed by Vlasto, since he had been a schoolmate of the new political leader. This Ralli was not related to the prominent merchant family of that name in New York.

The Greek-Turkish War of 1897 underscored the importance of the Great Idea on the daily lives of the Greek immigrants in New York. They volunteered for the armed forces and paid for their own return passsage to Greece. They contributed some of their meager savings to the nationalist cause of liberation. They did it again in 1912, 1913, 1916 and 1920 to 1921. They fought in the Balkan and World Wars. The New York Greeks had a very strong identity with the Greek nation and its aspirations.[97]

In the reaction in New York to Greek policy, the events of 1897 also showed the tensions within the Greek community in New York City. The wealthy, educated and prominent Greeks favored the cautious policies of the Glucksburg dynasty and the Greek government. The young, provincial immigrants, with nothing to risk except their lives and faith, favored the more aggressive policies of the National Society and the militant elements of the nationalist movement. All classes, however, were devoted to the basic dogma of the Great Idea. The various social groups differed with each other only on tactics of the nationalist movement.

8

Fraternal Associations

The first Greek immigrant fraternities were organized for specific community purposes and mutual assistance. Some were inclusive associations that included Greeks from all walks of life, such as the Brotherhood of Athena, church affiliated groups and the Panhellenic Union. There were also exclusive regional brotherhoods, *Topika Somaeia*, which included only members from a specific village, township, pro~ince or region, such as the Macedonian Society of Alexander the Great, Epirus Society, Pan-Cretan Society of Phoenix, Lacedaemonian Society and the Naupactian Brotherhood. The latter type also included occupational societies, such as the Retail Florists' Association, Coney Island Brotherhood and the Confectioners' Society.

The purposes of these immigrant fraternities were to (1) promote and protect Greek national interests, (2) ensure the economic and health needs of the immigrants, (3) provide social, philanthropic and recreational activities, (4) reinforce regionalism, by aiding local communities in their native land and (5) support religious activities, by organizing and supporting immigrant churches.

Most immigrant fraternities supported all these purposes. The differences were only in the degree of assistance. The regional societies, *Topika Somateia*, served all the principal purposes but with a greater emphasis on the regional activities. The national, occupational and church affiliated associations supported all the objectives except those that stressed a narrow regionalism. In the instance of the latter, aid was rendered whenever any specific region, province or township suffered from the calamities of nature, such as earthquakes and floods. The organizations also assisted in the construction of churches and schools in a particular village or town.

The first important association, the Brotherhood of Athena, was founded in 1891 on the recommendation of Prince George of Greece during his brief sojourn in New York. The young prince suggested to the immigrant leaders that the creation of an inclusive fraternal organization would greatly benefit the Greeks in New York.[1] This mutual benefit association lasted until the late 1890s. Solon J. Vlasto was the president of the group during its brief but influential existence. The maximum membership numbered about 450 immigrants, of whom the majority resided in the Greater New York area, including Brooklyn, Long Island and urbanized New Jersey. The wealthy merchants, such as Ralli, Negreponte, Fachiri and others, were not members of this association. The Brotherhood of Athena was primarily an organization sponsored by the newer and poorer immigrants.

The principal aims of the fraternity were religious, social and philanthropic. The establishment of a Greek church was one of its paramount goals. Adjustment of the newcomers to the emerging American urban society was an important objective of both the Brotherhood of Athena and of Solon J. Vlasto. The brotherhood constructed a temporary bridge, which enabled the immigrants to cross over into a new society, while at the same time conserving the ideals and traditions of Christian Hellenism.[2]

The principal officers during the association's life were Vlasto, George Giatras, John Poulides, John Samaras, Apostolos Rigas, Peter Minekakes and Menelaus Constantinides. The association's leaders represented the more successful entrepreneurs of the provincial immigrants. With the exception of Vlasto, the majority were identified with the restaurant, hotel, florist, confectionery and cigarette manufacturing business.[3] The fraternity met at various locations throughout the lower Manhattan area. One of the more popular meeting places was Cosmopolitan Hall, 11-15 East Broadway on the corner of Catherine Street, in the center of the Greek district.[4] The meetings provided the immigrants with the opportunity to discuss their problems, learn about American life and meet their friends and compatriots. For the recreation of its members and friends, the fraternal society sponsored picnics at Glendale Park in Long Island.[5]

The *Atlantis*, Vlasto's creation, implemented the work of the brotherhood. The pages of the *Atlantis* served as a medium for the solicitation of funds and new members. Notices regarding meetings were published in the newspaper. A highly active member and treasurer of the society, John Poulides, used the *Atlantis* as a dues-collection medium. Frequent requests for fees and dues from the membership appeared in the newspaper. The offices of *Atlantis* at 2 and 4 Stone Street and Poulides' cigarette business establishment at 84 Beaver Street served as the unofficial headquarters of the fraternal association.[6]

In its philanthropic mission, the Brotherhood aided its sick and needy brethren. The sick were sent to French Hospital in Chelsea. The institution served the early immigrants and residents. The *Atlantis* reported that at least 36 Greek immigrants were treated at French Hospital between November 1, 1894 and May 1, 1895.[7] The hospital director, Dr. Josef Thoron, had strong bonds with the Greek community. He was born in Crete of a French father and a Greek mother. A staunch philhellene, he assisted the early Greek-American physicians, such as Eugenios Caravias, Alexios Alexiou and Abraham Sekouris, in establishing their practices in New York. These medical practitioners served on the staff of French Hospital for many years and they cooperated with the several immigrant fraternal associations in meeting the needs of the Greeks in New York.[8]

At the turn of the century, another organization, *Ta Patria*, was formed in Greece to protect the national interests and social institutions of the Greeks, in the kingdom and overseas. The new organization had ambitious plans in spreading its influence among the immigrants in the United States. The association, however, was never able to establish itself in New York. The *Atlantis* believed that the society would fail because it did not understand the basic causes of the threat to Christian Hellenism, especially in the United States. There was an implicit inference that the organization, *Ta Patria*, might face competition from the *Atlantis* if it attempted to establish itself in America. The editors reiterated Vlasto's view that political incompetence was the reason for Greece's difficulties.[9]

During the late nineteenth century, xenomania in general and Francomania in particular, became an obsession of the wealthy and educated classes in Greece. French instead of Greek was spoken in the homes of many wealthy Greeks. The adoption of French words, expressions and manners became widespread and gradually filtered down to the lower classes.[10] The Great Idea and xenomania became rival forces, competing for the loyalty of the Greeks in Europe. The Great Idea accepted the worthiness of the national heritage and the Greek Orthodox Church, while xenomania rejected them as backward and provincial. Many of the educated classes preferred to emulate the fashion of the Paris salons with their tradition of materialism, secularism, agnosticism, and eventually, atheism.

On the other hand, the Greek provincial immigrants from Greece and Asia Minor were very proud of their humble rural origins. They were devoted to the cause of the Great Idea.

Therefore, all the Greek fraternal associations in New York were nationalist, religious and traditionalist. The New York immigrants and their several societies rejected xenomania as an anti-Greek attitude.[11]

An overseas-based organization, such as *Ta Patria*, did not assume any real leadership role in New York or the United States. In fact, very little reference is ever made to it today by any of the writers, historians and commentators. Actually, such organizations did not understand the fundamental problems of the rural immigrants in an emerging industrial society. Actually, they were interested in serving the national interests of the Greek nation in Europe, if not the state itself.

In the early years of the twentieth century, the national movement among the New York Greeks was not as well organized as it was during the period of the Greek-Turkish War of 1897. Moreover, the interests of the Greek immigrants were not protected by any large national organizations as were the Germans, Irish, Scandinavian, Italian and Polish newcomers. The principal medium for the dissemination of the Greek nationalist ideology and the leading spokesman for the Greek immigrants was the *Atlantis*. The newspaper continued its regular departments, "Enslaved Greece," "The Defense of Hellenism in Macedonia," and "Letters from Constantinople." Its book department not only sold Greek translations of the works of William Shakespeare, Alexander Dumas and Jules Verne, but also Bibles, religious texts and inexpensive books and pamphlets on Greek folklore and patriotic themes.[12] In this manner the immigrant was made aware of the continuous nationalist struggle.

As Prince George of Greece left the germ of creating a local fraternal society in New York, the Brotherhood of Athena, in 1891, so did the Boston educator of the blind and deaf, Michael Anagnos, plant the seeds for a large nationwide association to represent the interests of the Greek immigrants and the overseas nationalist movement in America. In 1903 Anagnos discussed his plan with his Boston compatriots. The result was the formation of the National Union in that city. Anagnos died, however, in 1906, before the final plans could materialize for a national organization. The impulse toward organizing such an association was also motivated by the founding of the Panhellenic Federation of Egypt in 1906.

The influence of the two organizations drove many Greek immigrants to seek the organization of a national association of Greek immigrants in the United States. Finally, in a three-day conference, October 16–18, 1907, held in the basement hall of the Holy Trinity Church at 152 1/2 East 72nd Street, a new immigrant fraternal association was established, the Panhellenic Union.[13] The Panhellenic Union's objectives were to make the immigrant into a worthy American citizen, adjust the newcomer to a new environment in an industrialized and urban America and, finally, support the aims of the Greek national movement.[14] The new group was also to counteract the propaganda activities of the Bulgarians, Serbs, Russians and Young Turks.[15] The five specific objectives of the Panhellenic Union were clearly stated in its constitution of 1910:[16]

(1) To cultivate among its members and through them among all Greeks residing in the United States and Canada the spirit of mutual aid and of love of nationality.
(2) To instill veneration and affection for the laws and institutions of their adopted country and the cultivation of friendly relations between the Greeks and American citizens.
(3) To teach the English and Greek languages, to preserve the Greek Orthodox religion and to develop and propagate moral tenets among the Greek compatriots residing in the United States and Canada.
(4) To procure pecuniary and other aid for the members of the Union and those dependent upon them, and, as far as its means will permit, to extend its protection to the Greek immigrants and workers.
(5) To secure the moral and material assistance of the Union toward the great needs of the Nation.

The initiation membership fee was $1.00. In addition, the monthly dues for each member was also $1.00. The union's charter included general welfare provisions for the assistance of needy members. Funds were authorized in the amounts of $5.00 per week for a total of three weeks to all needy or unemployed members of the Panhellenic Union. Hospitalized members, without means of support, were entitled to receive $10.00 for a period of ten weeks.[17] Death benefits were issued to dependents based on the years of membership in the Union: 1 year, $50; 2 years, $100; 4 years, $125; 6 years, $150; 8 years, $175 and 10 or more years, $200. Furthermore, provisions were made for the organization of social centers for Greek workers and immigrants.[18]

The national headquarters of the new association was established in Boston in honor of the initial activities of the late Michael Anagnos. Nevertheless, the New York chapter known as New York District No. 2 was the most important group in the United States. In 1907, the officers of the New York District No. 2 were Pandia Ralli, president (a member of the prominent New York Ralli family); Reverend M. Kourkoules, vice-president; G. Nicholas, general secretary; N. Flotorides, special secretary; N. Galanos, treasurer; John Counes, Dr. K. Nikas and S. Kalamanides, councilors. There was also a Brooklyn chapter of the union.[19]

The Panhellenic Union, the *Atlantis*, the local parishes and the responsible elements of the Greek immigrant community in New York and the United States were deeply troubled over the Greek government's shortsightedness in not providing professional and permanent diplomatic and consular services to protect the interests of the Greek immigrants. All consular posts were honorary. They were filled by leading and wealthy merchants in the several cities, such as Demetrius J. Botassi in New York, John M. Rodocanachi in Boston and Nicholas M. Benachi and A. G. Nicolopoulo in New Orleans. With a quarter of the working force of Greece emigrating to the United States, there was a concerted effort to compel the Greek government to fill its vacant diplomatic post in Washington. Alexander Skouze, Greek foreign minister, informed Vlasto that the Greek government was seriously considering the appointment of an envoy to the United States. He also indicated the assignment of professional consular officials to important American cities.[20] In 1907 the *Atlantis* disclosed that the Greek consul in San Francisco initiated a head tax of $1.00 per month on all Greek workers, especially those employed by the Southern Pacific Railway. It was this arbitrary and independent action by unsupervised consular officials that the *Atlantis* fought; and, therefore, the newspaper favored the appointment of an envoy who would protect the interests of the Greek immigrants.[21]

As a result of this pressure, Lampros Coromilas, a distinguished economist and former consul-general of Salonika was appointed minister plenipotentiary to Washington. After his arrival at the new post, Coromilas visited the important Greek communities in the United States. His preachments on the Great Idea and his concentrated efforts to strengthen the Panhellenic Union gradually polarized the New York Greeks into two rival groups. Misunderstandings, tactlessness and conflict over leadership tactics between Coromilas and Vlasto recreated the tense atmosphere of 1897. A decade earlier it was rivalry between Vlasto and Botassi. In 1908 it was conflict between Vlasto and Coromilas over the administration and purposes of the Panhellenic Union. In reality, the fundamental question was always who was to lead and represent the interests of the Greek immigrants in the New World.

The Panhellenic Union appeared as the most threatening challenger to the hegemony of Vlasto and the *Atlantis*, representing, as it did, the older merchant group. The potential rivalry of the Union was fully realized by the dynamic publisher. The new fraternal association, the *Atlantis* advised, must not only support the Greek national interests but must protect the immigrant from ruthless and unscrupulous exploiters.[22] The newspaper stressed that the Panhellenic Conference in Chicago had to emphasize that the immigrant must be "a good citizen . . . and not an undesirable person in the United States."[23]

In a leading editorial, the *Atlantis* wrote that the Panhellenic Union must serve and "live for all Greeks." The association's motto should be, added the editor, "All for one and one for all." The editorial commented that Pan-Slavism had destroyed the Greeks in Russia. "The Greeks of Romania . . . exist no more; the Greeks of Bulgaria and Eastern Rumelia . . . no longer exist. . . . The only Greeks that the nation can look to with hope are those in America."[24]

In a letter dated November 18, 1908, Vlasto wrote D. Manousopoulos, president of the Panhellenic Union, that the *Atlantis* would always serve Hellenism in America and overseas. Vlasto emphasized that he had the right to speak out against injustice, to tell the truth and to serve the immigrant community.[25]

In the controversy over the policies and purposes of the union, the perennial question of Greek currant exports to the United States was reintroduced by Vlasto. It became the center of a bitter feud between the publisher and the diplomat. The currant exports were always a convenient issue on the basis of which to condemn the Greek government and its officials. It served to strengthen Vlasto's position among many of the immigrants. Just as Vlasto and the *Atlantis* had denounced, more than a decade earlier, the Greek minister, John Gennadius, and the consul-general, Demetrius Botassi, for alleged ineptitude, Vlasto now launched similar attacks on the new envoy, Lampros Coromilas. The *Atlantis* wrote that "it would have been one thousand times better if the Greek legation vacancy in Washington was not filled."[26] In a signed feature article, "The Story of the Promotion of the Currant in America," Vlasto chastized the Greek diplomat for not creating new ideas and initiating effective sales campaigns in the United States.[27]

Moreover, the *Atlantis* attacked Coromilas too severely for carrying out an alleged "ecclesiastical revolution." The envoy was accused of appointing non-canonical clergy and actively supporting the movement for the creation of a Greek diocese in the United States. He was also denounced by the *Atlantis* for allegedly supporting a capitation or head levy tax on Greek immigrants. Tensions were high and partisanship was volatile. Once again the New York immigrant community was divided into factions. Vlasto and the *Atlantis* opposed Coromilas and the leadership of the Panhellenic Union. On the other hand the vestry and considerable portion of the Holy Trinity parish rallied to the support of Coromilas.[28]

In his efforts to save the social and economic structure of Greece, Coromilas favored immigration restriction. He also wanted to prevent the exploitation of the immigrant in New York and the United States. The envoy claimed that many immigrants were living in poverty and lacked the adequate social amenities to maintain a healthy and decent livelihood. The meaning of the diplomat's remarks were exaggerated. Coromilas was portrayed by the *Atlantis* as an insensitive and arrogant aristocrat who was contemptuous of the downtrodden.[29]

The Vlasto-Coromilas feud was quickly brought to a close by a military revolt in Greece in May 1909. One of the results of the military coup was the recall of the Greek envoy to Athens in 1910. He was appointed to the post of Finance Minister in the reformist government of Eleutherios K. Venizelos.[30]

The attacks on Gennadius, Botassi and Coromilas by Vlasto represented challenges to the political, social and economic establishment of the Greek kingdom. Whenever Greek officials and strong fraternal associations attempted to secure effective leadership and control over the immigrants, they became involved in personal bitter conflicts with Vlasto and the *Atlantis*. Vlasto was a complex and ambitious leader. He continuously contested the Greek leadership. His primary objectives were to be the unchallenged leader of the Greek immigrants in the United States. At the same time, he wanted to protect the Greek newcomers in their adopted land. The dynamic publisher was not, however, a staunch supporter of powerful fraternal associations. The Brotherhood of Athena declined because of internal factionalism and personality conflicts among the leadership. The Panhellenic Union gradually declined afer the successful Balkan Wars of 1912 to 1913.

There were, however, other fraternal associations and social organizations in New York to aid the unfortunate and poor immigrants. The Ladies Philoptochos Societies and the parishes of the Holy Trinity and Annunciation churches involved themselves in varied philanthropic activities. In 1908 a gymnastic group was established to widen the athletic and recreational interests of the New York Greeks.[31] In 1911 the *Atlantis*, Retail Florists' Association and the Confectioners' Society raised $31,000 for the establishment of a children's home and school, the Greek-American Institute in the Bronx. The institute was to provide for the education and the care of destitute immigrant children.[32]

The fraternal associations had a very beneficial role in the New York immigrant community. They aided the immigrants to find employment, housing and friends in a strange city. They helped the newcomers to adjust their lives to an emerging urban society. In addition they provided the bonds of national identity and unity and encouraged mutual assistance.

The Immigrant Church

The most prominent and permanent institution of the Greek immigrants was the Greek Orthodox Church. The first Greek-speaking or Hellenic Orthodox Church established in the United States was the parish of the Holy Trinity in New Orleans. A group of wealthy cotton merchants and shippers founded the church in 1865. There was a demand to establish a Greek church in New York in the latter half of the nineteenth century. On his visit to New York in 1891, Prince George of Greece encouraged the handful of Greek immigrants to organize a Greek church. The immigrants wanted the church because it would minister to their religious faith and support their ethnic identity. The primarily male character of the early immigrants, a considerable portion of whom were married with families in Greece and Asia Minor, reduced the demand for priests to perform the Holy Sacraments. As each year passed, however, there was an increasing need for the Greek clergy because of the slow but steady arrival of wives and families from overseas. Finally, the increased number of deaths among the immigrants accelerated the demand for the Greek clergy.[1]

The immigrants were neither ardent joiners nor attenders of churches. They attended the church services whenever they felt the need, especially during Holy Week, Easter, Christmas, Epiphany and the Feast of the Annunciation. The church parishes in New York and the United States were usually much larger than the enrolled membership. The latter represented that section of the laity that was interested in active participation in parish affairs. Therefore, it was not uncommon for a parish with 50 enrolled members to minister to the needs of a community that may have numbered several thousand. The enrolled members had the power to vote for and be elected as parish trustees. Ths problem of Americanization within the church did not occur until the immigrants' children grew to adulthood in the succeeding generations.

One of the major obstacles to the establishment of Greek-speaking Orthodox churches in New York was the existence of state legislation in 1871 that granted Russian diplomatic and consular officials tremendous powers over all Greek Orthodox churches. These included Greeks, Russians, Ukrainians, Georgians, Serbs, Syrians, Roumanians, Bulgars and Montenegrins.[2]

The most important objective of the Brotherhood of Athena was the establishment of a Greek Orthodox Church in New York to minister to the spiritual needs of the Greek immigrants. In addition to the religious aspect, the brotherhood wanted to maintain the immigrants' Greek ethnic identity. Church and nation were indivisible in the Greek tradition.

The Greek-speaking Orthodox Christians from Greece, however, were under the jurisdiction of the Autocephalous Church of Greece; the immigrants from the Ottoman Empire, under the Ecumenical Patriarchate of Constantinople; and the newcomers from Cyprus, under the primacy of the Autocephalous Church of Cyprus. The matter was further complicated by amendments to the Religious Corporation Law of New York in 1895, which stipulated that "a certificate of incorporation of an unincorporated Christian Orthodox Catholic Church of the Eastern confession shall be executed and acknowledged by the envoy extraordinary and minister plenipotentiary, and the consul-general of Russia to the United States." The amendments further added that the "envoy extraordinary and minister plenipotentiary and the consul-general of Russia . . . by virtue of office, be the trustees of every incorporated Christian Orthodox Catholic Church of the Eastern Confession in this state." The revisions of the Religious Corporation Law also granted the trustees of any such church the power to fix and change the salaries of the clergy. In other words, New York state law made these Russian officials very powerful forces in each incorporated Orthodox Christian parish, be it Russian, Ukrainian, Serb, Bulgar, Montenegrin, Syrian or even Greek.[3]

These laws retarded the organization of the Greek church. The New York Greeks did not incorporate their parishes as Greek Orthodox churches in the state until after the Russian Revolution of 1917. Instead, the two Greek parishes, Holy Trinity and Annunciation, were incorporated as independent religious communities as permitted by the Religious Corporation Law of New York. The Greek parishes' certificates of incorporation clearly indicated that the organizations did not have any hierarchic ties with the historic Orthodox Christian sees of Constantinople, Greece, Cyprus, Moscow or with any other Orthodox ecclesiastical jurisdiction. The absence of any uniform Orthodox Christian hierarchy in the United States, with the exception of the Russian Church, led to numerous difficulties until after World War I when ecclesiastical jurisdiction, among the Orthodox Christians, was defined and organized along the lines of the traditional language communities.

In 1891, under the leadership of Solon J. Vlasto, the Brotherhood of Athena petitioned the Holy Synod of Greece for an ecclesiastical diploma for the creation of a Greek Orthodox parish in New York. The fraternal association also requested a clergyman to minister the Greeks. By the end of the year, the first rector of the new parish of the Holy Trinity arrived, Archimandrite Paisios Pherentinos.[4] The first divine liturgy was celebrated by the new rector in January 1892.[5] The regular religious services were held in a Protestant church on West 53rd Street near Eighth Avenue. The first baptism was held on January 10, 1892, with the christening of Theodore and Lycourgos, children of George Thomas from Chios.[6]

The parish priest of the Holy Trinity Church also acted as an itinerant clergyman performing the several sacramental ceremonies and rites in other communities of the United States, in Coney Island, Brooklyn; Tampa, Florida; Hoboken and Patterson, New Jersey; Philadelphia, Pennsylvania; Boston and Springfield, Massachusetts.[7]

An Episcopal clergyman and philhellene, Reverend Dr. Thomas J. Lacey, described the genesis of a Greek parish as a community. He wrote that "when Greeks settle in a locality they organize a 'community' made up of all the Greeks in the district, with officers, executive committee and financial obligations. Its first care [was] to make provision for religious services."[8] The New York experience of the Greek immigrants supported this generalization as manifested by the establishment of the churches of the Holy Trinity and Annunciation.

The Holy Trinity parish not only served the religious needs of its Greek immigrants but also performed services for non-Greek Orthodox Christians. On June 7, 1892, Carlo Maria Livio Dante Oriola, child of Domenico Oriola, an Italian-Albanian, was baptized in the parish church. The godfather was a physician, Dr. Vicenzo Caputo.[9] On May 21, 1892, Nina Milovitch and Milo Boruontich of Dalmatia were married by the Greek rector.[10] In April of the same year, another Dalmatian couple from the Habsburg Monarchy were married by the Holy Trinity rector.[11]

Although the Greek immigrants married women of their own faith and ethnic origin, there were mixed marriages recorded in the community. John Zepos married an Irish girl, Annette Conklin, in May, 1892; A. N. Giannaros married Mary Dana, a native American, in June 1892; Athanasius Paraschilles married Ann Dower, a German girl, in June 1892; and Paul Negriostin married Louisa Fenwich, a native American, who was an Episcopalian.[12]

On October 8, 1895, the *Atlantis* reported the marriage of Dr. Leonidas D. Kourkoulas with Nolda Herzog, daughter of Dr. Sophia Herzog of Vienna. The newspaper stressed that the bridegroom was a graduate of the medical school of New York University. The wedding was performed at 530 Garden Street.[13] The Holy Trinity Book of Sacraments indicated that the Greek consul-general, Demetrius Botassi, officiated as the best man at many marriages and godfather at numerous baptisms.

An important social event for the Greek parish of the Holy Trinity was the marriage of Demetrius Kallias of Mytilene and Nancy Fish Barnum, widow of the famous circus promoter, P. T. Barnum, on August 8, 1895.[14] Nancy Barnum met Kallias, a very wealthy Greek in the Imperial Ottoman Service, while traveling in Europe. In the law offices of George P. Ingersol, 40 Wall Street, the marriage contract was signed and a civil ceremony was performed by a city alderman. The religious ceremony was held in the Holy Trinity Church, and the nuptial breakfast was served at Delmonico's.[15] A year later the marriage ended in tragedy with the death of Kallias in Constantinople. Bereaved, Mrs. Kallias went into retirement at Iranistan, the late P. T. Barnum's estate in Bridgeport, Connecticut.[16] Mrs. Kallias was a substantial contributor to the parish and its needs. In the exonarthex of the Holy Trinity Cathedral, the name of Mrs. Kallias is inscribed in gold on a marble plaque as the first great benefactor of the parish.

Another important event that aroused the interest of the New York press and the Greek immigrants was the visit of the Very Reverend Dionysios Latas, Bishop of Zante. He was the first Greek bishop to visit New York and the United States. The prelate was invited by various Protestant bishops to attend the Ecclesiastical Congress that convened in Chicago during the International Exposition of 1893.[17]

Bishop Latas was greatly impressed with New York and the United States. He informed the press that "this is indeed a most wonderful country. . . . I have always admired the free institutions and progress of the United States." The Greek prelate preached at the newly-formed Greek Orthodox Church of the Holy Trinity which, "reminded [him] of the little church [he] preached in years ago." *The New York Times* evaluated Bishop Latas as a man with liberal views who initiated reforms within his church and who opposed the persecution of Jews. The bishop supported the ideas of religious toleration and understanding at the ecclesiastical conference in Chicago.[18]

The significance of the bishop's trip to the United States was the further stimulation of cordial relations between the Greek immigrants and the Protestant community in New York. The friendly reception accorded to the Greek prelate by the New York press and the several public officials inspired a sense of pride, recognition and self-respect among the immigrants. It helped to induce affection on the part of the immigrants toward their adopted city, New York. Moreover, it stimulated greater inter-church relations between the Protestant Episcopal and Greek churches.

Need for space caused the removal of the Holy Trinity congregation from West 53rd Street to 77-79 Greenwich Street, where, as was customary, the church leased quarters. In 1899, the rector, Reverend Phiamboli, appealed for funds for restoring and renovating the church edifice at 77-79 Greenwich Street near Rector Street. The editors of the *Atlantis* wrote that the Greek immigrants were "the only group that lacks churches and priests." Vlasto was pressing for more religious facilities and clergy to minister to the needs of the New York Greeks.[19] The pages of the *Atlantis* were also used to inform communicants of the needs, services and activities of the local parish. Reverend Phiamboli called a community conference to discuss the needs of the Greek church in May 1899. All New York Greeks were invited to attend the meeting.[20]

At the turn of the century, the parish was located at 138 East 27th Street. The Holy Trinity Church had a precarious existence between 1899 and 1904 because nine rectors officiated at the church. The clergy of the parish came from Greece and the Ottoman Empire. The rectors were Archimandrite Paisios Pherentinos, 1891 to March 1894; Archimandrite Agathodoros Papageorgopoulos, 1894 to 1899; Reverend Panagiotis Phiamboli, 1899 to 1900; the fourth, fifth and sixth pastors were clergy, now unknown, who sporadically celebrated the divine liturgies from 1900 to 1901. The seventh rector was Archimandrite Anthimus Ioannides, 1901; Reverend Dorotheos Bakaliaros acted as the eighth pastor for only a few months in 1901. Reverend Leonidas Adamakos held the rectory from 1901 to 1903. The tenth rector of the Holy Trinity parish was Reverend Zysimus Typaldos. He held the post from March 1903 until November 1904.[21] The eleventh rector, Reverend Methodius Kourkoules, was assigned to the parish in November 1904. Reverend Kourkoules remained as the pastor and, later, as the Dean of the Cathedral until his death in 1941. He laid the solid foundation of the community during the earlier years of his office.[22]

In 1904 the Holy Trinity Church moved to new quarters at 151-53 East 72nd Street, between Third and Lexington avenues. The edifice was a former Protestant Episcopal church in Gothic style. The property was purchased for $65,000. The initial down payment of $5,000 was donated by Mrs. Kallias who was married in the church in 1895. In addition to her generosity, Anthony Ralli and other members of the firm of Ralli Brothers contributed substantial funds for the purchase and renovation of the property.[23] The church remained in those quarters until the building burned in the night of January 17, 1927.

Whenever the Greek-speaking or Hellenic Orthodox Church was not available to the Greeks, they attended the brethren Orthodox churches, either Russian or Syrian. Such a church was the Russian Church that was located at 207 East 18th Street.[24] The Greek newspaper reported that the Orthodox Christian community in the city numbered 3,500 members, including Russians, Montenegrins and Bulgars. Another Greek Orthodox Church for Syrian immigrants was formed at 77 Washington Street.[25] In the celebration of the Orthodox Christmas (O.S.), and disregarding their national rivalries, Greek, Syrian and Slav immigrants sometimes celebrated their Christmas holidays together.[26]

Disagreement, real or imaginary, on social, political and personality leadership matters in 1891 caused the organization of the second Greek church in New York. The new parish, Annunciation
Church, was placed under the jurisdiction of the Ecumenical
Patriarchate of Constantinople. The congregation was formally
organized in 1893, and the Very Reverend Archimandrite
Callinikos Dilveis was sent from Europe to administer the new
parish. The first divine liturgies and sacramental rites were cele-
brated in the Judson Memorial Church on Washington Square
South.[27] The new church later occupied the premises of a
Protestant church, 329-35 West 30th Street, from 1908 to 1910.
After numerous shifts, the church purchased a building at 310
West 50th Street in 1915.[28] The clergy of the Annunciation
Church were Archimandrite Dilveis from 1893 until the end of the
year when he transferred to the Greek parish in Lowell,
Massachusetts. The second rector was the Reverend Leonidas
Adamakos who assumed the pastorate until 1908. Later in the year,
Reverend Nicholas Lazaris became the rector until his death in
January 1933.[29]

The Greek Orthodox Church was an integral part of Greek life.
A basic difference between the Greek immigrants and the
American community was the latter's adherence to the notion of
the separation of church and state. In the nineteenth century the
typical Greek immigrants, influenced by their national tradition
and religious heritage, did not accept an artificial separation
between daily living and religion. All life, political, economic,
social and spiritual, was to be lived within the framework of the
Orthodox Church and its teachings. If the Greeks erred in their
ways, as many of them probably did, they had the path of repentance open to them. The church would help them to change for
the betterment of mankind and themselves.[30] In the hearts of the
immigrants, the church was a divinely ordained institution, essential for the salvation of man and the preservation of civilized society. The church encouraged the progressive impulses of its followers and frowned on the regressive escapism of the ignorant and
superstitious. A British contemporary, William Miller, was
impressed that the Greek church had always played "an important
part in the national life."[31]

Although passionately devoted to the church for its teachings and its historic mission of national renaissance, the Greeks were demanding of their clergy. Bishops and priests were regarded as mere human personalities, mortal and fallible. When the immigrants chastised the clergy and condemned the administration of ecclesiastical affairs, they were actually denouncing the fallible and mortal holders of the priestly office and never the church eternal. They attacked individuals but never dogmas.

The centuries of isolation from Western European thought insulated them from the influence of materialism and rationalism. Moreover, clericalism and Erastianism were alien ideologies. In the early twentieth century, the immigrants became exposed to the doctrines of atheism, agnosticism, secularism and free-masonry in New York. Their children became influenced by these liberal doctrines through the public schools, the press, the masonic lodges, literature and technology. An American clergyman of the Greek Orthodox Church, Reverend Eusebius P'Stephanou considered masonry as a threat to the Orthodox Church in America. He stated that masonry deals with "religion and worship and makes it mandatory for the Orthodox to avoid Masonry and all lodges of a similar character. . . ." Nevertheless, some New York Greeks became Masons and regarded the organization as purely a fraternal society. They did not know that Orthodox Christianity and masonry were regarded by the church as incompatible movements.[32]

The Orthodox Church of the Greek immigrants should not be compared to the Orthodox Church in Russia, which was influenced and dominated by Czar Peter I and his successors. Czar Peter I, an ardent admirer of the Western Enlightenment, reduced the Russian Church to subservience by appointing lay Procurators of the Holy Synod, completely responsible to the imperial will.[33] Bernard Pares reflected that Peter's action "thus began a secularization which was to have fatal results later."[34] B. H. Sumner said that Peter was "Erastian and anti-ritualist . . . and that Peter . . . required the subordination of the church to his conception of right governance." Sumner added that Peter was "involved in struggle with the schismatics, who regarded him as Anti-Christ and the official church as apostate."[35] It was the suspicion and distrust of Russian policy in the Balkans and Palestine that made the Greek immigrants isolate themselves from their Slavic Orthodox Christian brethren in New York. This was one of the fundamental reasons for the parallel and separate development of the Greek and

Slavic churches in the New World.[36]

Another basic difference between the immigrants and the native Americans was their concept of salvation within the church. The Western Christian emphasized "the pardon of sins of an individual reconciled to God through the passion and death of His Son." Nicolas Zernov, an Orthodox theologian, stresses that "Christ crucified, Christ dying on the Cross, is the usual picture of the Saviour seen by Westerners." The crucifix has become, claims Zernov, the symbol of their Christianity, and those Protestants who object to the use of it express the same ideas by the test that "Christ died for sinners."[37]

In the Orthodox Christian Church, salvation is interpreted as a new grant of life, "holiness and immortality, bestowed upon redeemed mankind through Christ's victory over death." The resurrection is the essence of salvation. Hence, the Feast of the Resurrection was the most important holiday for New York Greeks and other Orthodox Christians. Once again a difference existed between the native New Yorkers and the Greek newcomers concerning the celebration of Easter. This very important holiday was not usually celebrated by both groups at the same time. In maintaining the historical sequence of Easter, the First Ecumenical Synod (Nicaea) in 325 A.D. decreed that the resurrection would be celebrated "on the first Sunday after the full moon which falls after the Spring Equinox, always after the Jewish Passover." The Greek Orthodox Church never celebrates Easter before or simultaneously with the Jewish Passover as it is sometimes done by the Western churches. Christmas was celebrated by the Greek immigrants as the commemoration of the nativity of Jesus Christ.[38]

After the turn of the century, the parish of the Holy Trinity met hard times. The enrolled membership drastically dropped. There was sharp antagonism toward Reverend A. Papageorgopoulos (opposed to Vlasto) that divided the parish into several rival factions. As there was no permanently assigned rector during this time, Reverend Papageorgopoulos may have attempted to manipulate the unstable situation. The factional differences seemed to be based on personality conflicts within the Greek leadership and resentment, real or imaginary, between the wealthy patrician merchants and the newcomers. There was little conclusive, if any, evidence to show any fundamental cleavage among the New York Greeks. The ultimate leadership of both groups was always upper class of common aristocratic origins: Vlasto and Ralli.

There was, however, a strong nucleus within the parish that desired reconciliation and unity. A meeting was called to reorganize the parish and restore harmony among the Greek immigrants. Seventy persons were present at this church meeting held in December 1900. The participants of the gathering at the Holy Trinity Church included the Greek consul-general, Demetrius Botassi, Anthony P. Ralli, Pandelli Fachiri and the Reverend A. Papageorgopoulos. Alexander Evangelides was requested to act as secretary of the meeting, but he declined because of an eye ailment.

Anthony Ralli reported on the church finances. The current expenditures amounted to $3,509.59, while the revenues were listed as $2,914.56. The deficit was $595.03. In the previous year, the parish deficit was in the amount of $237.77. The current deficit was incurred because of the decoration and refurnishing of a new church edifice. The meeting underscored the basic problem facing the Holy Trinity Church: very limited enrolled membership. There were few active parishioners. The Church of the Holy Trinity had only 45 enrolled members out of a possible 6,000 Greeks in New York. The other important consideration was dissatisfaction among some of the parishioners, mostly provincial immigrants, with Reverend Papageorgopoulos' exercise of his pastoral obligations.[39]

In the early years, the wealthy merchants, such as the Ralli, Galatti, Fachiri, Negreponte and later the Calvocoressi, appeared to have been the more active and influential elements of the church. In time, as their numbers increased through the years, wealthy merchants and cigarette manufacturers of provincial origins assumed a more effective leadership role in parish affairs. They gradually replaced the patrician merchants on the vestry. The Greek immigrants usually supported and elected the more successful merchants and shopkeepers to manage their church and fraternal affairs. Unskilled workers and laborers, rarely, if ever, were elected to any responsible position by the parishioners.

In a feature article, "The Greek Community: The Present Condition—And What Can Be Done," published in the *Atlantis*, in 1900, the paper reiterated its proposal for a strong community leadership based on discipline, organization, direction and purpose. It also demanded the effective use of concerned clergy in fulfilling its obligations to the laity. The newspaper stressed that the church hierarchy in Europe, either the Ecumenical Patriarchate of Constantinople or the Church of Greece, establish a Greek diocese, and maintain discipline and order through ecclesiastical supervision. The newspaper hoped that the Greek church authorities would take a more active interest in the pastoral needs of the immigrants in America. The principal feature article was written by the editor of the *Atlantis*, Socrates Xanthakes, who emphasized the importance of active and intelligent lay participation in parish affairs. The newspaper article included an extended list of the parish committee, which also included Soterios Anargyros, Constantine Galanopoulos, Constantine Contopoulos and Alexander Evangelides.[40]

At a later meeting of the vestry, K.T. Kazantzin was elected president, J. Bombolin, treasurer. Once again, Alexander Evangelides declined the office of secretary, which was later accepted by C. Phassoularides. The problem of the limited church membership was reviewsd. A motion was introduced to evaluate the status in the community and parish of Reverend A. Papageorgopoulos. A parishioner emphasized that the New York church "must be the model of parishes." The provincial immigrants urged the meeting to submit a petition to the Holy Synod of Greece to send another priest to New York. One immigrant complained that "the poor, the masses give more than the well-to-do." There was no evidence to substantiate the charge. Some poor immigrants had this attitude. On the other hand, some of the wealthy parishioners claimed that they provided most of the financial resources and personal effort while the poor only complained and rarely participated in any church and fraternal activities. The final important business was completed with the creation of a special *ad hoc* committee to raise funds and enroll new members. The members of the group were Messrs. Loucatos, Poulides, Bombolin, Tragides, Drivas, Patras, Lyras, Vlachos, Ianopoulos, Lekas, Tombros, Minekakes and Katechakes. The committee members represented the newer and more affluent immigrants. No member of the patrician families was represented in this group.[41]

In a letter to Vlasto, K. T. Kazantzin, the vestry president, complained about the newspaper's critical comments on the administration of the parish affairs. In reply to that letter, Socrates Xanthakes, editor of the *Atlantis*, stressed that the controversy over the ability of the rector was unworthy and irrelevant to the more important problem of the systematic development of the church. With reference to the charges of incompetence leveled at Reverend A. Papageorgopoulos, Xanthakes stated that a "man is innocent until proven guilty." The editor remarked that the vestry must determine which was more important to the parish, removing a rector or collecting funds and establishing a sound foundation for the Greek church.[42] After a continuing bitter controversy, Reverend A. Papageorgopoulos severed all personal ties with the New York Greek community, leaving his apartment for an unknown destination.[43] The clergyman's sudden departure was lamented by some of the New York immigrants because there were no Greek services in the city.[44]

In spite of these difficulties, the parish diligently worked to solve the fundamental problem and restore the parish on a tranquil and harmonious basis. Numerous meetings were called. The laity volunteered for parish chores and duties. Presiding at one of the meetings, Demetrius Botassi sagaciously suggested that after the *ad hoc* committee completed its initial mission of reestablishing the solvency of the parish, it should resign. With the primary goals established, the *ad hoc* committee should prepare for a citywide parish election and surrender its powers and functions to a newly elected body.[45]

At the committee meeting, presided over by Demetrius Botassi, the following persons were selected: D. Tryforos, N. Dotoraton, G. Drivas, J. Logothetes, J. Zacharias, J. Bombolin and M. N. Katrevan. The conference desired a 20-man commmittee to register new parishioners and collect funds. Thirteen extra members were appointed by the group to assist in the community canvas and registration drive.[46] In several days, the *ad hoc* committee was expanded to include 22 members, who selected Nicholas Lelys, Eias Tombros and Nicholas Christatos. The committee received contributions in the amount of $425.00.[47]

In a later meeting of the parish council, the decision was made to call a general meeting on the evening of May 13, 1901 in order to vote for a new parish constitution and discuss the expansion of the parish boundaries to include the Greeks in Manhattan, Brooklyn and New Jersey. By this time the *ad hoc* committee had collected $1,162.25 for the benefit of the church.[48] The successful efforts of the committee were evidenced by the publication of a list of 330 church members in the *Atlantis*.[49]

The individual and group participation of the laity was dynamic and effective in creating a viable parish. The lay participation and control of the administrative affairs of the church was an integral part of the Greek Christian tradition. In an editorial, the *Atlantis* recommended that new elections be scheduled quickly. Moreover, the new vestry should avoid petty factionalism and encourage group cohesiveness. The parish elections were scheduled for Sunday, May 26, 1901.[50]

At the time of the election there were 1,415 enrolled members who elected 11 trustees. Once again the elected trustees represented the affluent provincial immigrants, florists, cigarette manufacturers, confectioners and others.[51] According to traditional procedures, the laity elected a board of trustees. At a later date, the trustees elected their own officers.[52]

At a succeeding meeting, in which ten of the eleven trustees were present, the election of the executive officers took place. The results were: G. Tragides, president; N. Lelys, treasurer; Stavros Visvinis, secretary. In addition, the trustees unanimously elected Demetrius Botassi as the honorary president of the council of trustees.[53] By the first year of the twentieth century, the Holy Trinity parish had laid the foundations for the permanence of the Greek Orthodox Church in New York. Furthermore, the provincial newcomers, and not the patrician merchants, were in effective control of the parish organization. A special committee of the Holy Trinity Church purchased land for 50 grave sites at Mr. Olivet Cemetery in Maspeth, Long Island. The original purchase order for sites was issued by the parish on March 31, 1898.[54]

In a comprehensive two-column editorial, "The Greek Clergy in America," the *Atlantis* reviewed the limitations and vicissitudes of the Hellenic Orthodox Church in the New World. The editorial expressed the view that the clergy, as represented by Reverend Papageorgopoulos, late rector of the Holy Trinity Church in New York, and the late Reverend Michael Karidis, former pastor of the Holy Trinity Church in New Orleans, who committed suicide in New York in June, 1901, were weak pillars of the immigrant society.[55] The newspaper blamed the ecclesiastical hierarchy of Greece and its Holy Synod as being remiss in their pastoral obligations in not selecting stable clergymen for duty among the immigrants in the United States. The Greek newspaper underscored the need for qualified priests who could function in an expanding urban society.[56]

In the first decade of the twentieth century, the Greek immigrants faced the threat of Russian domination of the Hellenic Orthodox Church. The New York Greeks were apprehensive concerning the attempts of Russian Archbishop Platon to reduce the Hellenic Orthodox Church to a tool of the Pan-Slav goals of Russia. The threat of Russian domination influenced the structural and legal organization of the Greek parishes in New York.[57] The Greek immigrants were suspicious of the use of Greek-educated Syrian clergy for the baptism of infants and other sacramental rites. The Greek newcomers regarded this clergy as a wedge that would open the door to Russification.[58]

In order to avoid domination by the Russian Orthodox Church, which was recognized as the Greek Orthodox Church in New York under the state laws of 1871 and 1895,[59] the Greek parish had purchased their church building through a legal corporation of which three American citizens were trustees: Peter Minekakes, Kyriakoulis Tsiklakos and Constantine Vlachos.[60] In the evening of the Orthodox Christian Good Friday in 1904, the presiding Russian prelate appeared and laid claim to the property of the Holy Trinity Church. The threat was dissipated by the claim that the newly purchased edifice had been bought in the name of the parish trustees, and not in the name of the Greek Orthodox parish of the Holy Trinity. Thus, technically, the church property belonged to these three indivduals.

In the face of this crisis the parish had three alternatives: (1) to accept Russian domination, (2) to continue the status quo and maintain the parish in the name of three private persons, or (3) to seek separate legal status under state law. The third alternative was overwhelmingly supported. An *ad hoc* committee was established that included Reverend Methodius Kourkoules, parish rector, Constantine Galanopoulos, president of the parish trustees, and Solon J. Vlasto, publisher of the *Atlantis*. With sustained vigor and skill, Vlasto and the committee launched a campaign that achieved success on June 3, 1905 when the Holy Trinity Church was incorporated as an independent religious community under the state laws as the Hellenic Eastern Christian Orthodox Church. In the statute of incorporation, it was specifically stated that the new legal and independent entity was to "distinguish the said 'Hellenic

Eastern Christian Church of New York' from the so-called Church of Russia and the Church of Greece."[61] In other words, it was organized as a new church body. If it had used the terminology of Greek Orthodox Christian Church, it would have been placed under the jurisdiction of the Russian Church and the Russian consul-general. The action of the Holy Trinity Church set the precedent for the other Greek churches in the state. The second Greek parish in New York, Annunciation Church, followed the identical procedure and incorporated itself as an independent religious entity on April 10, 1909.[62] Therefore, by 1910, at least two independent religious bodies existed in New York without a hierarchy that could enforce order and discipline.

The Greek community continued to fear the possibility of "religious and social propagandizing," through the Russian dominated church that would alienate the Greek immigrants from their tradition and loyalties. Individuals, fraternal associations and the parishes recommended that the Holy Synod of Greece send a bishop and qualified priests to America to organize the churches into a diocese. Dismay and concern were voiced over the appointment of a Greek-educated Syrian bishop under Russian auspices.[63] The threat of the expanding influence of the Russian Church was due to the dearth of Greek clergy and lack of ecclesiastical organization in the United States.[64] Reverend Joachim Alexopoulos stressed the urgent necessity for the creation of a Greek diocese in America.[65]

The continued fear of Russian domination was justified. The Russian episcopate found the opportunity to act against the independent Hellenic parishes when the Turkish government followed traditional anti-Christian and anti-Greek policies.[66] The Young Turk Revolution, 1908 to 1909, increased the persecution of the subject nationalities, Greeks, Armenians and other Christian minorities.[67] With the sustained onslaught on Christian Hellenism, the Russian imperial policy-makers felt that they could force the Ecumenical Patriarch of Constantinople to transfer his powers, prerogatives and privileges over the Greek diaspora in the Americas to the Holy Synod of the Russian Church.[68] His Holiness, Joachim III, Ecumenical Patriarch, however, transferred temporarily his powers over the Greek immigrants in the Western Hemisphere to the Holy Synod of the Church of Greece in March 1908. In 1918 the Ecumenical Patriarchate of Constantinople regained its authority over the Greek immigrants.[69]

Undaunted by the turn of events, the Russian ecclesiastical authorities initiated legal and legislative action in New York. New York State legislator, Artemus Ward, Jr., and friend of Russian Archbishop Platon, sponsored a bill, passed on March 10, 1909, which amended the religious corporation laws in New York State so as to place all Orthodox Christian churches under Russian ecclesiastial jurisdiction and control.[70] At this juncture, Vlasto and the editors of the *Atlantis* telegraphed Governor Charles Evans Hughes, contending that the bill was a violation of the basic liberties of the Greek churches inasmuch as "His Holiness" had transferred "all his rights over all Greek churches to the Holy Synod of Greece." The counsel to the governor replied that Hughes would "give a hearing on the proposed measure."[71] Thereupon, Vlasto prepared a model petition for all Greeks to send to Charles E. Hughes on the pending bill.[72] It read:

We, the undersigned Greeks belonging to the Holy Greek Catholic Apostolic Church of the Eastern Confession, protest against the Act passed by the Legislature becoming a law, and such a law will deprive us of our Constitutional rights and will tend to place our Churches under the direct control of the Czar of Russia. We, therefore, beg your Excellency to give due consideration to our protest.

Thousands of telegrams and letters were sent to the Executive Mansion in Albany protesting the act. The protests came from all parts of the United States, from New York, Massachusetts, Illinois, California, New Jersey, New England and other regions of the country. Vlasto and the *Atlantis* planned their effective campaign as a national rather than a statewide protest.

On May 5, 1909, Vlasto wrote Governor Hughes that all Orthodox churches were autocephalous bodies that accepted the spiritual authority of the Ecumenical Patriarch of Constantinople. He added that the Greeks had "nothing to do with Russia, Russian things." Vlasto reviewed the early beginnings of the Holy Trinity Church in the early 1890s when a small group of wealthy Greek merchants, including the Ralli, Fachiri, Livieratos families and himself, had planned the establishment of the first Greek parish in New York.[73]

The sustained and well directed *Atlantis* campaign succeeded. In May, Governor Charles E. Hughes vetoed the controversial bill.[74] In a headline, "Great Triumph of Hellenism against Panslavism," the *Atlantis* acclaimed Hugh's veto as a guaranty of the Greek immigrants' rights and liberties. The newspaper emphasized that the United States was "neither Turkey nor Palestine" and, therefore, not easily influenced by the "pressures of Czarist Russia."[75]

Throughout the ecclesiastical controversy, the position of the Greek minister in Washington, Lampros Coromilas, seemed to be ambivalent and enigmatic. It was reported by some critics that Coromilas allegedly did not favor the appointment of a Greek bishop and the creation of a diocese in the United States. The *Atlantis* candidly remarked, however, that the Greek envoy secretly wanted the appointment of a bishop to protect the rights of the immigrants. According to widespread rumors and allusions, the inactivity and reluctance of the Holy Synod of Greece in selecting a bishop and establishing a diocese was in deference to the will of Queen Olga of Greece who was also a Grand Duchess of Russia. The critics of the Glucksburg dynasty claimed that Queen Olga's personal sympathies and aspirations were with the aims of Pan-Slavism and not with the mission of the Great Idea.[76]

The Russian threat never was eliminated until the Bolshevik Revolution of 1917. The Lay Procuratorship of the Holy Synod, created by Peter the Great, was abolished. The Russian Patriarchate was reestablished in 1918. Freed from Russian interference, the Greek Orthodox Archdiocese of North and South America was formed on October 20, 1918 with Bishop Alexander of Rodostolos as Synodical Supervisor.[77] The Greek Orthodox Archdiocese was placed under the jurisdiction of the Ecumenical Patriarchate of Constantinople.[78] The archdiocese was granted its certificate of incorporation from the state of New York on September 17, 1921. The County Document, file number T650, was executed by Archbishop Meletios Metaxakis, as president, and the Reverend Archdeacon Germanos Polyzoides, as clerk.[79] The clerical trustees were Bishop Alexander of Rodostolos, Reverend Methodius Kourkoules, Reverend Demetrius Callimachos, Reverend Stephanos Makaronis and Reverend Germanos Polyzoides. The lay trustees were Leonidas Calvocoressi, Panagiotes Panteas, George Kontomanlis and Alexander Alexion. All the lay trustees were prominent men with provincial origins, except Leonidas Calvocoressi. The latter was the last representative of the patrician gentry to hold an important position in the Greek parish of the Holy Trinity. Calvocoressi was associated with the merchant banking firm of Ralli Brothers. Nevertheless, the provincial immigrants formed the most prominent element within the Greek church in New York.

10

The Immigrant Press

The establishment of the Greek language newspaper, *Atlantis*, was one of the most important landmarks in Greek immigrant history in New York and the United States.[1] The *Atlantis* and the entire Greek immigrant press belonged to the group of foreign language newspapers that reached the new urban peoples "whose occupations [were] predominantly commercial—the Greeks, Armenians, Chinese, Syrians . . . and the Jews."[2] It was founded in 1894 by Solon J. Vlasto, as a small weekly newspaper with offices at 2 and 4 Stone Street. In a few years it became a semi-weekly and ended up as the leading national Greek daily. The national circulation rose from 3,400 in 1900 to 6,000 in 1904.[3] At the end of the first decade of the twentieth century, the newspaper boasted a circulation of more than 17,014 with an editorial staff of five. By 1913 the circulation had increased to an estimated 20,000 to 25,000.[4]

The *Atlantis*, which has been in continuous operation since the nineteenth century, has continued to exist up to the present time as the second or perhaps, the third oldest Greek daily newspaper in the world.[5] Vlasto's newspaper became an incorporated enterprise in January 1904.[6] Exclusive of the merchant banking and cotton exporting firms of Ralli Brothers and Fachiri & Co., the *Atlantis* became the largest and most profitable Greek business in America during this period.[7]

The newspaper also published the *Atlantis Illustrated Monthly*, which had an estimated national circulation of 12,000 in 1913. This was a well edited periodical of 30 to 40 pages. It covered the news of the United States, Greece, Greek-Americans and the world. The Greek magazine was perhaps "most resembling *Collier's* in appearance."[8] Down through the years the *Atlantis* recorded the social history of the Greek immigrants in New York and the United States. It functioned as the chronicle of Greek immigration in the Western Hemisphere.

Although there were other short-lived newspapers established, the *Atlantis*, and later the *Ethnikos Kyrix*, founded in 1915, were the only newspapers to become dailies with national circulation on a permanent basis. Among the regular departments that appeared in the pages of the *Atlantis* were "Greeks in America," "Athens," "American Affairs," "Greece," "Economic Affairs," and "Enslaved Greece." The first department described the activities of Greek immigrants in New York and America. It has survived to the present day. It reported on the everyday life of the immigrants, reporting regularly on marriages, betrothals, baptisms, deaths, funerals, religious memorial services, arrivals and departures from and to Greece and Asia Minor. Not only did the departments report on such routine social events, but on occasion, they aroused bitter controversy.[9]

In addition to brief notices, the newspaper published small human interest items, such as those that reflected the sorrow of the early immigrants when some of their brethren died in a foreign land and far away from their relatives. Typical was the announcement of the death of Demetrius Lampesis in March 1895. The greatest tragedy that had befallen Lampesis was his burial in New York, and not in his native Greece.[10] The death of a young child was deemed the greatest misfortune. Pathos and compassion were reflected in the death notice of Calliope, daughter of George Kouris, who passed away after a brief three-day illness.[11]

The quality of literary style and editing was very high. The puristic, literary language used by the newspaper was suited more for an urban educated class than the unschooled provincial newcomers. Sociologist Robert Park stated that the *Atlantis* wrote editorials that the readers could not comprehend.[12] He added that the purist language was used because of the dialectical differences and not from any desire to preserve the literary and historic quality of the Greek language.[13] The sociologist did not provide any conclusive evidence to support these two generalizations.

On the contrary, the evidence seems to indicate that the *Atlantis* probably had a definite purpose of uplifting the cultural, literary and educational standards of the Greek immigrant in New York and the United States. The high quality of editing and literary language matched and even surpassed that of several newspapers published in Greece during this period. These high standards were maintained up to and beyond World War II. The immigrant newspaper was also an effective educator of the newcomers. It raised the educational level of the Greeks by developing their reading facility. The newspaper introduced the Greek words of an urban society to the immigrants. Inasmuch as the vast numbers of Greeks came from a rural-agrarian society, they learnad the Greek words for skyscrapers, suspension bridge, elevated railroad, building elevator, subway and bus.

As a teacher of American politics, the *Atlantis* informed its readers about the American methods of government, political campaigning and the intricate system of the College of Presidential Electors. In 1897 the newspaper published an informative series of articles on the American constitutional system. The series was entitled: "By What the United States Is Governed: Patriotism." In this respect, the newspaper acted as an interpreter of American government to the immigrants who were interested in becoming naturalized citizens.[14]

Politically, the *Atlantis* was highly critical of the Glucksburg dynasty of Greece and the radical elements in American politics during the period, 1894 to 1910. In many ways, The American progressives of the periods, Solon J. Vlasto and the *Atlantis* shared similar views. They denounced the exploitation and championed the rights and hopes of the unprotected. The *Atlantis* always followed a policy based on nationalism, capitalism, constitutionalism and moderation. Toward the beginning of the second decade of the twentieth century, the newspaper gradually espoused the cause of its former Greek antagonists. It became the most influential royalist-Glucksburg organ in the Western Hemisphere.[15] Today, it still represents the royalist, nationalist and moderate conservative interests in Greek politics. In American politics, it has consistently supported the system of free enterprise and the moderate wing of the Republican Party.[16]

In 1911 there were about 2,000 naturalized citizens in the New York Greek immigrant community. According to sociologist Henry P. Fairchild, almost all of them adhered to the tenets of the Republican Party because they believed that its policies "were most favorable to the commercial advancement of the nation." The New York Greeks had a political club with Republican affiliations on

Sixth Avenue.[17] The attachment of the New York Greeks to the Republican Party may be explained as a result of (1) strong influence of the *Atlantis* in interpreting party policy to the immigrants, (2) the existence of friendly relations between the party and the New York Greeks, (3) the appeal of the party given the commercial outlook of the Greek immigrants. In addition, the Democratic Party and the Tammany organization did not actively seek out the support of the New York Greeks during this period. Fairchild reported that Marxist socialism found "no followers among the people of this race in the United States."[18]

In the presidential election of 1896, the *Atlantis* vigorously supported the candidacy of William McKinley. The Republican Party was regarded by the publisher and editors as the party with the most "stable basis and set purpose." The newspaper stressed that the Democrats were torn by intense factionalism over personality conflicts and monetary policies. The editors wrote that the election of William Jennings Bryant "would be a danger to the United States economy."[19] In another feature article published before the election, the newspaper emphasized that severe economic consequences would result from Bryant's silver policy.[20] The Greek-American naturalized citizens were encouraged to vote "the Republican Party line for progress and stability."[21]

In a preelection survey, the *Atlantis* wrote that there were very few basic differences between the major political parties in the United States. All parties supported the federal constitution, the free enterprise system and the other fundamental democratic institutions of the country. The Greek editors added, however, that the Democratic Party "suffered because of the silver issue" and from Bryant's ideas and leadership. The newspaper reaffirmed its loyalty to the principles of economic and political liberty as manifested in the Republican Party. With the Republican triumph, the *Atlantis*, in large headlines, announced the election results with "Glad Tidings for the McKinley Victory." It commented that the American public was not "so naive as to be fooled by Bryant's rhetoric."[22] The political objectives, which were highly valued by the publisher and editors of the *Atlantis*, were progress, stability and responsibility.[23]

The *Atlantis* threw its support to McKinley's bid for re-election in 1900. In this campaign, the newspaper published detailed articles exploring the major issues of the election: the silver issues and imperialism and colonialism in the Far East and the Caribbean. Although staunchly Republican and dedicated to McKinley's policies, the *Atlantis* had reservations concerning colonialism and imperialism. The editorial staff felt that overseas economic and territorial expansion was not fully compatible with the American political tradition.[24] Nevertheless, as expected, the victor in the November election made the *Atlantis* very "joyous."[25]

In 1904 the Greek language newspaper supported the heir to the assassinated president, Theodore Roosevelt. It regarded the young political leader as progressive and friendly to immigrants, especially the Greek newcomers. As usual, Roosevelt's success at the polls pleased the *Atlantis*. The continuous Republican triumphs reinforced the *Atlantis*' support of the party.[26]

By 1908 the editor and publisher of the newspaper accepted William Howard Taft as the logical successor to Theodore Roosevelt. The newspaper felt that Taft would continue the enlightened Republican progressive policies. In an editorial entitled, "The Strength of the People," it lauded both the Republicans and Taft:

It was not only the triumph of Taft and Roosevelt in yesterday's election; it was the triumph of the Republican party; it was the triumph . . . of the American people . . . the people want tranquility, they want peace, they want commercial, agricultural and industrial advancement; they do not want demagogues and seditionaries, imposters, office seekers or pseudo-patriots at its head.

The *Atlantis* favored the fundamental aspects of the Square Deal, its attack on "bad trusts," its concern for the public welfare. The newspaper was impressed with the Square Deal's dedication to economic progress. Nevertheless, it was Roosevelt's policy of protecting the community and the individual from the onslaught of the huge organizations such as the trusts, corporations and labor unions that greatly influenced the newspaper.[27]

The presidential election of 1912 coincided with the Balkan Wars. The Greek victories against the Turks during the autumn of that year removed most of the presidential campaign from the front pages of the *Atlantis*. Preoccupied with the triumphs of the Great Idea in the Balkans, the *Atlantis* followed a cautious policy in the national election. Although Republican in its views, the Greek language newspaper regarded William Howard Taft as well as Woodrow Wilson as the spokesmen for the old line chieftains of their respective parties. The *Atlantis* was very sympathetic to

Theodore Roosevelt, whom it regarded as the leader of a "great popular movement." With Wilson's minority victory, the newspaper promised its loyal support to the new president on behalf of the progress of the United States.[28]

In municipal politics, the *Atlantis* was the avowed foe of Tammany Hall and the local Republican political bosses. It staunchly aided the efforts of Seth Low and urban reform in the election of 1897. In a front-page editorial supporting the mayoral candidacy of Low, the newspaper stressed the candidate as a capable, educated, statesmanlike person who would enhance the status of the city and improve the economic status of New York.[29] The *Atlantis* editors stated that a Low victory would mean support for "order, self-government of the city . . . independent of national and state questions." According to the *Atlantis*, Low's triumph would mean a victory for the forces of responsible and healthy political leadership.[30]

However, the election of 1897, in bringing in Robert Van Wyck as mayor, witnessed the victory of "Boss" Croker and Tammany Hall. The editors compared the municipal victory of Tammany to that of the Greek leader, Deliyannis, who reintroduced instability into Greece's political and economic life. The newspaper sharply criticized the Tammany election slogan, "To Hell With Reform," as a deliberate affront to public decency, responsible government and municipal reform.[31]

The influence of the *Atlantis* was in large measure a reflection of the activity of the publisher Solon J. Vlasto. It should not be forgotten that Vlasto was a member of a Greek aristocratic family with wealthy connections in France, England and Greece. His family and class never had any contempt for commercial and professional activity. On the contrary, the Vlasto family had a long tradition of involvement in economic undertakings for many generations.

Vlasto's social and economic outlook was similar to that of the wealthy and socially prominent families of Boston, Philadelphia and New York, such as the Winthrops, Roots, Stimsons and Roosevelts. His political orientation was greatly influenced by the Republican progressivism of the American urban middle class. The publisher did not show any strong leanings toward either the new class of industrialists or to the factory working class. Nevertheless, he was a staunch opponent of human exploitation by padrones, political and labor bosses, irresponsible entrepreneurs and indifferent managers. He supported individual responsibility in business and government. He opposed corruption and bossism. In other words, Vlasto had little in common with the Tammany political chieftains and the mass political organizations in New York. In fact, during the mayoralty election, the symbol of the Citizens Union appeared on the front pages.

An example of this progressive patrician attitude appeared during the 1897 election. Although supporting McKinley Republicanism, gold and Low urban reformism, the *Atlantis* took a very kindly view of the deceased mayoral candidate, Henry George. In a sympathetic feature story and obituary, the Greek editors, reflecting Vlasto's views, considered that "after Low, George was the enemy of the tyranny of Croker and Platt." The newspaper expressed strong opposition to Henry George for his revolutionary economic and single-tax theories, but thoroughly praised him as a man of integrity, strength and compassion.[32]

Vlasto was often involved in leadership controversies in the immigrant community—first with the patricians and later with the Panhellenic Union. Factionalism broke out during the first decade of the twentieth century, with Vlasto and the *Atlantis* on one side and Lampros Coromilas, Greek Minister to the United States, the Panhellenic Union, the largest Greek fraternal organization, on the other. The basic problem was the leadership issue. Who was going to lead and represent the Greek immigrants in New York and the United States? Vlasto or Coromilas? *Atlantis* or the Panhellenic Union? In the long run, Vlasto and the *Atlantis* won. Coromilas returned to Greece in a few years and the Panhellenic Union was dissolved after the Balkan Wars. There was also a limited rivalry among the three important cities for leadership: New York, Chicago and Boston. Inasmuch as New York was the center of the Greek newspaper industry, it exerted a far greater influence than the other two cities.

A steamship agent, John Booras, published a weekly, *Thermopylae*, in 1900, which was later merged with another newspaper, *Simaea*, in 1906 to become *Thermopylae-Simaea*. This newspaper ceased publication in 1907. *Simaea* had been founded by Constantine Phassoularides in 1905. The establishment of other Greek newspapers represented opposition to Vlasto's almost monopolistic control of the Greek press.[33]

The newspaper that most seriously rivaled the *Atlantis* for a very brief time was the *Panhellenius Ephimeris*.[34] It was established on April 7, 1908 by Socrates Xanthakes, a former editor-in-chief of the *Atlantis*.[35] By 1910 its national circulation rose to 9,262, but it never achieved the strength of the *Atlantis*.[36] It opposed the personal ambitions and policies of Solon J. Vlasto and supported Coromilas. The new publication was dedicated to the goals of the Panhellenic Union and the ideals of the Great Idea. It considered the *Atlantis* as self-centered, divisive and obstructive to the unity of the immigrant community in New York and America.

The financial backers of the opposition newspaper were prominent and affluent members of the vestry and parish of the Holy Trinity Church. They included the rector, Reverend Methodius Kourkoules, Peter Minekakes, Demetrius Polymeris and Constantine Galanopoulos. Unable to withstand a long and sustained competition with the *Atlantis*, *Panhellenius Ephimeris* ceased publication in April, 1913.

The last important newspaper to be established in New York during this period was the *Phruros*. It was published by C. Sakellarakos in the latter part of 1909. Lacking a continued popular interest and sagging in circulation, the *Phruros* stopped publishing in the early months of 1910.[37]

Vlasto triumphed in these various newspaper wars because he understood the nature of Greek immigration and its position in the American environment. He was victorious in his struggles during the years from 1894 to 1910 because the *Atlantis* had solid financial foundations and because both the publisher and editorial staff were geared to combating competition.

Vlasto's personal sympathies and animosities, as fully reflected in his newspaper, *Atlantis*, can be best summarized in this period as follows: (1) support for the Republican Party in American national politics, especially for the progressive elements, (2) admiration for William McKinley, Theodore Roosevelt and William Howard Taft as among the best presidents of the United States,[38] (3) opposition to Tammany Hall and all forms of bossism in New York municipal politics, (4) opposition to the Glucksburg dynasty of Greece for its alleged indifference to the national movement and public welfare,[39] (5) dedication to the national liberation of the Greek nation as manifested in the ideals of the Great Idea,[40] (6) adherence to the aims of the political policies of Demetrius Ralli in Greek politics,[41]

(7) sympathy for the goals of the *Ethnike Hetaireia*,[42] (8) championship of the rights of the poor provincial immigrants who began to settle in New York and the United States between 1894 and 1910, and (9) resentment toward the influence of the prominent Greek families in New York, such as the Ralli, Galatti, Negreponte, Fachiri and Botassi families. Vlasto's resentment toward these affluent families during the 1890s probably was personal and not political and economic, for although the politics of these prominent Greek families is not known, it is likely that they shared Vlasto's adherence to urban middle-class progressivism and Republican politics. In the final analysis, the *Atlantis* mirrored the personal, economic, social and political views of its founder and publisher, Solon J. Vlasto.

11

Conclusion

By 1910 the New York Greeks' efforts bore fruit. The community was firmly established in New York. The immigrant institutions were flourishing. The Holy Trinity Church was the most influential parish in the social, cultural and religious life of metropolitan New York and its surrounding suburbs. For all practical purposes, the immigrant newspaper, *Atlantis*, was the most important opinion-forming organ in the country despite the challenges of the Panhellenic Union and the *Panhellenius Ephimeris*. The particularist and regional associations, the confectioners' and retail florist societies were thriving. The institutions which placed their indelible stamp on the community in its early formative stages were the *Atlantis*, Holy Trinity and Annunciation churches, Panhellenic Union and the Brotherhood of Athena. Only the *A'lantis* and the two parishes remain today.[1]

The year of 1910 closed the decade that recorded the largest influx of newcomers from Greece and the Ottoman Empire. The declining influence of the wealthy cotton merchants was clearly evident. The rapid ascendancy of the provincial immigrants was a striking development. The succeeding generations saw the molding of the New York community in the image and attitudes of the newer immigrants. The stalwarts, friends and foes, who formed the nucleus of the Greek colony were Solon J. Vlasto, Theodore Ralli, Anthony P. Ralli, Demetrius Botassi and the Reverend Methodius Kourkoules, but newer elements were assuming significant influence. Vlasto, however, was the most dynamic contributor in the formation of the community and its attitudes. In projecting future studies in immigrant history, Marcus Lee Hansen, referring to the role of the immigrant newspaper as "the mouthpiece of their respective groups," called Solon J. Vlasto, of the

Greek paper *Atlantis*, one of the "leading journalists" among American immigrant groups.[2] The year 1910 closed an important chapter in the life of S. J. Vlasto, but there were many more written before the resolute and enigmatic publisher passed away in 1927.

The origins of the Greek immigration to New York City were deeply rooted in the social history of the nineteenth century. Economic factors were not the only cause. The pioneers, as their descendants called them, were not a downtrodden people who came to America to escape persecution and poverty in Greece. Restlessness in a slowly changing rural society, disillusionment with the political establishment and the desire to seek rapid changes were prominent factors. The expansion of education and urbanization of Greece from 1870 to 1910 encouraged the rural population to demand the social amenities of the emerging industrial-urban society of the twentieth century. It was not poverty itself that had induced emigration but rather the frustration that it inflicted upon the ambitious and energetic. It was the sense of injustice pressed upon those who felt that their own talents and hopes went unrewarded and unrecognized by the contemporary Greek society. The immigrants rejected the Greek establishment for its mishandling of the national movement.

Moreover, the dogma of the Great Idea gave them direction and purpose in national life. Tacit submission to fatalism was rejected. Independent initiative and self-interest were the impulses of the era. The pioneers, serious in purpose, built a way station in New York with the fruits of their labor. In essence, the harvest of the golden trees was their love of God, country and family.

Notes

Chapter 1

Prologomena

1. Great Britain, Foreign Office, Protocol No. 23, Respecting the Sovereignty of Greece, February 3, 1830, 17 *British and Foreign State Papers*, 191ff. Hereafter this series will be cited as *B.F.S.P.*; Sir Edward Hertslet, ed., *The Map of Europe by Treaty* (4v. London, 1875-91), II, 841. Hereafter cited as Hertslet; Treaty between Great Britain, France and Russia, Regarding the Pacification of Greece, London, July 6, 1827, *ibid.*, II, 769-74; Protocol between Great Britain, France and Russia, Regarding the Boundaries of Grece, Poros, December 12, 1828, *ibid.*, II, 798; Paulos Karolides, *Historia Tis Hellados* (Athens, 1925), p. 730; Sir John A.R. Marriott, *The Eastern Question: An Historical Study in European Diplomacy* (London, 1940), pp. 11, 524, 533-38, 544. Cf. Great Britain, Foreign Office, *Lausanne Conference on Near Eastern Affairs, 1922-1923: Records of Proceedings and Draft Terms of Peace* (London, 1923); Edgar Turlington, "The Settlement of Lausanne," *American Journal of International Law*, XVIII (October, 1924), 696-706.

2. Arrangement between Great Britain, France, Russia and Turkey, Regarding the Greek Boundary for the Definitive Settlement of the Continental Limits of Greece, Constantinople, July 21, 1831, Hertslet, II, 903-8; 23 *B.F.S.P.* 934; London Convention of May 7, 1832, Hertslet, II, 895; Edward S. Forster, *A Short History of Modern Greece, 1821-1957*, Third Edition, Revised and Enlarged by Douglas Dakin (New York, 1958), pp. 12ff.; Spyridon Trikoupis, *Historia Tis Hellinikis Epanastaseos* (4v. London, 1860), I, 4; C.W. Crawley, "Modern Greece, 1821-1939," *A Short History of Greece From Early Times to 1964* (Cambridge, 1965), pp. 96-97.

3. Family Compact Between Bavaria and Greece, Munich, November 1, 1832, Hertslet, II, 913-14; Convention between Great Britain, France, Russia and Bavaria, London, May 7, 1831, *ibid.*, II, 894-95; Crawley, pp.

98-99; Forster, pp. 10-11. The first sovereign ruler of Greece was a former minister of Czar Alexander I, Count John Capodistrias (1776-1831). He was elected president of the Greek state in April, 1827 and assassinated on October 19, 1831. The Bavarian prince was selected after Prince Leopold of Saxe-Coburg rejected the Crown of Greece. Trikoupis, IV, 238-40.

4. Hertslet, II, 800; Marriott, p. 525; Prince Andrew of Greece, *Towards Disaster: The Greek Army in Asia Minor in 1921*. Translated from the Greek by H.R.H. Princess Andrew of Greece (London, 1930), pp. 7ff.; Ferdinand Schevill, *The History of the Balkan Peninsula* (New York, 1933), p. 344.

5. Ernest Christian Helmreich, *The Diplomacy of the Balkan Wars, 1912-1913* (Cambridge, Mass., 1938), pp. 418-42; Edward Crankshaw, *The Fall of the House of Habsburg* (New York, 1963), p. 371; Prince Nicholas of Greece, *My Fifty Years* (London, 1926), p. 154; Eleutherios K. Venizelos, *The Vindication of Greek National Policy, 1912-1917* (London, 1918), p. 80ff.; Eleutherios K. Venizelos, *La Politique de la Grèce* (Paris, 1916), pp. 167, 168; Alexander A. Pallis, *Greece's Anatolian Venture and After: A Survey of the Diplomatic and Political Aspects of the Greek Expedition to Asia Minor, 1915-1922* (London, 1937), pp. 5-6, 12ff.; King Constantine of Greece, *A King's Private Letters* (London, 1925), p. 72; King Constantine to Princess Paola of Saxe-Weimar, Smyrna, June 18, 1921, *ibid.*, p. 190.

6. Steven Runciman, *The Great Church in Captivity* (Cambridge, 1968), pp. 378-79; J.C. Voyatzidis, "Le grand Idée," *Le Cinq-Centième Anniversaire de la Prise de Constantinople, 1453-1953, L'Hellenisme Contemporain*, 2ème serie, 7ème année, fascicule hors serie (Athens, 1953), p. 281. There is also a Greek version of the previous work, *He Pentakosiosti Epeteios Apo Tis Aloseos Tis Konstantinoupoleos* (Athens, 1953); Dionysios A. Zakythinos, *Byzantion, Kratos Kae Koenonia, Historike Episcopisis* (Athens, 1951), p. 150; D.M. Nicol, "The Fourth Crusade and the Greek and Latin Empires, 1204-61," *The Cambridge Medieval History*, IV, *The Byzantine Empire*, Part I, Second Edition (Cambridge, 1966), 327-28.

7. Voyatzidis, p. 282; Anthony Bryer, "The Great Idea," *History Today*, XV (March, 1965), 159, 160-61.

8. Charles Diehl, *L'histoire de l'empire byzantin* (Paris, 1924), p. 216; Charles B. Eddy, *Greece and Greek Refugees* (London, 1931), p. 25; Andreas M. Andreades, *Les effets économique et sociaux de la Guerre en Grèce, Histoire économique et Sociale de la Guerre* (Paris, 1929), p. 105; John Campbell and Philip Sherrard, *Modern Greece* (New York, 1968), pp. 83, 84ff., 93ff.; John Mavrogordato, *Modern Greece: A Chronicle and a Survey*,

1800-1931 (London, 1931), p. 44, hereafter cited as *Modern Greece*; Voyatzidis, p. 285; Bryer, p. 163; William Miller, *The Last Greek Empire* (London, 1926), p. 126; William Miller, "The Last Athenian Historian: Laonikos Chalkokondylas," *Journal of Hellenic Studies*, XLII (1922), pp. 36ff. The name of Laonicos Chalcocondyles varies in several titles and countries. It is also rendered as Chalcocondylae, Chalcocondylaes, or in its abbreviated form, Chalcondyles. Cf. Laonici Chalcondylae, Athenienis, Historiarum (libri x Paris, MDCL). This Greek-Latin version is located in the New York Public Library.

9. George Zoras, *Ae Pro Kae Meta tin Alosin Diamorphotheisae Ideologikae kae Politikae Katheythynseis, 1453-1953*. Spudastirion Byzantinis Kae Neohellenikis Philologias, University of Athens (Athens, 1953), pp. 22, 24, 33; A. Ellissen, ed. "Threnes Tis Konstantinoupoleos," *Analekten der Mittel und Neugrieschen Literatur* (Leipzig, 1857), pp. 665-71 cited in *ibid.*, p. 16. Romania was the land of the Christian Romans or the Hellenic Byzantine Empire. It does not refer to the modern Balkan state of Rumania which received its name in the nineteenth century.

10. Anthimos A. Papadopoulos, "O Pontus Dia Ton Aeonon," *Pontic Archives*, I (1928), 23, 29, 30, 31; George Zoras, *Peri Tin Alosin Tis Konstantinoupoleos* (Athens, 1959), pp. 157-283, *passim*.

11. Zakythinos, *Byzantion, Kratos Kae Koenonia, Historike Episcopiesis*, p. 150; Steven Runciman, *The Fall of Constantinople* (Cambridge, 1965), pp. 190-91.

12. James Rennell Rodd, *The Customs and Lore of Modern Greece* (London, 1892), p. 205; Zakythinos, *Byzantion, Kratos Kae Koenonia, Historike Episcopiesis*, pp. 29ff.; Mavrogordato, *Modern Greece*, pp. 44, 48; Roander A.H. Bickford-Smith, *Greece under King George* (London, 1893), pp. 318, 322, 335ff.; Lewis Sergeant, *New Greece* (London, 1878), pp. 189, 219, 233, 403ff.; Lewis Sergeant, *Greece in the Nineteenth Century* (London, 1897), pp. 344, 363; Leften S. Stavrianos, *The Balkans Since 1453* (New York, 1958), pp. 467-68; Schevill, pp. 343-44.

13. Christopher M. Woodhouse, *The Story of Modern Greece* (London, 1968), p. 115; Mavrogordato, p. 18; Rodd, pp. 218, 219; Christopher M. Woodhouse, *The Greek War of Independence* (London, 1952), p. 26. The editors of the *Atlantis* published a popular and brief account of the Greek revolutionary leaders, *He Epanastasis tu Eikosiena* (New York, 1910), I, *passim*; *Atlantis*, ed., *Historia Tis Hellados* (New York, 1909), pp. 51-52. Cf. Theodore Kolokotrones, *The Klepht and the Warrior. Sixty Years of Peril and Daring, An Autobiography*. Translated by Mrs. Edmonds. A Preface by J. Gennadius, Greek Envoy to the Court (London, 1892). There is also a Greek version of the above book, *O*

Kolokotrones (Athens, 1892). Theodore Kolokotrones was one of the most famous leaders in the Greek War of Independence. His name was a household toast. His exploits were the envy of every young boy in Greece. Kolokotrones was probably the most popular hero of the New York Greeks from 1887 to 1910.

14. Eddy, p. 236; Alexander A. Pallis, "Effets de la Guerre en Grèce," *Effets Économique et Sociaux de la Guerre en Grèce*, p. 147; Alexandros Mazarakes-Ainianos, *Historike Melete, 1821-97* (2v. Athens, 1950), I, 307, 326. General Mazakares-Ainianos served as a junior lieutenant in the Greek army during the Greek-Turkish War of 1897.

15. The Eastern Christian community in Syria was divided among the Greek Orthodox, Maronites, Jacobites, Melkites and a handful of Nestorians. The Orthodox Christian Patriarchate transferred its see from Antioch to Damascus in 1268.

16. Philip Pandely Argenti, *Chius Vincta, or the Occupation of Chios by the Turks, 1566, and Their Administration of the Island, 1566-1912* (Cambridge, 1941), p. cxxvii; Aron Hill, *The Present State of the Turkish Empire* (London, ca. 1709), p. 311.

17. Alexander George Paspates, *Poliorkia kae Alosis Tis Konstantinoupoleos Ypo ton Othomanon en etei 1453* (Athens, 1890), p. 229; Sir Edwin Pears, *The Destruction of the Greek Empire* (London, 1903), pp. 382-83; Jacques Visvisis, "L'administration communale des Grecs pendant la domination turque," *Le Cinq-Centième Anniversaire de la Prise de Constantinople, 1453-1953*, p. 219. The official style of the highest Orthodox Christian ecclesiastical leader is Bishop of New Rome, Archbishop of Constantinople and Ecumenical Patriarch. Traditionally, he is referred to as the Ecumenical Patriarch of Constantinople.

18. Sir George Young, *Corps de Droit Ottoman* (7v. Oxford, 1905-6), II, 14ff.; Theodore Papadopoullos, *Studies and Documents Relating to the History of the Greek Church and People under Turkish Domination. Bibliotheca Graeca Aevi Posterioris*, X (Brussels, 1952), pp. 3-4ff.; Sir Charles N. Elliot, *Turkey in Europe* (London, 1908), p. 302; George X. Carapanayotis, *L'Autonomie de la Nation Grecque sous le protectorat turc* (Athens, 1912), pp. 112ff.; Count Josef von Hammer-Pugstall, *Histoire de l'Empire Ottoman*. French translation by J.J. Hellert (18v. Paris, 1835-43), II, 543; Sir Paul Rycaut, *The Present State of the Ottoman Empire* (London, 1668), p. 100; Prince Demetrius Cantemir, *The History of the Growth and Decay of the Ottoman Empire*. Translated by N. Tindal (London, 1734), pp. 101-20.

19. G. Georgiades Arnakis, "The Greek Church of Constantinople

and the Ottoman Empire," *Journal of Modern History* XXIV (September, 1952), 238-39.

20. William Miller, *The Ottoman Empire and Its Successors, 1801-1927* (Cambridge, 1927), pp. 21ff.; William Eton, *A Survey of the Turkish Empire* (London, 1801), p. 98; Trikoupis, I, 97, 119; Nicolae Iorga, *Byzance après Byzance* (Bucharest, 1935), pp. 168, 175-77, 186, 214; Rycaut, p. 103; Na'ima, *Annals of the Turkish Empire: 1591-1659*. Translated by Charles Fraser (London, 1832), I, 60. Na'ima published the annals ca. 1747 in Constantinople.

21. Ogier Ghiselin de Busbecq, *The Epistles of A.G. Busbequius*. Translated from the Latin (London, 1694), p. 57. Cf. *The Life and Letters of Ogier Ghiselin de Busbecq*. Translated by Charles T. Forster and F.H.B. Danieli (2v. London, 1881).

22. Ray Stannard Baker, "Seen in Turkey," *The Outlook*, LXXII (October, 1902), 26.

23. Ecumenical Patriarchate of Constantinople, *The Black Book of the Sufferings of the Greek People in Turkey: From the Armistice to the End of 1920* (Constantinople, 1920), pp. 100ff.; Eton, p. 335; New York *Atlantis*, 1896-1910, *passim*. The newspaper published regular departments under varying titles such as "Enslaved Greece" and "Turkish-dominated Greece." It disseminated information concerning the Greek nationalist movement and the depredations of the Turks in Macedonia and Asia Minor; New York *Ethnikos Kyrix*, 1915-23, *passim*. Margaritu Evangelides, *Aetia Tis Metanasteuseos Ton en Kaukaso Hellenon Tu Pontu* (Athens, 1900), p. 2; William J. Stillman, *The Cretan Insurrection: 1866-68* (New York, 1874), p. 29. Cf. Carroll N. Brown and Theodore P. Ion, *Persecutions of the Greeks in Turkey Since the Beginning of the European War, American-Hellenic Society Publications*, No. 3 (New York, 1918).

24. Panagiotis Bratsiotis, *The Greek Orthodox Church*. Translated by Joseph Blenkinsopp (Gary, IN, 1968), p. 18; Bryer, p. 163; Visvisis, p. 219.

25. Runciman, *The Fall of Constantinople*, pp. 154, 155-56; Arnakis, pp. 242-43; Charles A. Macartney, *National States and National Minorities*. Issued under the auspices of the Royal Institute of International Affairs (London, 1934), pp. 6-8; Elliott Grinnell Mears, *Modern Turkey* (New York, 1924), pp. 35ff.; Henry Pratt Fairchild, *Immigrant Backgrounds* (New York, 1927), pp. 62-64; Roderic H. Davison, "Turkish Attitudes Concerning Christian-Muslim Equality in the Nineteenth Century," *American Historical Review*, LIX (July, 1954), 844-45; Robert W. Seton-Watson, *The Rise of Nationality in the Balkans* (London, 1917), p. 21; Visvisis, p. 234.

26. Trieste *Nea Hemera*, March 17, 1907-May 25, 1907 and February 19, 1908-March 23, 1908. A Greek writer, Achilles Kallistratos, wrote a series of articles concerning the rights, immunities and prerogatives of the Ecumenical Patriarchate. The Greek language newspaper, *Nea Hemera*, was the leading organ of the influential Greek commercial community in Trieste and the Habsburg Empire. The above newspaper files are located in the Library of the Royal Parliament in Athens, Greece. Cf. Young, II, 12-69, *passim*; Papadopoullos, pp. 26-39; Argenti, *Chius Vincta*, pp. cxli, cxciv; Carapanayotis, pp. 41-46, 47ff.; Avrilios Spatharis, *The Ecumenical Patriarchate: A Many Century Old Institution* (Athens, 1959), pp. 11ff.; Thanassis Aghnides, *The Ecumenical Patriarchate of Constantinople: In the Light of the Treaty of Lausanne* (New York, 1964), pp. 9, 19, 21, 25; Philip Newman, *A Short History of Cyprus*, Second Edition (London, 1953), pp. 172, 176; Stavrianos, pp. 103-5; Schevill, pp. 327-28.

27. Runciman, *The Fall of Constantinople*, p. 156.

28. *Roum* or *Rum* is the Turkish corruption of the word Roman. Orthodox Christian Greeks were called Romans by the Turks because they were the descendants of the Christian Roman Empire in the East, i.e. Byzantine Empire. Two other words derived from *Roum* are *Romaic* and *Romeios*. The former refers to the colloquial Greek dialect, while the latter refers to a Greek person of provincial origins. The contemporary Turks continue to call the Ecumenical Patriarch as the *Rum* Patriarch or Roman Patriarch. Greece and the contemporary Greeks are called *Yunanistan* and *Yunanli*, i.e. Ionia and the Ionians.

29. Argenti, *Chius Vincta*, p. cxxx; Carapanayotis, p. 113; Nicholas S. Kaltchas, *Introduction to the Constitutional History of Modern Greece* (New York, 1940), pp. 27-28.

30. Great Britain, Foreign Office, *Report on Smyrna, Report on the Civil Staff of the Late Hospital*, November 1, 1856 (London, 1857), p. 36. The report is located in the Gennadius Library, American School of Classical Sudies, Athens, Greece.

31. Iorga, pp. 79, 234-35.

32. Jeanne Z. Stephanopoli, "L'École, facteur du reveil national," *Le Cinq-Centième Anniversaire de la Prise de Constantinople, 1453-1953*, p. 252.

33. A.H. Lyberer, "The Ottoman Turks and the Routes of Oriental Trade," *English Historical Review*, CXX (October, 1915), 581.

34. Runciman, *The Great Church in Captivity*, pp. 196, 360.

35. Traian Stoianovich, "The Conquering Balkan Orthodox

Merchant," *The Journal of Economic History*, XX (June, 1960), 234, 235; Woodhouse, *The Greek War of Independence*, p. 30.

36. Runciman, *The Great Church in Captivity*, pp. 196, 197; Iorga, pp. 66-67.

37. Stoianovich, p. 241.

38. *Ibid.*, pp. 232, 240.

39. Angeliki Hadjimichali, "Aspect de l'organization économique des Grecs dans l'empire ottoman," *Le Cinq-Centième Anniversaire de la Prise de Constantinople, 1453-1953*, p. 268.

40. Iorga, pp. 114-15.

41. Nicolas G. Svoronas, *Le Commerce de Salonique au XVIIIe Siècle* (Paris, 1956), p. 193; Hadjimichali, p. 272; Runciman, *The Great Church in Captivity*, pp. 360-61.

42. Hadjimichali, pp. 271, 275.

43. *Ibid.*, p. 273.

44. Stoianovich, p. 271; Runciman, *The Great Church in Captivity*, p. 361.

45. Stoianovich, p. 271.

46. Argenti, *Chius Vincta*, pp. clxv, clxvii-clxix, 216, 217ff., 220ff., 231-46; Mavrogordato, *Modern Greece*, p. 20; Alexander M. Vlasto, *Chiaka* (2v. Hermoupolis, 1840), II, 229, 230ff.; Trikoupis, IV, 219, 269; William Miller, "The Genoese in Chios, 1346-1566," *English Historical Review*, CXX (July, 1915), 418, 420, 428; Woodhouse, *The Greek War of Independence*, p. 41; Woodhouse, *The Story of Modern Greece*, p. 85; Stoianovich, p. 250.

47. Philip P. Argenti, ed. *Libro d'Oro de la Noblesse de Chio* (2v. London, 1955), *passim*. The detailed genealogical tables in volume II clearly establish the intermarriages and intimate blood relationship among all the noble families.

48. *Trow's New York City Directories*, 1850-1910, *passim*.

49. Runciman, *The Great Church in Captivity*, pp. 361-62ff. Cf. Eugene Rizo-Rangabe, ed. *Livre d'Or de la Noblesse Phanariot par un Phanariot* (Athens, 1892), *passim*.

50. Stoianovich, p. 309.

51. Alexander C. Sturdza, *L'Europe Orientale et le Role Historique des*

Maurocordato, 1660-1830 (Paris, 1913), pp. 81, 82, 85, 86; Runciman, *The Great Church in Captivity*, p. 362; Iorga, pp. 113ff., 120ff.; Theodore Blancard, *Les Mavroyenni: Essai d'Etude Additionelle à l'Histoire Moderne de la Grèce, de la Turquie et de la Roumanie* (Paris, 1893), pp. 1, 2ff., 14ff.; Theodore Blancard, *Les Mavroyenni: Histoire d'Orient de 1700 à nos jours* (2v. Paris, 1909), I, 11ff.; Scarlatos D. Byzantios, *He Konstantinoupolis He Perigraphi* (3v. Athens, 1862-90), I, 572, 573-74; Woodhouse, *The Greek War of Independence*, pp. 27, 41ff. The family name of Mavroyenni is sometimes rendered as Mavrogenni or Mavrogheni. The family name of Soutstos is sometimes rendered as Soutso, Soutzo or Soutzos. The family name of Mavrocordato is sometimes rendered as Mavrocordatos, Maurocordato or Mavrogordato.

52. P.A. Argyropoulos, "Les Grecs au Service de l'Empire Ottoman," *Le Cinq-Centième de Anniversaire de la Prise de Constantinople, 1453-1953*, pp. 155ff.; N. Vlachos, "Le relation des Grecs Asservis avec l'État Musselman Souverain," *ibid.*, p. 135; Konstantinos Paparrigopoulos, *Historia Tu Helleniku Ethnus*. Eleutheroudakis Revised Edition (8v. Athens, 1925), V. Pt. 2, 80, 89, 93; M. Villeman, *Lascaris, les Grecs du Quinzième Siècle* (Paris, 1825), p. 154.

53. Bryer, p. 164.

54. Marriott, p. 200; Runciman, *The Great Church in Captivity*, p. 365; Forster, p. 4; Argyropoulos, pp. 155, 156, 163; Sturdza, *L'Europe Orientale et le Rôle Historique de Maurocordato, 1660-1830*, p. 87.

55. Forster, p. 3; Runciman, *The Great Church in Captivity*, p. 368; Marriott, p. 5.

56. Argyropoulos, p. 161; Marriott, pp. 200-201; Runciman, *The Great Church in Captivity*, p. 365.

57. William Miller, *A History of the Greek People, 1821-1921* (London, 1922), p. 9; Hereafter cited as Miller, *Greek People*; Argyropoulos, pp. 167-77; Bratsiotis, p. 20; Blancard, *Les Mavroyenni: Histoire d'Orient de 1700 à Nos Jours*, I, 11ff.; Blancard, *Les Mavroyenni: Essai d'Etude Additionelle à l'Histoire Moderne de la Grèce, de la Turquie et de la Roumanie*, pp. 1, 2ff., 14 ff,; Byzantios, I, 573-74, 538, II, 110-12, 114, 388ff.; Alexander C. Sturdza, *Regne de Michel Stourdza, Prince Regnant de Moldavie, 1834-1849* (Paris, 1907), pp. 136, 265, 287; Prince Nicolas Soutzo, *Memoires du Prince Nicolas Soutzo, Grand Logothete de Moldavie, 1798-1871* (Vienna, 1899), pp. 3, 4ff.; Woodhouse, *The Story of Modern Greece*, p. 116. Cf. Eugene Rizo-Rangabe, ed., *Livre d'Or de la Noblesse Phanariote et des Familles Princière de Valachie et de Moldavie* (Athens, 1904), *passim*; Eugene Rizo-Rangabe, ed., *Livre d'Or de la Noblesse Ionienne* (4v. Athens, 1925-27), *passim*.

58. Blancard, *Les Mavroyenni: Histoire d'Orient de 1700 à nos Jours*, p. 559; Miller, *Greek People*, p. 586. After the Balkan Wars the Princely Assembly of Samos had proclaimed union with Greece in 1913. Therefore, all Greeks from Samos in New York City were regarded as Turkish subjects and listed in the statistics of Turkey-in-Europe in the several census reports until 1920.

59. Runciman, *The Great Church in Captivity*, pp. 407ff. The name of Musurus may be rendered as Moussouros, Mousouros and Mousuros.

60. William Miller, *The Ottoman Empire and Its Successors 1801-1927, With an Appendix, 1927-1936* (London, 1936), pp. 380, 387, 395. The name Karatheody is sometimes rendered as Caratheodri, Caratheodory or Karatheodori.

61. Runciman. *The Great Church in Captivity*, pp. 407-408.

62. Notis Botzaris, *Visions Balkaniques dans la Préparation de la Révolution Grecque, 1789-1821, Études d'Histoire Économique, Politique et Sociale*, XXXVIII (Geneva, 1962), 71, 86; Stephanopoli, pp. 243-44; Iorga, pp. 201ff., 214; Runciman, *The Great Church in Captivity*, pp. 392-93, 396.

63. Forster, pp. 8-9; Miller, *Greek People*, pp. 11-12; Botzaris, 83ff., 93ff.; Marriott, p. 203.

64. Botzaris, pp. 72, 73ff. It is interesting to note that the first Panhellenic brotherhood established in the 1890s in New York City was called the Brotherhood of Athena.

65. New York *The Evening Telegram*, April 21, 1897; *The New York Times*, April 22, 1897. These newspapers claimed that Solon J. Vlasto, publisher of the New York Greek newspaper, *Atlantis*, and his younger brother, Demetrius Vlasto, were active agents of the *Ethnike Hetaireia* in New York.

66. Botzaris, pp. 225-6; Marriott, pp. 195ff.

67. Woodhouse, *The Greek War of Independence*, pp. 47-51; Marriott, pp. 204ff., 212ff.; Trikoupis, I.

68. Andreas M. Andreades, *Meletae Epi Tis Synchronu Hellenikis Demosias Oeconomias, Erga*. Kyriakos Varvaressos, G.A. Petropoulos, J.D. Pintos, eds. (4v. Athens, 1939), II, 184. Hereafter cited as *Erga*.

69. Demetrius Bikelas, *Seven Essays on Christian Greece* (London, 1890), p. 267.

70. Forster, pp. 10ff.; Argenti, *Libro d'Oro de la Noblesse de Chio*, I, ix;

Philip P. Argenti, *The Massacre of Chios* (London, 1932), *passim*; Philip P. Argenti, *The Expedition of Colonel Fabrier to Chios* (London, 1933), *passim*; Reverend T.S. Hughes, "An Address to the People of England in the Cause of the Greeks, Occasioned by the Late Inhuman Massacres on the Island of Scio," *The Pamphleteer*, XXX (1822), 167, 168ff., 188; Christophorus Plato Castanis, *The Greek Exile or a Narrative of the Captivity and Escape of Christophorus P. Castanis During the Massacre on the Island of Scio by the Turks Together with Various Adventures in Greece and America* (Philadelphia, 1851), pp. 23, 24ff.

71. Mavrogordato, *Modern Greece*, pp. 20-22.

72. *Report of the American Board of Commissioners For Foreign Missions, 1827*, p. 47; *ibid.*, *1833*, p. 40.

73. United States Treasury Department, *Tables Showing the Arrivals of Alien Passengers and Immigrants in the United States from 1820 to 1888* (Washington, 1889), p. 8. Hereafter cited as the *Treasury Tables, 1820-88*. The immigrant figures for the Ionian Islands and Thessaly were included with those of Greece after 1863 and 1881, respectively.

74. *Report of the American Board of Commissioners for Foreign Missions, 1823* p. 128; *ibid.*, *1824*, pp. 112-113; *ibid.*, *1827*, p. 48; *ibid.*, *1831*, p. 43.

75. *Ibid.*, *1827*, p. 43; *ibid.*, *1831*, p. 37; *ibid.*, *1835*, pp. 40, 42; *ibid.*, *1837*, p. 52; *ibid.*, *1840*, pp. 84-85.

76. John M. Francis to Hamilton Fish, Athens, May 24, 1873, *Papers Relating to Foreign Relations of the United States, 1873*, p. 483. The series hereafter are cited as *Foreign Relations* and the document as *Francis-Fish, May 24, 1873*. John Francis traveled through the provinces of Greece in 1873. He was accompanied by Charles S. Francis, his son, George Constantine Francis, former United States consul in Patras, and Ellis H. Roberts, a New York congressman.

77. Lewis Sergeant, *New Greece*, pp. 104ff.; Karolides, p. 793; Forster, p. 16; Marriott, pp. 366-70; Protocol Between Great Britain, France and Russia: Termination of the Bavarian Order of Succession to the Throne of Greece, May 16, 1863, Hertslet, II, 1535-36. An eye witness account of the insurrection at Hermoupolis, Syros, was recorded by Christodules Evangelides. Cf. Unpublished Manuscript, Diary of Christodules Leonidas Miltiades Evangeles, New-York Historical Society (4v. 1834-39), III, inserted manuscript dated April 4, 1862.

78. George M. Trevelyan, *History of England*. Third Edition (London, 1945), p. 587; Marriott, pp. 365-66; Forster, pp. 17-18; Rizo-Rangabe, *Livre d'Or de la Noblesse Ioniènne*, I, p. 11; Protocol of Conference

Between the Plenipotentiaries of Great Britain, France, Russia and Denmark, Relative to the Succession to The Throne of Greece, and to the Annexation of the Ionian Islands to That Kingdom, Hertslet, II, 1539; Treaty Between Great Britain, France, Russia and Greece respecting the Union of the Ionian Islands to the Kingdom of Greece, London, March 29, 1864, *ibid.*, III, 1589-95; Greek Decree, Cession of the British Protectorate over the Ionian Islands, Athens, March 20, 1863, *ibid.*, II, 1530; Article IV of the Treaty of July 13 and November 14, 1863, *ibid.*, II, 1547; Treaty of March 29, 1864, *ibid.*, II, 1591.

79. Sergeant, *New Greece*, p. 89; Schevill, p. 388; Forster, pp. 19, 56-57; Karolides, p. 800; Trikoupis, II, 222-23, IV, 238-40; Paparrigopoulos, VI, 315; Alexandre Couclelis, *Les Régimes Gouvernementaux de la Grèce à Nos Jours* (Paris, 1925), pp. 14, 18, 20, 83-94, 95ff.; Alexandre Svolos, "L'influence des Idées de la Révolution Française de la Guerre d'Indépendance," *Révolution Française*, n.s., No. 4 (Paris, 1935), pp. 341, 345-47; the text of the constitution of 1864 is found in 56 *B.F.S.P.* 572; the constitutions of January, 1822 and May, 1827 are found in 9 *ibid.*, 620 and 15 *ibid.*, 1069, respectively; Samuel Gridley Howe, *A Historical Sketch of the Greek Revolution* (New York, 1828), pp. 445-52. A revolutionary and poet, Constantine Rhegas Velestinlis drafted a model constitution for a proposed Greek Republic that was based on the French constitutions of 1793 and 1795, cited in Botzaris, pp. 103-205. Cf. Apostolos Daskalakis, *Les Oeuvres Rhegas Velestinlis* (Paris, 1937), pp. 75-125.

80. Marriott, pp. 318-26, 341-46; Carapanayotis, pp. 224-27; H.A. Munro-Butler-Johnstone, *The Turks: Their Character, Manners and Institutions As Bearing in the Eastern Question* (London, 1876), pp. 24, 43-45; Carlton J.H. Hayes, *A Generation of Materialism: 1870-1900. The Rise of Modern Europe*, edited by William L. Langer (New York, 1941), pp. 25-34, 231, 278; Turkish Firman, Granting Immunities and Favours to Ottoman Subjects, December 12, 1875, Hertslet, IV, 2414; Preliminary Treaty of Peace Between Russia and Turkey, San Stefano, March 3, 1878, *ibid.*, 2672-94; Treaty Between Great Britain, Austria-Hungary, France, Germany, Russia and Turkey for the Settlement of the Affairs of the East, Berlin, July 13, 1878, *ibid.*, 2759-98; British Order-in-Council Defining the Powers and Jurisdiction of Great Britain over the Island of Cyprus, Balmoral, September 14, 1878, *ibid.*, 2804-9, 2844; 69 *B.S.F.P.* 720; Sergeant, *Greece in the Nineteenth Century*, pp. 281, 283, 297; Roander A.H. Bickford-Smith, p. 339; Forster, pp. 28-29.

81. Runciman, *The Great Church in Captivity*, pp. 208-220ff., 259ff., 378, 379, 382-83, 390, 392-398ff.; Botzaris, pp. 17, 18ff., 71ff., 177-81; Bryer, pp. 166-67.

82. Patrick Leigh Fermor, *Roumeli: Travels in Northern Greece* (New York, 1962), pp. 106, 107-13.

83. New York *Pan-Hellenic Union*, July 1, 1914; *New-York Daily Tribune*, February 26, 1897 and September 25, 1906; Karolides, p. 225; Stavrianos, pp. 467-68; Alexander Rhizos-Rhankabes, *Greece: Her Progress and Present Condition* (New York, 1867), p. 19; New York *Atlantis*, 1894-1923, *passim*; New York *Ethnikos Kyrix*, 1915-23, *passim*; Bickford-Smith, pp. 318-22; Sergeant, *Greece in the Nineteenth Century*, pp. 55, 75, 282, 344, 363.

84. George Zoras, *Ae Pro Kae Meta Tin Alosin Diamorphotheisae Ideologikae Kae Politikae Kateythynseis: 1453-1953*, pp. 22, 24, 33; Ellissen, pp. 665-71 cited in *ibid.*, p. 16; Zakythinos, *Byzantion: Kratos Kae Koenonia Historike Episcopisci*, pp. 29ff.; Papadopoulos, 17; Rodd, pp. 205, 218, 219, 223; George T. Zoras, *E Xeniteia en Ti Helleniki Poeisei* (Athens, 1953), pp. 20-21ff.; Runciman, *The Fall of Constantinople*, pp. 189-191. Cf. Dionysios Zakythinos, *E Alosis Tis Konstantinupoleos Kae Tin Turcocratia* (Athens, 1954); Zoras, *Peri Tin Alosin Tis Konstantinupoleos*; Alexander Soutsos, *Turcomachos Hellas*, Sixth Edition (Constantinople, n.d.); *Nea Helleniki Anthologia* (New York, 1913). The last work, an anthology of modern Greek poetry, was edited and published by the *Atlantis*; Bryer, pp. 159, 163, 167-168.

85. Kenneth C.M. Sills, Letter to the Editor, dated September 27, 1913, "Greek Americans," *The Nation*, XCVII (October, 1913), 309-10.

86. F.R. Welles, Letter to the Editor, dated July 8, 1914, *ibid.*, XCIX (July 23, 1914), 102.

Chapter 2

The Newcomers

1. Theodore P. Saloutos, "The Greeks in the United States," *South Atlantic Quarterly*, XLIV (January, 1945), p. 69.

2. U.S. Census, *Ninth*, 1870, pp. 340, 342, 376, 390; *ibid.*, *Thirteenth*, 1910, *Population*, I, 815, 824; *ibid.*, III, 213, 217ff. The federal census reports in 1830 and 1840 listed all Greeks from the various states in the category of "Other Countries."

3. New York State, Secretary of State, *Census of the State of New York*, 1855, pp. 132, 177.

4. *Ibid.*, 1865, pp. lxxii, lxxiv, 131, 164.

5. *Ibid.*, 1875, pp. 30, 56. The succeeding New York State Census sur-

veys of 1892, 1906 and 1925 listed only three categories, (1) total population, (2) citizens and (3) aliens. The confidential information concerning names, addresses, occupations was not published nor is it available to the historian.

6. Theodore Saloutos, *The Greeks in the United States* (Cambridge, 1964), p. 44.

7. Rev. Thomas J. Lacey, *Our Greek Immigrants* (New York, 1918), p. 13. The Serbs, Bulgars and Montenegrins were other Europeans that had great religious homogenity during this period. Cf. J.P. Xenides, *The Greeks in America* (New York, 1922), pp. 54, 67; Unpublished doctoral dissertation, Robert Augustus Georges, Greek-American Folk Beliefs and Narratives: Survivals and Living Tradition, Indiana University, 1964, p. 46, University Microfilms, Inc., Ann Arbor, Michigan.

8. U.S. Census, *Thirteenth*, 1910, *Population*, I, 781. Cf. *ibid.*, *Fourteenth*, 1920, *Population*, II, 685, 687; *ibid.*, *Fifteenth*, 1930, II, 225.

9. Leland Gordon, *American Relations with Turkey: 1830-1930* (Philadelphia, 1932), p. 306.

10. *Ibid.*, p. 307.

11. *Ibid.*, pp. 308-309. Cf. U.S. Census, *Thirteenth*, 1910, *Population*, I, 968, 975.

12. U.S. Census, *Compendium of the Eleventh Census of the United States*, 1890 (2v. Washington, 1892), I, 475ff., 515, 582, 666; *ibid.*, *Special Report on Religious Bodies*, 1906 (2 pts. Washington, 1910), I, 29, 240, 340ff.

13. *Ibid.*, 1916, I, 450ff.

14. *Ibid.*, *Thirteenth*, 1910, *Population*, I, 959. Cf. *ibid.*, *Fourteenth*, 1920, *Population*, II, 965, 968; *ibid.*, *Fifteenth*, 1930, *Population*, II, 341, 342-43.

15. *Ibid.*, *Thirteenth*, 1910, *Population*, I, 980.

16. *Ibid.*, 975.

17. *Ibid.*, 975, 980, 1011. The Bureau of the Census adopted the term, *foreign stock*, to indicate "combined total of three classes, namely (1) the foreign born persons, (2) native children of foreign parentage, i.e., those having both foreign born parents, (3) natives of mixed parentage, i.e., those persons having one native and the other a foreign born parent. In other words, immigrants and their native born children.

18. *Report of the American Board of Commissioners for Foreign Missions*, 1831, p. 34; *ibid.*, 1870, p. 16; Eddy, pp. 27-28; reminiscences of Nicholas A. Contopoulos; F.W. Hasluck, "The Crypto-Christians of Trebizond,"

Journal of Hellenic Studies, XLI (1921), pp. 199, 202; Robert M. Dawkins, *Modern Greek in Asia Minor: A Study of the Dialects of Sille, Cappadocia, and Pharasa With Grammar, Texts, Translations and Glossary* (Cambridge, 1916), pp. 1, 2ff., 38ff.; Karl Dieterich, *Hellenism in Asia Minor*. Translated by Carroll N. Brown, *American-Hellenic Society Publications*, No. 4 (New York, 1918), pp. 31-32. Microfilm copies of the newspaper, *Anatoli*, are located in the Newspaper Division of the New York Public Library.

19. Sarah Searight, "The Turkey Merchants: Life in the Levant Company," *History Today*, XVI (June, 1966), 418; Alfred C. Wood, *A History of the Levant Company* (Oxford, 1935), p. 244.

20. U.S. Census, *Twelfth*, 1900, *Population*, I, 915, 919, 943, 951.

21. *Ibid.*, *Thirteenth*, 1910, *Population*, I, 1065, 1068, 1083.

22. *Ibid.*, *Special Report: Occupations at the Twelfth Census*, 1900, pp. 65ff., 71, 346ff., 634ff. Not only Greeks but also Armenians, Syrians, Maronites, Serbs, Arabs and Albanians were included in the same category of "Other Countries."

23. *Ibid.*, *Thirteenth*, 1910, *Population: Occupation Statistics*, IV, 494ff., 571.

24. *Annual Reports of the Commissioner-General of Immigration*. 1899-1910, *passim*.

25. Thomas Burgess, *Greeks in America* (Boston, 1913), pp. 52-53; Seraphim G. Canoutas, *O Hellenismos en Ameriki* (New York, 1918), pp. 162-63 n; Thomas J. Lacey, *A Study of Social Heredity As Illustrated in the Greek People* (New York, 1916), p. 48; Henry P. Fairchild, *Greek Immigration to the United States* (New Haven, 1911), p. 120; Saloutos, *The Greeks in the United States*, p. 126; John Lampridu, *Ae Hellenikae Apokiae* (Athens, 1895), *passim*.

26. Lacey, *Our Greek Immigrants*, pp. 4, 6; Theodore Saloutos, *The Greeks in America: A Student's Guide to Localized History* (New York, 1967), p. 8; U.S.A., Works Progress Administration, *The HIstorical Record Survey, Inventory of Church Archives in New York City of the Eastern Orthodox Churches and the Armenian Church in America* (Washington, 1940), p. 114. Hereafter cited as *Inventory of Church Archives*.

27. *New York Daily Tribune*, May 10, 1896.

28. New York *The Sun*, February 20, 1897; New York *Atlantis*, November 24, 1899; *Annual Reports of the Commissioner-General of Immigration*, 1899-1913, *passim*; United States Immigration Commission,

Reports of the Immigration Commission (41v. Washington, 1911), IV, *Emigration Conditions in Europe*, pp. 391ff. Hereafter cited as *Emigration Conditions in Europe*; *ibid.*, III, *Statistical Review of Immigration: 1820-1910, Distribution of Immigrants*: 1850-1910, 14ff.; Hereafter cited as *Distribution of Immigrants*: 1850-1900; Emmanuel Repoulis, *Meleti Meta Schediu Nomu Peri Metanasteuseos* (Athens, 1912), pp. 7ff.

29. Fairchild, *Greek Immigration to the United States*, pp. 150-51.

30. U.S. Census, *Special Report on Religious Bodies*, 1906, I, 29, 100, 240, 340, 516ff.; *ibid.*, 1916, I, 486ff.

31. Great Britain, Parliament, *Sessional Papers*, XXVI (London, 1923), "Turkey No. 1 (1923) Lausanne Conference on Near Eastern Affairs, 1922-1923, Convention Concerning the Exchange of Greek and Turkish Populations, signed at Lausanne the 30th of January, 1923," 817-18; League of Nations, 32 *Treaty Series* (1925), 76-77; League of Nations, *Official Journal* (November, 1923), pp. 1468; Eddy, pp. 13-14, 43-45, 248, 252.

32. Stephen P. Ladas, *The Exchange of Minorities; Bulgaria, Greece and Turkey* (New York, 1932), pp. 377, 378, 390.

33. *Ibid.*, p. 384.

34. U.S. National Archives, Index to Passenger Lists of Vessels Arriving at New York, 1820-1846. National Archives Microfilm Publication, Microcopy No. 261, Roll No. 18.

35. Lacey, *Our Greek Immigrants*, p. 3.

36. Athens, *Neon Asty*, December 15, 1901; *ibid.*, January 31, 1905; advertisement, New York *Atlantis*, June 3, 1903; *ibid.*, June 4, 1906; *Levant Trade Review* (June 11, 1911), p. 19; C. Christophi, *Genèse de l'émigration orientale* (Athens, 1916), pp. 7ff., 18, 20.

37. U.S. Census, *Eighth*, 1860, pp. xxii, xxxi.

38. *Ibid.*, *Ninth*, 1870, pp. 340, 342; *ibid.*, *Tenth*, 1880, I, 776.

39. *Ibid.*, *Ninth*, 1870, *Statistics of Population*, p. 390.

40. *Ibid.*, *Compendium of the Tenth Census*, 1880, I, 486, 550.

41. Maurice S. Thompson, "Notes on the Social and Economic Conditions in Greece," *Sociological Review*, VI (July, 1913), 215-16; Henry P. Fairchild, "Causes of Emigration From Greece," *Yale Review*, XVIII (August, 1909), 176, 182-83; Nicos J. Polyzos, *Essai sur l'émigration Grecque, Étude Démographique, Economique et Sociale* (Paris, 1947), pp. 48, 55ff.; Xenides, pp. 105ff.; Burgess, pp. 20-21; Saloutos, *The Greeks in the United States*, p. 29.

Chapter 3

The Merchants

1. Argenti, *Libro d'oro de la Noblesse de Chio*, I, 50-51, 78-80, 101-04, 129-31; B. Efthimiou, *Skiagraphia Ton Apodemon Hellenon Tis Amerikis Kae Historia Tu Kathedriku Neas Yorkes* (New York, 1949), pp. 38-39; Rizo-Rangabe, *Livre d'or de la noblesse Phanariote par un Phanariote, passim; Society List and Club Register* (New York, 1886-87), p. 92; *Social Register of New York, 1890*, p. 130; *ibid., 1895*, p. 211. Cf. Constantine Kerofilas, *Une famille patricïenne, Les Vlasto* (New York, 1932). Alexander, P. Ralli, *A Pedigree of the Rallis of Scio, 1700 to 1892* (London, 1896). The latter book was privately printed and circulated among the members of the Ralli family. A copy of this book is located in the Gennadius Library of the American School of Classical Studies in Athens, Greece.

2. *Dictionary of American Biography* (22 v. New York, 1937-58), II, 640; Canoutas, p. 28; *The New York Times*, March 21, 1898; New York *The Sun*, March 21, 1898; *New York Daily Tribune*, March 21, 1898; New York *Atlantis*, March 24, 1898.

3. William Cullen Bryant, *Poems* (New York, 1868), pp. 184-85; Solon J. Vlasto, *Historia Ton Henomenon Politeion Tis Amerikis*, Revised Edition (New York, 1919), pp. 274 n, 274-75; Vlasto's history of the United States was first published in 1908; G. Stone to Christodules Evangeles, Saratoga Springs, October 4, 1833, miscellaneous Julia Ward Howe Papers, New-York Historical Society. Evangeles was elected as the second president of the Philomathein Society of New York University in 1833.

4. Evangeles Diary, II, n.d., autobiographical sketch appears before the entry of March 1, 1838; *ibid.*, August 17, 1834; *ibid.*, August 18, 1834. Several undated autobiographical outlines appear in the above volume in the handwriting of Evangeles. Traditionally, the Orthodox Christian Greek assumes his father's first name as his own middle name for identification, e.g., Nicholas, son of Anastasios Contopoulos, became Nicholas A. Contopoulos; Theodore, son of Pandias Ralli, became Theodore P. Ralli; Paul, son of Stephen Galatti, became Paul S. Galatti; and Alexander, son of Christodules or Christopher Evangelides, became Alexander C. Evangelides.

5. *Ibid.*, June 2, 3, 5, 7, 1835.

6. *Ibid.*, June 11, 1835.

7. Daniel F. Allen to Christodules Evangelides, Boston, August 21, 1850, miscellaneous Christodules Evangeles Papers, New-York Historical Society; Copy of letter, William Cullen Bryant to Moses Grinnell, New York, May 31, 1869, Diary of Alexander C. Evangelides, New-York

Historical Society (1864-69); Christos Evangelides, *Kanonismos Tu Helleniku Lydeiu* (Athens, 1877), pp. 7ff.

8. Verplanck Papers. Christodules Evangelides' command of written English was not excellent. His letters and diary contain misspelled words. He was actually translating from Greek to English because the syntax of the sentences and use of prepositions were Greek.

9. Julia Ward Howe, *Is Polite Society Polite?* (New York, 1895), p. 80; I.H. Hill to Christopher Evangelides, Athens, July 8, 1843; Miscellaneous Julia Ward Howe Papers, New-York Historical Society; I.H. Hill to Christopher Evangelides, Athens, April 29, 1844, miscellaneous J.W. Howe Papers. In his letter, Hill informed that Evangelides' circulars on educational views were sent to P. Schilizzi, a partner in the banking firm of Thomas Ralli & Co. in Constantinople; Julia Ward Howe to Christopher Evangelides, Rome, April 11, 1844, miscellaneous J.W. Howe Papers, New-York Historical Society; I.H. Hill to Christopher Evangelides, Athens, October 29, 1845, miscellaneous J.W. Howe Papers, New-York Historical Society.

10. Copies of letters, Alexander C. Evangelides to William Cullen Bryant, New York, May 30, 1869; Alexander C. Evangelides to William Cullen Bryant, New York, June 1, 1869, A.C. Evangelides Diary; *Manual of the Common Council, City of Brooklyn* (New York, 1886), pp. 23, 42; *Third Annual Report of the Civil Service Commission of the City of Brooklyn, 1886*, p. 12.

11. Julia Ward Howe, *Reminiscences, 1819-1899* (New York, 1899), pp. 313, 441; *D.A.B.*, I, 261; Babes Malafouris, *Hellenes Tis Amerikis: 1528-1948* (New York, 1948), pp. 52ff.; Canoutas, pp. 66, 73, 108; New York *Atlantis*, June 29, 1906. Cf. *Michael Anagnos: 1837-1906* (Boston, 1906). The Perkins Institute published the above work as a tribute to the deceased educator.

12. Evangeles Diary, IV, November 16, 1836; for George M. Colvocoresses (1816-72), see *D.A.B.*, IV, 326-27 and *New York Herald*, June 5, 1872. The Greek and British branches of the family used the original name, Calvocoressi; George M. Colvocoresses to Henry August Wise, Litchfield, Conn., January 29, 1867, Henry August Wise Papers, L.B. 13, No. 107, New-York Historical Society. Colvocoresses became an admiral in the United States Navy; Canoutas, pp. 26-27, 30-31, 66, 73-74; Malafouris, pp. 39-49; for E.A. Sophocles, see *D.A.B.*, XVIII, 397.

13. Evangeles Diary, II, November 17, 1836; Canoutas, p. 95.

14. John Rodocanachi (1828-1906) was appointed Greek Consul of Boston in 1865. He was also a member of the New York Cotton

Exchange. Upon his death, Rodocanachi bequeathed funds to Greek Churches in Boston and Greek Schools in Smyrna. Pandia Ralli was commissioned as the Greek Consul-General in London. The Greek government used these successful merchants as their consular officers in New York, New Orleans, Boston, London and other trade centers.

15. *Burke's Genealogical and Heraldic History of the Peerage and Knightdom, Privy Council and Order of Precedence.* Ninety-seventh Edition (2v. London, 1939), II, 2033. Hereafter cited as *Burke's Peerage.* Other members of the family were Pandia (1791-1865); Augustus Stephen (1797-1878); Thomas Stephen (1798-1880) represented the family firm in Constantinople; Eustratios Stephen (1800-1880) was assigned to Manchester; Baron Ambrose Ralli was resident in Trieste and John Ralli conducted the family business in Odessa.

16. *Ibid.,* 2032-33.

17. Canoutas, pp. 31, 101; Basil Zustis, *O En Ameriki Hellenismos Kae E Drasis Autu* (New York, 1954), p. 37; Efthimiou, p. 38. Reverend Efthimiou was the Dean of the Hellenic Archdiocesan Cathedral of the Holy Trinity from 1941 to 1953. The Holy Trinity Church was transformed into the Cathedral of the Holy Trinity Church in 1918.

18. *Wilson's Business Directory of New York City, 1857,* p. 118. Hereafter cited as *Wilson's Directory;* Zustis, pp. 38-40.

19. Canoutas, p. 32. Ralli Brothers continued trading in New York with the firm of Munzinger & Pitzipios in 1869.

20. There are no available records for the Fachiri firm and its affiliated and successor companies. Information was gathered from the annual reports of the several commodity exchanges, directories, newspaper accounts, newspaper obituaries, social club directories as well as the work of Seraphim Canoutas, a contemporary of Anthony P. Ralli, Pandia A. Ralli, Solon J. Vlasto and other important personalities in the Greek community during the first decade of the twentieth century.

21. Cf. Volume 46, Manuscript Population Schedules, *Tenth Census,* 1880.

22. New York *Atlantis,* August 25, 1899; *Annual Reports of the New York Cotton Exchange, 1885-87, passim.; ibid., 1888,* pp. 21ff.; *ibid., 1891-1897, passim.; ibid., 1906,* pp. 19, 21; *Annual Report of the New York Produce Exchange, 1887,* p. xlix; *ibid., 1890,* p. xlix.

23. New York *Ethnikos Kyrix,* August 12, 1916; *The New York Times,* August 14, 1916.

24. *Annual Report of the New York Cotton Exchange, 1870,* p. 29; *ibid.,* *1871,* p. 29; *ibid., 1872,* p. 28; *ibid., 1875,* p. 27.

25. *New-York Daily Tribune,* September 25, 1896. Theodore Fachiri died in Liverpool, England, on September 24, 1896. See obituaries, *The New York Times,* September 25, 1896; *Annual Report of the New York Cotton Exchange, 1897,* p. 5; New York *Atlantis,* September 26, 1896.

26. *Social Register of New York, 1891,* pp. 83, 195; *ibid., 1893,* pp. 114, 241; *ibid., 1901,* p. 68; *Dau's New York Blue Book, 1915,* p. 248.

27. The New York Club, *Club Constitution, By-Laws and House Rules, 1867,* p. 25; *ibid., 1885,* pp. 46, 51; *ibid., 1889,* pp. 20, 21, 32; *ibid., 1894-5,* pp. 17, 23.

28. *New York Herald,* December 1, 1876.

29. *Ibid.,* March 22, 1887.

30. The first citation in a business directory of S.J. Vlasto as an importer at 2 Stone Street was in *Wilson's Directory, 1888,* p. 589; *New York Journal of Commerce,* March 21, 1887; *New York Herald,* March 22, 1887; *The New York Times,* March 23, 1887. Solon J. Vlasto retired in the early 1920s. He left the United States and died at his home, outside of Paris, France on September 30, 1927. See obituaries, New York *Atlantis,* September 30, 1927; New York *Ethnikos Kyrix,* September 30, 1927; New York *The Herald-Tribune,* September 30, 1927; *The New York Times,* September 30, 1927. Demetrius J. Vlasto died in New York on May 17, 1944. See obituaries, *The New York Times,* May 19, 1944; New York *Atlantis,* May 18, 1944; New York *Ethnikos Kyrix,* May 18, 1944. Cf. Constantine Kerofilas, *Une Famille Patriciènne, Les Vlasto* (New York, 1932).

31. New York *The Evening Post,* March 12, 1897.

32. William H. Boyd, *New York City Tax Book, Being a List of Persons, Corporations and Co-Partnerships, Resident and Non-Resident Who Were Taxed According to the Assessor's Book,* 1856 and 1857 (New York, 1857), pp. 162, 169, 174, 231. Hereafter cited as *Boyd's Co-Partnership and Residence Directory.*

33. George M. Trevelyan, *English Social History* (London, 1942), pp. 389-90, 559.

34. *The New York Times,* Ocotober 20, 1855.

35. Trevelyan, *English Social History,* pp. 200, 216, 217, 323. To secure currants, raisins and wines of Zante, Crete and Chios were major objectives of the Levant Company founded in 1581. The word currant is

derived from Corinth, one of the major producing regions, just as Malmsey wine is a corruption of Monemvasia in the Peloponnesus, renowned in the middle ages for its distinctive wines.

36. Elijah Helm, "The British Cotton Industry," *British Industries*, edited by W.J. Ashley (London, 1907), pp. 81, 85; Canoutas, pp. 31, 100-102 n. The merchant banking firms of Ralli Brothers and P.P. Rodocanachi were founded in their present forms in 1820 and 1860, respectively. See *The Bankers' Almanac and Yearbook, 1960-1961* (London, 1961), pp. 196, 198. The Ralli company was first organized as Ralli & Petrokokinos from 1818 to 1825. After 1826 the firm was permanently established as Ralli Brothers. In 1961 the company was reorganized. By January, 1962 Ralli Brothers, Ltd. was controlled by Sir Isaac Wolfson's General Guarantee Corporation. The Ralli family is not associated with the firm any longer. See London *The Times*, January 23, January 27, August 9 and August 25, 1962.

37. *The New York Times*, October 20, 1855.

38. *Rode's New York City Business Directory for 1854-1855* (New York, 1954), p. 122. Hereafter cited as *Rode's Directory*; *Wilson's Directory, 1852*, p. 80; *ibid., 1852-1853*, p. 80; *ibid., 1855*, p. 108; *ibid., 1855-56*, p. 108; *ibid., 1856-57*, pp. 111, 258, 261, 269, 296; *ibid., 1861-62*, p. 311; *ibid., 1863-64*, p. 284.

39. *Heller's New Orleans Business Directory for 1860 and '61 with Commercial Register of Business Men of New York City* (New York, 1860), pp. 17, 37, 38, 39; *Gardiner's New Orleans Directory for 1860* (New Orleans, 1859), pp. 411, 412, 413.

40. C.H. Brown, *Egyptian Cotton* (London, 1953), pp. 15, 137; C.N. Livanos, *John Sakellaridis and Egyptian Cotton* (Alexandria, Egypt, 1939), pp. 16, 17, 24-25, 27ff. The firm of Choremi, Benaki & Co. had a branch office in Boston. See Canoutas, p. 32.

41. These years indicate when the companies were first listed in business directories. *Wilson's Directory, 1865*, p. 300; *ibid., 1868*, pp. 368, 369, 377; *ibid., 1869*, p. 373; *ibid., 1873*, p. 76. The firm of Constantine Menelas was reorganized as Menelas & Mikas in 1877. Later, Menelas became an agent for Ralli Brothers. Most of the firms terminated their operations by 1900. Their activities were transferred to the development of cotton exports from Egypt and India.

42. *Duncan & Co.'s New Orleans Directory for 1866* (New Orleans, 1865), p. 55; *Gardiner's New Orleans Directory for 1866*, pp. 81, 365; *ibid., 1867*, pp. 58, 71, 325.

43. The following Greek merchants were members of the New York Produce Exchange from 1870 to 1910; L.M. Calvocoressi, Basil Eutichidi, Nicholas Eutichidi, Panteleon Fachiri, G.E. Franghiadi, Paul S. Galatti, Pantaleon Gunari, John C. Maximos, Constantine Menelas, G.N. Paspati, Aristides Paterachi, Pandia Ralli, Thomas Zizinia, Stamaty Covas, Christos D. Georgiades, A.Z. Vouros, Lucas E. Ralli, L. Argenti, Constantine P. Ralli, Solon J. Vlasto, George Pitzipios, Theodore P. Ralli.

44. *Annual Report of the Board of Managers of the New York Produce Exchange, 1873*, pp. 151, 157, 160, 173, 177, 179, 193; *ibid., 1875*, pp. 163, 186, 190, 193, 208; *ibid., 1887*, p. xlix; *ibid., 1890*, pp. xix, xlix.

45. The following Greek merchants were members of the New York Cotton Exchange from 1870 to 1910: Theodore Fachiri, charter member, Demetrius N. Botassi, John Contostavlos, John M. Calvocoressi, Basil Eutichidi, E.A. Fachiri, P.A. Fachiri, P.Y. Fachiri, Ambrose Fachiri, Pantaleon Gunari, Paul S. Galatti, Constantine Menelas, Paul P. Negreponte, Anthony P. Ralli, Alexander Ralli, Theodore P. Ralli, John M. Rodocanachi, Thomas Zizinia.

46. *Annual Reports of the New York Cotton Exchange, 1870-1898, passim.*

47. *Ibid., 1874*, p. 7; *ibid., 1876*, p. 8; *ibid., 1886-97, passim.*; *ibid., 1898*, p. 7; *ibid., 1888*, pp. 32ff.

48. *Ibid., 1915*, pp. 5, 12. Anthony P. Ralli was admitted to the exchange's membership on December 10, 1883, while Alexander A. Ralli was accepted on March 13, 1907.

49. *Annual Reports of the President and Directors of the Savannah Cotton Exchange, 1878-1892, passim.*

50. *Ibid., 1878*, pp. 14-16; *ibid., 1879*, pp. 15, 17, 19; *ibid., 1881-1889, passim.*; *ibid., 1890*, pp. 9, 11, 22; *ibid., 1891*, p. 11; *ibid., 1892*, pp. 29, 31. Thomas Zizinia died at his home, 271 West 71st Street on July 9, 1896. See *Annual Report of the New York Cotton Exchange, 1897*, p. 5; New York *Atlantis*, July 11, 1896.

51. *Memphis Cotton Exchange Directory and Book of Reference, 1892*, pp. 9, 33; *ibid., 1893*, pp. 11, 40; *ibid., 1898*, pp. 11, 37. Ralli Brothers was listed as a cotton buying concern with offices at 266 Front Street, Memphis.

52. New York *Atlantis*, January 3, 1906.

53. The material on succeeding pages in this chapter was being revised at the time of Mr. Contopoulos' final illness. Hence footnotes are not supplied.

54. [Anon.], *For the Establishment of the first Orthodox Church in New York, N.Y.* (New York, 1865), cited in Basil Zustis, *O En Ameriki Hellenismos Kae E Drasis Autu* (New York, 1954), p. 53. Basil Zustis was the archivist of the Greek Archdiocese of North and South America.

55. Zustis, p. 43; Canoutas, p. 161.

56. *Ibid.*, p. 165; Zustis, pp. 299, 321.

Chapter 4
The Provincial Influx

1. New York *Atlantis*, April 20, 1895; *ibid.*, June 22, 1895; *ibid.*, October 20, 1899; Athens, *Neon Asty*, April 4, 1902; Trieste *Nea Hemera*, July 13, 1907; *New-York Daily Tribune*, May 10, 1896; Saloutos, *The Greeks in the United States*, p. 23; Grace Abbott, *A Study of the Greeks in Chicago* (Chicago, 1909), p. 380; Percy F. Martin, *Greece of the Twentieth Century* (London, 1913), p. 161; Seraphim G. Canoutas and N. Helmis, Compilers, *Greek-American Guide and Business Directory*, First Edition (New York, 1907), p. 27; Hereafter cited as *Greek-American Guide*; William I. Cole, *Immigrant Races in Massachusetts: The Greeks* (Boston, 1919), p. 2; Nicholas G. Pieropoulos, *Meleti Peri Tis en Hellados Metanasteuseos Anaphorikos Kae ek Tis Eparchias Megalopoleos* (Athens, 1911), pp. 22ff. This study covers the movement from the Arcadian district of Megalopolis; Aristomenos Theodorides, *Peri Tis eis Amerikin Metanasteuseos: Kae Ton Aetion Autis* (Athens, 1907), p. 4. The lecture was given on June 10, 1907 at the Athens Parnassus Philological Society on the causes of the emigration to the United States. Cf. Andreas M. Andreades, ed. *E Helleniki Metanasteusis* (Athens, 1917). Andreades edited a symposium of seminar studies that dealt with the emigration from the various districts and provinces of Greece; John A. Booras, *Ae Ethnikae Thermopylae* (New York, 1910); George J. Chryssikos, *The Heritage of the Lacedaemonians and American Opportunities* (New York, 1938).

2. New York *Atlantis*, July 21, 1910; *ibid.*, July 22, 1910; *ibid.*, July 23, 1910; *ibid.*, July 25, 1910; Greece, Hypourgeion Ton Exoterikon, *Persecution of the Greek Population in Turkey* (London, 1918), pp. 1, 7ff.; Oscar S. Straus, *Under Four Administrations: From Cleveland to Taft* (New York, 1922), pp. 277-78. Straus was the United States Ambassador to Turkey in 1887-89, 1898-1900, 1909-11. Cf. Ecumenical Patriarchate of Constantinople, *Persecution of the Greeks in Turkey: 1914-1918* (Constantinople, 1919), *passim.*; Henry Morgenthau, *Ambassador Morgenthau's Story* (New York, 1918). Morgenthau was the American ambassador to Turkey from 1913-16; George Horton, *The Blight of Asia*

(Indianapolis, 1920). The author was the United States consul-general in Athens and later in Smyrna.

3. Troisième Assemblée Nationale à Athènes, *Les Persecutions antigrec-ques en Turquie de 1908 à 1921*. Translated and published by the Press Bureau of the Greek Foreign Ministry (Athens, 1921), p. 6.

4. The information in Table 5 was computed on data found in the New York *Atlantis*, November 24, 1899; *Emigration Conditions in Europe*, 391ff.; *Distribution of Immigrants: 1850-1900*, 14ff.; Repoulis, pp. 7ff. Emmanuel Repoulis (1863-1924) initiated the above study and proposed legislation for the control of Greek emigration. He was the minister of interior, 1910-15, minister of finance, 1915 and minister of interior in the Venizelist Provisional Government of Northern Greece in 1917.

5. *Brooklyn Daily Eagle*, March 5, 1892; *ibid.*, March 27, 1892; *New-York Daily Tribune*, March 2, 1892; *ibid.*, March 3, 1892; *ibid.*, March 5, 1892; *ibid.*, June 21, 1892; *The New York Times*, March 5, 1892; *New-York Daily Tribune*, November 27, 1893; *ibid.*, May 11, 1893; *ibid.*, December 26, 1893; *Brooklyn Daily Eagle*, July 5, 1893; *New-York Daily Tribune*, January 5, 1894; New York *Atlantis*, October 12, 1895; *Brooklyn Daily Eagle*, January 18, 1895; *The New York Times*, January 23, 1895; *ibid.*, June 11, 1895; *New-York Daily Tribune*, June 21, 1896; Forster, pp. 30ff.; Marriott, pp. 378ff.

6. Correspondence from John B. Jackson to Elihu Root, Athens, July 2, 1906, *Foreign Relations, 1906*, p. 800.

7. Theodorides, pp. 16, 20; Lampridu, pp. 85ff.

8. Greece, *Plythismu, 1870*, p. 1; *ibid., 1879*, pp. 1, 22ff.; *ibid., 1889*, pp. 1ff.; *ibid., 1896*, pp. 7ff.; *ibid., 1907*, pp. 7ff.; Andreades, *Erga*, II, 185-88; Repoulis, pp. 21, 37ff.

9. Pieropoulos, p. 13.

10. Repoulis, p. 35.

11. Pieropoulos, pp. 15, 16; *Plythismu, 1870, passim.*; *ibid., 1879*, pp. 4, 12, 17; *ibid., 1889, passim,*; *ibid., 1896*, pp. 8, 12, 14, 15, 18, 25, 27, 73; *ibid., 1907*, pp. 9, 15, 20ff.; Forster, pp. 252.

12. Repoulis, pp. 36, 37ff.

13. *Ibid.* pp. 40, 41; *Plythismu, 1879*, p. 32.

14. Emmanuel Stylianos Lykoudes, *Oe Metanastae* (Athens, 1903), p. 14; Xenides, p. 38; Saloutos, *The Greeks in the United States*, p. 31; Maldwyn Allen Jones, *American Immigration* (Chicago, 1960), p. 202;

The New York Times, September 9, 1889; Theodorides, p. 13; Fairchild, *Greek Immigration to the United States*, pp. 74, 76; Theodore A. Burlemi, *History of Currants and of the Currant Vine* (Manchester, 1911), p. 18; Athens *Ta Patria* (June 8, 1903), No. 13, p. 2; London *The Times*, April 22, 1901; New York *Atlantis*, March 12, 1899; Correspondence E. Alexander to Walter Q. Gresham, Athens, November 19, 1894, *Foreign Relations, 1894*, p. 292; Great Britain, Foreign Office, Report for the Years 1891-1894 on the Trade and Navigation of Greece, *Diplomatic and Consular Reports*, No. 1591 (1894), p. 2; Hereafter the British series are cited as *D.C.R.*; Report for the Year 1895-96 on the Finances of Greece, *ibid.*, No. 1782 (1896), pp. 1, 13; Report for the Year 1899 on Trade and Commerce of the Morea and the Provinces of Acarnania and Aetolia, *ibid.*, No. 2408 (1899), p. 6; United States, Bureau of Manufacturers, *Reports from the Consuls of the United States on the Commerce, Manufacturers of the Consular Districts*, No. 141 (June, 1892), p. 346; *ibid.*, No. 71 (November, 1896), pp. 423-24. Hereafter cited as *Consular Reports*; United States, Bureau of Manufacturers, *Commercial Relations of the United States With Foreign Countries During the Years 1888 and 1889*, No. 70, p. 95. Hereafter cited as *Commercial Relations*.

15. Nicholas J. Cassavetes, "L'avenir de l'hellenisme d'Amérique," *Les Études Franco-Grecques*, III (April, 1920), p. 86; Fairchild, *Greek Immigration to the United States*, p. 60; Canoutas, pp. 136, 137ff.; Protestant Episcopal Church in the United States, Domestic and Foreign Missions Department, *The People of the Eastern Orthodox Churches: The Report on the Greeks* (Springfield, Mass. 1913), p. 19. Hereafter cited as the *Protestant Episcopal Report on the Greeks*; Xenides, p. 78; Alexander Krikou, *E Metanasteusis: Pleonektimata-Meionektimata Synepeiai* (Athens, 1950), p. 25. Krikou visited the United States during World War I. Theodore Geannakoulis, "Eisagogi Stin Historia Ton Hellinoamerikanon," New York *Argonautis* (Winter, 1959), pp. 166-67. Geannakoulis was born in Pista, Corinth, 1896 and he emigrated to America in 1913. Christos Damiris, *Peri Tis Ek Zakinthu Metanasteuseos*. Phrontistirion tu Kathygitu Tis Demosias Oekonomias, No. 3. (Athens, 1912), p. 6; Fairchild, "Causes of Emigration from Greece," 176, 182-83.

16. Saloutas, *The Greeks in the United States*, p. 29.

17. Martin, p. 162.

18. K.N. Gergaga, *E Metanasteusis ek tu Nomu Euboeas: Meleti Statistiki Kae Koenoniki* (Chalcis, 1912), p. 25.

19. *Annual Report of the Commissioner-General of Immigration*, 1907, p. 60; Lykoudes, p. 14; Michael Dendia, *Hellenikae Paroekiae Ana Ton Kosmon* (Athens, 1919), p. 91; Repoulis, pp. 152-55; Salopoulos, p. 6;

Jones, p. 191; Edward A. Ross, *The Old World in the New* (New York, 1914), p. 190.

20. United States Industrial Commission, *Report of the Industrial Commission on Immigration and Education*, XV (1901), pp. 430ff.; Lykoudes, p. 31; Saloutos, *The Greeks in the United States*, pp. 28ff.

21. Salopoulos, p. 7.

22. *Report of the Industrial Commission on Immigration and Education*, XV, p. 8.

23. *Ibid.*, p. xli.

24. *Ibid.*, p. 83.

25. New York *Atlantis*, July 18, 1896; Jason Georgakopoulos and E. Papachelas, "O Hellin en Ameriki," Andreades, ed., *E Hellinikin Metanasteusis*, pp. 3-39; Basil B. Melas and Leander M. Melas, "Antidrasis Kata Tis Helliniki Metanasteuseos eis Amerikin," *ibid.*, pp. 40-59.

26. New York *Atlantis*, May 16, 1896.

27. *Ibid.*

28. Konstantinos D. Maniakes, *America and Greece* (Athens, 1899), p. 4.

29. *Emigration Conditions in Europe, The Emigration Situation in Greece*, p. 401. The Immigration Commission reported that the economic factor was a more legitimate motive in Austria-Hungary, Italy and Russia. In those states the commission ascertained that emigration was very often an economic necessity, while it was not in Greece.

30. Dendia, p. 90.

31. Greek Parliament, *E Ekthesis Tis Epitropis Tis Bules Kae E Schetiki Protasis Nomu* (Athens, 1906), p. 10. The committee investigated the extent and character of the Greek emigration with the purpose of initiating protective legislation. No important legislation, however, resulted from its findings.

32. Alexander Krikou, *E Thesis tu Hellinismu en Ameriki* (Athens, 1915), p. 40. Krikou toured the United States and he viewed the immigrants' hopes for quick wealth with skepticism. He believed that unrestricted immigration was detrimental both to the United States and Greece.

33. Repoulis, p. 127.

34. Phanis Michalopoulos, "O Apodimos Hellinismos," Athens *Ethnos* (December 15, 1950) as quoted by the author in "E Metanasteusi-O

Neoteros Apoekismos Stin Ameriki," *Nea Hestia*, LVIII (December, 1955), 87.

35. John A. Levandis, *The Greek Foreign Debt and the Great Powers: 1821-1898* (New York, 1944), p. 44.

36. "Greece; Report of Finances of Greece for the Year 1906," *D.C.R.*, No. 3821, pp. 12-13; Charles S. Wilson, Chargé d'Affaires, to Elihu Root, Athens, July 24, 1906, *Foreign Relations, 1906*, I, p. 810.

37. John B. Jackson to Elihu Root, July 2, 1906, *ibid.*

38. New York *Atlantis*, February 10, 1903; Athens *Neon Asty*, December 11, 1905; New York *Atlantis*, June 4, 1906; *ibid.*, June 9, 1906.

39. *Ibid.*, April 13, 1906.

40. *Ibid.*, June 15, 1906.

41. Fairchild, *Greek Immigration to the United States*, p. 81; *Morton Allen Directory of European Passenger Steamship Arrivals*, 1893-1930 (New York, 1931), pp. 96, 103, 111, 128, 135, 143.

42. United States Department of Commerce and Labor, Bureau of Manufacturers, "Greece, 1907," *Consular Reports, Annual Series*, No. 10, pp. 7ff.

43. Fairchild, *Greek Immigration to the United States*, p. 66.

44. *Morton Allen Directory*, p. 130; New York *Atlantis*, January 28, 1908; *ibid.*, September 26, 1908.

45. *The New York Times*, February 17, 1909; New York *Atlantis*, February 17, 1909.

46. Burgess, pp. 22-23; Xenides, p. 81.

47. Fairchild, *Greek Immigration to the United States*, p. 81.

48. New York *Atlantis*, January 28, 1908; *ibid.*, October 12, 1902; *ibid.*, April 11, 1902; *ibid.*, June 3, 1903; *ibid.*, December 22, 1903; *ibid.*, June 4, 1906; *ibid.*, June 4, 1909; Athens *Skrip*, June 10, 1907.

49. United States, Department of Commerce and Labor, Bureau of Manufacturers, "Turkey-in-Asia, Trade for the Year of 1907," *Consular Reports, Annual Series*, No. 30, p. 13. Cf. *Levant Trade Review* (June 11, 1911), p. 19.

50. United States, Department of Commerce and Labor, Bureau of Manufacturers, "Turkey," *Consular Reports, Annual Series*, No. 1, 1907, pp. 17, 35. Cf. *Morton Allen Directory, Adler's Directory* (New York, 1940), *passim.*

51. United States, Department of Commerce and Labor, Bureau of Manufacturers, "Greece, 1907," *Consular Reports, Annual Series*, No. 10, 1907, p. 7.

52. S.T. Cooke, "The Greeks in the United States," *Eastern and Western Review*, III (November, 1910), 1.

53. Elias K. Zioga, *O Hellenismos Tis Amerikis: Autos O Agnostos* (Athens, 1958), pp. 4, 23ff.; Arnold J. Toynbee, *Nationality and the War* (London, 1915), pp. 365-78; Arnold J. Toynbee, *Turkey: A Past and a Future* (London, 1917), p. 2; Madison Grant, *The Passing of the Great Race* (New York, 1916), pp. 165-66; Carlton J.H. Hayes, *Essays on Nationalism* (New York, 1926), pp. 69, 117.

Chapter 5
The Immigrant Society

1. Martin, *Greece of the Twentieth Century*, pp. 163, 164; Fairchild, *Greek Immigration to the United States*, p. 151; Cooke, "The Greeks in the United States," 1; Canoutas, pp. 117ff.; Hypurgeion Ton Exoterikon (Greek Foreign Affairs Ministry). *Deltion Tu Epi Ton Exoterikon Meros Deuteron. Meletae Kae Ektheseis*, No. 12. *Ektheseis Peri Tis Hellinikis Metanasteuseos: Kae Peri Tu Emporiu en Taes Henomenaes Politeias Tis Amerikis Kata To Etos 1911* (Athens, 1912), p. 5; Burgess, pp. 26, 60, 61-62.

2. Bayrd Still, *New York City, A Student's Guide to Localized History* (New York, 1965), p. 43.

3. Report For the Year 1903 on the Trade and Commerce of the Morea, and Province of Aetolia and Acarnania, *D.C.R.*, No. 3156 (1904), pp. 17-18.

4. Fairchild, *Greek Immigration to the United States*, pp. 148, 149.

5. Xenides, p. 85.

6. *New-York Daily Tribune*, May 10, 1896.

7. Fairchild, *Greek Immigration to the United States*, pp. 152, 153.

8. This account of the favorite recipes, menus and cooking methods of the New York Greeks during the period is based on the reminiscences of the earlier and later immigrants to New York. They were waiters, cooks, restaurateurs and customers. The best Greek meals were served at the Athens Restaurant, 30 E. 42nd Street, near Grand Central Station, during the first decade of the century.

9. As other Orthodox Christians from Eastern Europe, such as the Roumanians, Carpatho-Russians, Ukrainians, Russians and Serbs, the Greeks considered Easter as their most sacred holiday. St. Basil's Feast corresponded with New Year's celebration. Hence, there was great joy during the day. The Greeks prepared a braided yeast cake topped with almonds for the great holiday. Moreover, the Greeks served a traditional Easter soup, *mageritsa*, after attending midnight Resurrection services. The soup was made with marrow bones, lamb offals. Its broth was later blended with whipped yokes and lemon juice.

10. *New-York Daily Tribune*, May 10, 1896.

11. Burgess, p. 151.

12. *Greek-American Guide*, 1907, p. 161; *ibid.*, 1909, p. 164; *ibid.*, 1910, p. 160; *ibid.*, 1912, p. 317; Fairchild, *Greek Immigration to the United States*, pp. 148, 152; Saloutos, *The Greeks in the United States*, p. 85.

13. Christine Avghi Galitzi, *A Study of Assimilation Among the Roumanians in the United States*. Columbia University *Studies in History, Economics and Public Law*, No. 315 (New York, 1928), p. 89. Cf. Theodore Saloutos, *They Remember America* (Berkley, 1956), pp. 66-70.

14. Canoutas, p. 212; *Greek-American Guide*, 1910, p. 162; Burgess, pp. 53, 56-57.

15. Xenides, pp. 46, 49, 89, 90.

16. *New-York Daily Tribune*, May 10, 1896.

17. Zotos, pp. 53, 55.

18. [Reminiscences of early immigrants and Nicholas A. Contopoulos, 1907–1910.

19. Fairchild, *Greek Immigration to the United States, passim.*

20. Prescott Farnsworth Hall, *Immigration: And Its Effects Upon the United States* (New York, 1906), *passim.*

21. Grant, pp. 163, 165-66.

22. *The New York Times*, June 30, 1891.

23. Zustis, p. 56.

24. New York *The World*, July 1, 1891; *New-York Daily Tribune*, July 1, 1891; New York *The Evening Post*, July 1, 1891; *Brooklyn Daily Eagle*, July 1, 1891; *The New York Times*, July 1, 1891; New York *The Sun*, July 1, 1891; *New York Herald*, July 1, 1891; *New York Evening Telegram*, July 1, 1891.

25. *New York Herald,* July 1, 1891.

26. New York *The Evening Post,* July 1, 1891.

27. *New-York Daily Tribune,* July 1, 1891. The presence of the Russian diplomat in the reception committee was a courtesy afforded to the prince's mother, Queen Olga, a Grand Duchess of the Imperial House of Russia.

28. *New York Herald,* July 2, 1891.

29. *The New York Times,* July 2, 1891; *New-York Daily Tribune,* July 2, 1891; New York *The World,* July 2, 1891; *Brooklyn Daily Eagle,* July 2, 1891.

30. *New York Herald,* July 3, 1891.

31. *The New York Times,* July 3, 1891; *New-York Daily Tribune,* July 3, 1891.

32. *New York Evening Telegram,* July 3, 1891; *New-York Daily Tribune,* July 4, 1891; *New York Herald,* July 4, 1891.

33. New York *The Sun,* July 3, 1891; *New-York Daily Tribune,* July 3, 1891; New York *The World,* July 3, 1891.

34. *Ibid.,* July 4, 1891.

35. New York *The Sun,* July 4, 1891.

36. *Brooklyn Daily Eagle,* April 6, 1893.

37. *New-York Daily Tribune,* April 6, 1893.

38. *New York Herald,* April 6, 1893.

39. New York *The World,* April 6, 1893.

40. *The New York Times,* April 6, 1893.

41. *New-York Daily Tribune,* April 9, 1894; New York *The World,* April 9, 1894.

42. *The New York Times,* April 9, 1894.

43. New York *Atlantis,* April 13, 1895; *New-York Daily Tribune,* April 8, 1895.

44. New York *Atlantis,* July 10, 1895.

45. *Ibid.,* July 6, 1895.

46. *The New York Times,* April 6, 1897.

47. *Ibid.*, April 21, 1894; *ibid.*, April 22, 1894; *ibid.*, April 23, 1894; *ibid.*, April 30, 1894; *New York Herald*, April 22, 1894.

48. *The New York Times*, April 29, 1894.

49. *New York Herald*, April 29, 1894.

50. *Ibid.*

51. New York *The Evening Post*, September 27, 1900.

52. New York *The Evening Telegram*, September 27, 1900.

53. New York *Atlantis*, September 28, 1900; *The New York Times*, September 28, 1900; New York *The World*, September 28, 1900.

54. *New-York Daily Tribune*, September 28, 1900.

55. *Ibid.*

56. New York *The Sun*, September 28, 1900.

57. Krikou, *E Thesis tu Hellenismu en Ameriki*, pp. 77, 78; New York *Atlantis*, September 22, 1908; *ibid.*, September 23 1908; *ibid.*, February 6, 1909. The Greek war vessel, *Miaoulis*, revisited New York in March, 1901.

58. *Ibid.*, December 28, 1898; *ibid.*, February 19, 1899; *ibid.*, February 20, 1899; Hall, p. 153; Fairchild, *Greek Immigration to the United States*, pp. 158-59; Cooke, p. 1.

59. New York *Atlantis*, May 26, 1899.

60. *Ibid.*, June 2, 1899.

61. *Ibid.*, October 20, 1899.

62. Reminiscences of early and later immigrants to New York City.

Chapter 6
Economic Foundations

1. Athens *Oe Kaeroe*, November 28, 1900; Athens *Asty*, November 14, 1900; *ibid.*, December 11, 1905; *Brooklyn Daily Eagle*, August 17, 1902; Dendia, p. 87; M. A. Triantaphylides, *Hellenes Tis Amerikis* (Athens, 1952), p. 7; Elia Kazan *America, America* (New York, 1962), pp. 159, 165, 182-85; Grace E. Marshall, *Eternal Greece* (Rochester, 1938), pp. 74-76; Mary Vardoulakis, *Gold in the Streets* (New York, 1945), pp. 78ff., 94ff.

2. New York *The Sun*, November 3, 1903.

3. Canoutas, p. 137.

4. New York *Atlantis*, June 11, 1897.

5. *The New York Times*, February 13, 1888; *ibid.*, September 9, 1889; Report for the Year 1888 on the Trade of Piraeus, *B.D.C.R.* (1888), p. 22; London *The Times*, June 18, 1900; *ibid.*, August 16, 1900; *ibid.*, January 2, 1900; *ibid.*, January 1, 1904; Athens *Neon Asty*, December 9, 1901; *ibid.*, August 25, 1902.

6. Nicholas Gkortzi, *Ameriki kae Amerikanoe* (Athens, 1907), pp. 68-69.

7. New York *Atlantis*, April 13, 1895; *ibid.*, January 14, 1898.

8. *Ibid.*, March 2, 1895; *ibid.*, March 16, 1895; *ibid.*, April 6, 1895.

9. Athens *Neon Asty*, August 4, 1902; *ibid.*, August 10, 1902; *ibid.*, August 17, 1902.

10. 61st Congress, 3rd Session, Senate Document No. 747 *Abstracts of the Reports of the Immigration Commission*, II (Washington, 1911), pp. 391-406; Cassavetes, pp. 88ff.; Dendia, pp. 88-89; Henry Pratt Fairchild, *Immigration* (New York, 1925), pp. 273-75; Saloutos, *The Greeks in the United States*, pp. 48-58; New York *Atlantis*, November 10, 1908; *ibid.*, December 26, 1908; *ibid.*, January 23, 1909.

11. Although the *Atlantis* used the Greek term which, on literal translation, means "body merchants," the term connotes either a "slave trader" or a procurer of persons for immoral purposes. From 1894 to 1910, the *Atlantis* mercilessly condemned the padrone system and endlessly worked for its abolition. The newspaper championed the cause of the tragic victims.

12. *The New York Times*, February 6, 1898.

13. Kazan, p. 190. Elia Kazan was born in Asia Minor and emigrated to the United States in his early childhood. The book, *America, America*, is partially based on the personal reminiscences of Kazan's family as early immigrants in New York.

14. *New York Herald*, February 6, 1898.

15. *Ibid.*

16. U.S. Immigration Commission *Abstract of the Report on the Greek Padrone System* (1911), pp. 9, 14.

17. *Ibid.*, p. 15.

18. Saloutos, *The Greeks in the United States*, p. 54; Malafouris, pp. 118ff.; Burgess, pp. 38-40; Canoutas, pp. 145-46; Xenides, p. 84.

19. John R. Commons, *Races and Immigrants in America* (New York, 1907), p. 47. There is no data on the extent of the padrone system in New York City. It formed only a small segment of the immigrant population.

20. *The New York Times*, February 6, 1898; *New York Herald*, February 6, 1898.

21. Zustis, pp. 53ff.; Canoutas, p. 164; Oscar Handlin, *The Uprooted* (New York, 1951), pp. 69-70.

22. Malafouris, p. 342; reminiscences of Nicholas A. Contopoulos, 1907-1910; *Greek-American Guide*, pp. 300-302. Cf. Socrates A. Xanthakes, *O Syntrophos tu Hellinos* (New York, 1903). Xanthakes, *Atlantis'* editor, published this guide for the Greek immigrants.

23. *The New York Times*, May 18, 1894; Peter Roberts, *The New Immigrants* (New York, 1912), p. 60; (Anon.), "Life Story of a Pushcart Peddler," *Independent* LX (February 1, 1906), 277, 278. Cooke, p. 1; Jacob Riis, *Battle with the Slum* (New York, 1902), p. 202; Bayrd Still, *Mirror for Gotham* (New York, 1956), p. 247.

24. *Ibid.*

25. *Ibid.*

26. New York *Atlantis*, July 6, 1895.

27. *Ibid.*, July 13, 1895.

28. *The New York Times*, May 5, 1900.

29. New York *Atlantis*, August 3, 1900.

30. *New York Herald*, September 11, 1900.

31. New York *Atlantis*, August 3, 1900; *New York Herald*, September 11, 1900; *New-York Daily Tribune*, September 12, 1900; *The New York Times*, September 11, 1900; New York *The World*, September 11, 1900.

32. New York *Atlantis*, September 14, 1900.

33. *New-York Daily Tribune*, September 16, 1900; New York *The Evening Post*, September 17, 1900.

34. New York *Atlantis*, September 19, 1900.

35. *Ibid.*, July 23, 1901.

36. *Ibid.*, July 30, 1901.

37. Athens *Neon Asty*, December 1, 1905.

38. New York *Atlantis*, August 13, 1901.

39. Reavis Cox, *Competition in the American Tobacco Industry, 1911-1932*, Columbia University *Studies in History, Economics and Public Law*, No. 381 (New York, 1933), pp. 326, 328-29, 335; Efthimiou, p. 41; Malafouris, p. 262; New York *Atlantis*, March 24, 1899; *Greek-American Guide, 1907-10, passim*.

40. *U.S. Tobacco Journal, The Century Issue, 1800-1900* (New York, 1900), p. 52.

41. John N. Bain, *Cigarettes in Fact and Fancy* (Boston, 1906), p. 23.

42. *Ibid.*; Xenides, p. 83; Burgess, p. 33; William W. Young, *The Story of the Cigarette* (New York, 1916), p. 65.

43. *Wilson's Business Directory, 1889*, p. 834.

44. *Twelfth Census, 1900, Manufacturers*, IX, Part III, *Special Reports on Selected Industries*, "Tobacco," prepared by John H. Garber (Washington, 1902), 637, 651, 671; *ibid.*, VII, 426.

45. United States Immigration Commission, *Reports of the Immigration Commission*, XV, *Immigrants in Industries*, Part 14: "Cigar and Tobacco Manufacturing" (Washington, 1910), pp. 35ff., 82.

46. *Ibid.*, pp. 16, 90; United States Bureau of Corporations, *Report of the Commissioner of Corporations on the Tobacco Industry* (3v. Washington, 1909-15), I, 30.

47. Richard B. Tennant, *The American Cigarette Industry, Yale Studies in Economics* (New Haven, 1950), p. 45.

48. *Trow's Business Directory, 1893*, p. 237; *ibid., 1897*, p. 242; *ibid., 1899*, p. 270; *Boyd's Co-Partnership and Residence Directory, 1899*, p. 134.

49. *Trow's Business Directory, 1894*, p. 242; *Trow's Co-Partnership and Corporation Directory, 1895*, p. 38.

50. New York *Atlantis*, March 16, 1895; *Trow's Business Directory, 1897*, p. 252.

51. *Ibid., 1895*, p. 228; *ibid., 1896*, p. 248; *ibid., 1897*, p. 252; *ibid., 1899*, pp. 270-71; *Trow's Co-Partnership and Corporation Directory, 1904*, p. 40.

52. Efthimiou, p. 41; Tennant, pp. 45-46, 52, 73-75, 79-81; Malafouris, pp. 262-66; *Trow's Co-Partnership and Corporation Directory*, 1904, p. 129; *Boyd's Co-Partnership and Residence Directory*, 1899, p. 211.

53. Xenides, p. 83. Euripides Kehaya, an immigrant from Pontus, Asia Minor, had prominent financial interests in the Standard Commercial Tobacco Company.

54. Malafouris, pp. 264-65. The firm of G.A. Georgopoulo & Sons, Inc. maintained a small establishment at 48 Stone Street in 1968. This small company was the last Greek cigarette manufacturing plant in New York. Cf. *Greek-American Guide, 1907-21, passim.*

55. *U.S. Tobacco Journal,* December 1, 1900.

56. *Ibid.,* December 22, 1900; New York *Atlantis,* March 16, 1895.

57. *Report of the Commissioner of Corporations on the Tobacco Industry,* I, 334.

58. New York *Atlantis,* July 28, 1899.

59. *Report of the Commissioner of Corporations on the Tobacco Industry,* I, 83. The Monopol Tobacco Works was formed on January 31, 1883.

60. *Ibid.,* I, 223.

61. *Ibid.,* 86ff.; *U.S. Tobacco Journal,* March 31, 1900; *ibid.,* November 10, 1900. The directors of the new subsidiary company were Soterios Anargyros, Martin D. Watts and James Gillien. On November 3, 1900 the S. Anargyros company registered another brand, *Egyptian Emblems.*

62. *Report of the Commissioner of Corporations on the Tobacco Industry,* I, 228, 334. The federal authorities did not classify the employees explicitly because ethnic Turks and ethnic Egyptians rarely emigrated to the United States. It is more than likely that the so-called "Turks" and "Egyptians" were Christian Greeks, Lebanese and Syrians born in the Ottoman Empire.

63. *Ibid.,* I, 230.

64. *U.S. Tobacco Journal,* January 5, 1901.

65. *Report of the Commissioner of Corporations on the Tobacco Industry,* III, 439, 440; Tennant, pp. 45, 53; Cox, pp. 326, 328-39. Cf. *United States* v. *American Tobacco Company,* United States District Court for Eastern Kentucky, Criminal No. 6670 (1941).

66. *Ibid.*

67. Tennant, p. 75.

68. Walter E. Weyl, "Pericles of Smyrna and New York," *The Outlook,* XCIV (February 26, 1910), 464.

69. *Ibid.,* 465.

70. *Ibid.,* 468.

71. *Trow's Business Directory, 1895,* p. 582.

72. *Ibid.*, *1897*, p. 242; Canoutas, pp. 149-50.

73. *Trow's Business Directory, 1893*, p. 403; *ibid.*, *1894*, p. 407; *ibid.*, *1895*, p. 328.

74. *Ibid.*, *1898*, p. 404. A considerable number of the immigrants became fruit dealers and peddlers during this period, 1890-1910; Weyl, pp. 464, 470.

75. New York *Atlantis*, March 2, 1895; *ibid.*, September 14, 1895. In 1901 S.J. Vlasto became the representative for the Bank of Mytilene and the Empedocles Bank of Greece; *ibid.*, August 9, 1901.

76. *Ibid.*, January 3, 1906.

77. John B. Jackson to Elihu Root, Athens, July 2, 1906, *Foreign Relations*, 1906, I, 809, 810; Charles S. Wilson to Elihu Root, Athens, July 22, 1906, *ibid.*, 812; Damaris, pp. 23, 24, 28-29; reminiscences of Nicholas A. Contopoulos; Greek Parliament, *E Ekthesis Tis Epitropis, 1906*, pp. 15, 50, 55-56. The parliamentary report also recommended the creation of an agency of the National Bank of Greece in the United States. This proposal was in the footsteps of the Italian government's initiative in creating a branch of the Banco di Napoli.

78. New York *Atlantis*, January 3, 1903; *ibid.*, March 13, 1909.

79. E.P. Despotopoulos and C. Anastasopoulos to Michael Contopoulos, Athens, September 24, 1964. The former are officials of the National Bank of Greece.

80. *Ibid.*

81. L.J. Ralli to Michael Contopoulos, London, September 23, 1964. L.J. Ralli is a director of G.&L. Ralli Investment and Trustee Co. Ltd., which represents the financial interests of the Ralli family after it sold the merchant bank, Ralli Brothers Ltd., to Sir Isaac Wolfson's interests in 1962.

82. Obituary, *The New York Times*, April 19, 1952; obituary, *New York Herald-Tribune*, April 19, 1952; *Social Register, 1951 New York* (New York, 1951), p. 106. L.J. Calvocoressis (1879-1952) was born in London and emigrated to New York in 1909. He married Eugène Ralli in 1910. He was a former president of the Board of Trustees of the Hellenic Cathedral of the Holy Trinity. Calvocoressis played an important role in the establishment of the Greek Archdiocese of North and South America.

83. Fairchild, *Greek Immigration to the United States*, p. 167.

84. Malafouris, pp. 271ff.

85. Burgess, p. 26.

86. Canoutas, p. 181; Malafouris, pp. 267, 268-70. After 1920 the New York fur industry moved to its present center on Eighth Avenue between West 23rd and West 30th Streets.

87. Roxane Cotsakis, *The Wing and the Thorn* (Atlanta, 1952), p. 17.

88. Canoutas, p. 145; Malafouris, p. 276.

89. New York *Atlantis*, May 30, 1896.

90. Fairchild, *Greek Immigration to the United States*, pp. 127, 151, 171; Xenides, p. 81; Burgess, p. 40. Canoutas, p. 158; reminiscences of Nicholas A. Conopoulos, 1907-12.

91. Canoutas, p. 151.

92. *Ibid.*, p. 159.

93. Xenides, p. 82

94. Dendia, p. 97; Xenides, p. 85.

95. Burgess, pp. 36-38.

96. Fairchild, *Greek Immigration to the United States*, p. 152.

97. Burgess, p. 37; Canoutas, p. 145 n.

98. Zustis, p. 41; Saloutas, *The Greeks in the United States*, p. 262; Malafouris, pp. 272-74.

99. Burgess, p. 35; Canoutas, pp. 143-44 n.

100. *Greek-American Guide, 1907*, p. 330.

101. Fairchild, *Greek Immigration to the United States*, p. 150. In 1907 the confectioners formed a mutual benefit society to protect their economic interests and support philanthropic and educational activities in New York.

102. Burgess, p. 35.

103. *Greek-American Guide, 1907*, p. 303. All the Greek business concerns were not included in the guides published from 1907 to 1910.

104. *Ibid., passim.*

105. Fairchild, *Greek Immigrants to the United States*, pp. 148, 150-51, 209. Cf. Paul H. Douglas, *Real Wages in the United States: 1890-1926* (Chicago, 1930), pp. 96, 205, 252.

106. Martin, *Greece in the Twentieth Century*, pp. 297-300; Fairchild, *Greek Immigration to the United States*, p. 248. Actually, the daily wages for laborers in Greece ranged from $0.35 to $0.96 during the working seasons. There was seasonal unemployment in the provinces.

107. Samuel Joseph, *Jewish Immigration to the United States: From 1881 to 1910*, Columbia University *Studies in History, Economics and Public Law*, LIX, No. 4 (New York, 1914), 141-43, 144.

108. Fairchild, *Greek Immigration to the United States*, pp. 209-10.

Chapter 7
The Involvement of New York Greeks in the Greek-Turkish War of 1897

1. New York *Atlantis*, June 6, 1896; *ibid.*, July 11, 1896; *ibid.*, February 16, 1897; *ibid.*, March 19, 1897; Forster, pp. 31-34.

2. W. Kinard Rose, *With the Greek Army in Thessaly* (London, 1898), p. 5. One of the largest palatial mansions in Athens belonged to the Benaki family, which made a fortune in the cotton trade in New Orleans in the nineteenth century. The family later transformed the mansion into the Benaki Museum of Hellenic Folk Arts.

3. Clive Bigham, Second Viscount Mersey, *With the Turkish Army in Thessaly* (London, 1897), p. 5.

4. Zotos, p. 81.

5. Miller, *Greek People*, pp. 104-105; Mazarakes-Ainianos, I, 267-68; Demetrius N. Botassi and Sir Charles W. Dilke, "The Uprising of Greece," *North American Review* CLXIV (April, 1897), 453-56; New York *Wall Street Journal*, April 10, 1897; *ibid.*, April 21, 1897; *Brooklyn Daily Eagle*, February 21, 1897; *ibid.*, February 24, 1897.

6. New York *Atlantis*, May 23, 1896; *ibid.*, May 30, 1896; *ibid.*, June 27, 1896.

7. *New-York Daily Tribune*, February 16, 1897.

8. *The New York Times*, February 10, 1897; *ibid.*, February 14, 1897; *ibid.*, February 16, 1897; *ibid.*, March 9, 1897.

9. New York *The World*, February 18, 1897.

10. *New-York Daily Tribune*, February 21, 1897.

11. New York *The Sun*, February 26, 1897.

12. *New York Herald*, March 3, 1897.

13. *Brooklyn Daily Eagle*, March 11, 1897.

14. *Ibid.*, March 6, 1897.

15. *New-York Daily Tribune*, March 8, 1897.

16. New York *Atlantis*, February 26, 1897.

17. *Ibid.*, March 5, 1897.

18. *Ibid.*, March 11, 1897.

19. *The New York Times*, March 11, 1897.

20. New York *The Sun*, March 11, 1897; New York *The World*, March 11, 1897.

21. *New York Herald*, March 11, 1897.

22. *Ibid.*

23. *Ibid.*

24. New York *The Evening Post*, March 11, 1897.

25. New York *The Sun*, March 12, 1897.

26. New York *The Evening Post*, March 11, 1897.

27. New York *Atlantis*, March 12, 1897; *ibid.*, March 19, 1897.

28. *New-York Daily Tribune*, March 12, 1897.

29. *Ibid.*

30. New York *The Evening Post*, March 12, 1897. Vlasto's letter to the editor was dated March 12, 1897. See *infra*, Appendix No. 5.

31. *New-York Daily Tribune*, March 12, 1897.

32. *Ibid.*

33. New York *The Sun*, March 13, 1897.

34. *The New York Times*, March 13, 1897.

35. *New-York Daily Tribune*, March 13, 1897.

36. *Ibid.*; New York *The World*, March 13, 1897.

37. *New-York Daily Tribune*, March 13, 1897. The speakers included Dr. R. S. Tharin, Dr. Achilles Rose and J. M. Rodocanachi, a former Greek consul of Boston.

38. *Ibid.*, March 13, 1897.

39. New York *Atlantis*, December 12, 1896.

40. New York *The Sun*, March 13, 1897.

41. New York *Atlantis*, April 2, 1897.

42. *Ibid.*, March 26, 1897; *Brooklyn Daily Eagle*, March 27, 1897.

43. *The New York Times*, March 27, 1897.

44. *New-York Daily Tribune*, April 4, 1897.

45. *Ibid.*, April 7, 1897.

46. *Ibid.*

47. *The New York Times*, April 23, 1897.

48. *Ibid.*

49. *New-York Daily Tribune*, April 24, 1897; *New York Herald*, April 25, 1897; New York *The Sun*, April 25, 1897; New York *The Evening Post*, April 24, 1897; New York *Atlantis*, April 30, 1897; New York *The World*, April 24, 1897.

50. *New York Herald*, April 29, 1897; *New-York Daily Tribune*, April 29, 1897.

51. New York *Atlantis*, May 4, 1897; *New-York Daily Tribune*, May 2, 1897.

52. *The New York Times*, April 21, 1897. For some unaccountable reason the vast majority of Greeks and Americans of Greek origin who bore and bear the name Demetrius called themselves *James* or *Jim*. The latter name in Greek is either *Jacob* or *Iakovos*. The same practice held true for Constantine, who was usually referred to as *Gus* or *Dean*; and for Basil, who was usually called *William* or *Bill*.

53. *Ibid.*

54. *Ibid.*

55. *Ibid.*

56. *Ibid.*

57. *Ibid.*

58. *Ibid.*

59. *Ibid.*

60. *Ibid.*

61. *New-York Daily Tribune*, April 22, 1897.

62. *Ibid.*, April 25, 1897; *The New York Times*, April 25, 1897; New York *Evening Telegram*, April 24, 1897; *Brooklyn Daily Eagle*, April 22, 1897.

63. *New York World*, April 24, 1897.

64. *New York Herald*, April 25, 1897.

65. *Ibid.*

66. *The New York Times*, April 26, 1897.

67. *New York Herald*, April 26, 1897; *The New York Times*, April 26, 1897.

68. *New-York Daily Tribune*, May 8, 1897.

69. Letter to the Editor, *The New York Times*, April 28, 1897.

70. *New-York Daily Tribune*, May 9, 1897.

71. *Ibid.*, March 21, 1897.

72. *New York Herald*, April 25, 1897. The committee members were the same wives of the wealthy brokers of the New York Cotton Exchange; *New-York Daily Tribune*, April 25, 1897.

73. *Ibid.*, April 28, 1897.

74. *Ibid.*, April 29, 1897.

75. *The New York Times*, April 20, 1897.

76. *New York World*, April 25, 1897.

77. *Ibid.*, April 30, 1897.

78. New York *The Evening Post*, May 3, 1897.

79. *New-York Daily Tribune*, May 7, 1897; *ibid.*, May 8, 1897.

80. *Ibid.*, May 12, 1897.

81. *The New York Times*, September 16, 1897; *ibid*, April 27, 1897.

82. *Ibid.*, April 26, 1897.

83. *New-York Daily Tribune*, April 30, 1897.

84. *Ibid.*, May 6, 1897; *ibid.*, May 5, 1897.

85. *Ibid.* May 9, 1897; *ibid.*, May 13, 1897; *ibid.*, May 17, 1897; *ibid.*, May 24, 1897; *ibid.*, June 1, 1897.

86. *The New York Times*, April 7, 1897; *New York Herald*, April 26,

1897; Charles Williams, "The Thessalian War of 1897," *Fortnightly Review*, LXVII (June, 1897), 967ff.

87. New York *Atlantis*, April 9, 1897.

88. *The New York Times*, April 26, 1897; *New-York Daily Tribune*, April 30, 1897. It was reported that the German warship, *Kaisirin Augusta* was dispatched to Greece to protect members of the Greek royal family. Crown Princess Sophie was the sister of Kaiser Wilhelm II.

89. *The New York Times*, April 19, 1897.

90. New York *Atlantis*, April 30, 1897.

91. New York *The Sun*, May 4, 1897; *New-York Daily Tribune*, May 3, 1897; *ibid.*, May 4, 1897; *ibid.*, May 14, 1897.

92. *New York Herald*, April 29, 1897.

93. *New-York Daily Tribune*, April 29, 1897.

94. New York *Atlantis*, May 25, 1897.

95. *Ibid.*, April 11, 1896.

96. *Ibid.*, April 30, 1897; *ibid.*, July 16, 1897.

97. John Mavrogordato, *Letters from Greece: Concerning the War of the Balkan Allies* (London, 1914), pp. 3, 4, 5.

Chapter 8
Fraternal Associations

1. Burgess, p. 53. There are no known records of the brotherhood available.

2. Zustis, p. 53; Canoutas, p. 164; Efthimiou, pp. 45-46; Saloutas, *The Greeks in the United States*, p. 126; Malafouris, pp. 191-92; *Greek-American Guide, 1907*, pp. 158, 165; *ibid., 1910*, p. 156; *ibid., 1912*, p. 313. In the same period Chicago Greeks founded the Lycourgos Society and the Boston immigrants established the Plato Society.

3. New York *Atlantis*, April 27, 1895; *ibid.*, August 10, 1895.

4. *Ibid.*, August 10, 1895.

5. *Ibid.*, July 27, 1895.

6. *Ibid.*, April 27, 1895.

7. *Ibid.*, June 8, 1895.

8. Zustis, pp. 55-56; *Greek-American Guide, 1910*, p. 162. The last of the early immigrant physicians, Dr. A. Sekouris died on July 17, 1953.

9. New York *Atlantis*, December 4, 1900.

10. The contemporary Athenians dubbed their city as the "Little Paris" of the Near East. In the Greek capital the French words, *au revoir, merci, pardon* and *s'il vous plaît* became accepted words in the speech pattern of the Athenians. Other words, *jambon, crème, ascenseur* and *allez et retour* were readily adopted while their Greek counterparts were quickly forgotten.

11. Bryer, pp. 159, 162ff.

12. Advertisements, New York *Atlantis*, 1894-1910, *passim*.

13. *Greek-American Guide, 1910*, pp. 398, 401; Burgess, pp. 63-67, 88, 89, 153, 159; Canoutas, pp. 214, 215, 221, 223; Lacey, *A Study of Social Heredity As Illustrated in the Greek People*, p. 60; Saloutos, *The Greeks in the United States*, pp. 246-47; Cooke, p. 3; Malafouris, pp. 194-96.

14. Canoutas, pp. 182, 215-16; New York *Atlantis*, October 11, 1907; *ibid.*, October 15, 1907; *ibid.*, October 16, 1907; *ibid.*, October 19, 1907. The member associations of the Panhellenic Union were primarily occupational and regional fraternities. Cf. Panhellenic Union, *Katastikon*, 1910, (New York, 1910), pp. 1, 2, 5ff. The pamphlet included the constitution of the fraternal association. The official crest of the Panhellenic Union was modeled on a double-headed eagle of Imperial Byzantium.

15. New York *Atlantis*, September 28, 1907.

16. Panhellenic Union, *Katastikon*, 1910, pp. 3, 4.

17. *Ibid.*, pp. 36, 37, 50.

18. *Ibid.*, p. 49.

19. *Greek-American Guide*, 1907, p. 295. There were approximately 18,000 active members in 125 chapters in the United States during the period 1909-10.

20. New York *Atlantis*, September 20, 1907.

21. *Ibid.*, October 7, 1908; *ibid.*, October 29, 1907; *ibid.*, November 1, 1907.

22. *Ibid.*, January 23, 1908; *ibid.*, July 7, 1908; *ibid.*, October 13, 1908.

23. *Ibid.*, October 10, 1908; *ibid.*, October 26, 1908; *ibid.*, October 27, 1908; *ibid.*, October 28, 1908.

24. *Ibid.*, October 28, 1908.

25. *Ibid.*, November 28, 1908.

26. *Ibid.*, December 2, 1908; *ibid.*, December 3, 1908.

27. *Ibid.*, December 5, 1908.

28. Canoutas, pp. 174, 175-76; New York *Atlantis*, January 16, 1909; *ibid.*, February 4, 1909; *ibid.*, February 6, 1909; Elihu Root to Lampros Coromilas, Washington, December 12, 1908, *Foreign Relations*, 1908, p. 400; reminiscences of Nicholas A. Contopoulos (1881-1948). The latter arrived in New York from Constantinople in 1907 and became a member of the Panhellenic Union.

29. New York *Atlantis*, February 5, 1909; Krikou, *E Thesis tu Hellenismu en Ameriki*, pp. 57ff.

30. Forster, pp. 44-45; Martin, *Greece of the Twentieth Century*, pp. 53-54, 122. Coromilas was married to the former Ana Cockrell, daughter of United States Senator Cockrell.

31. *Greek-American Guide, 1910*, pp. 164, 405; *ibid., 1912*, p. 320; *philo-ptochos* means "friends of the poor."

32. *Ibid., 1910*, p. 319; Burgess, p. 76; Xenides, p. 108; Efthimiou, p. 86.

Chapter 9
The Immigrant Church

1. *Inventory of Church Archives*, pp. 113, 114, 132-42; Alexander Doumouras, "Greek Orthodox Communities in America before World War I," *St. Vladimir's Seminary Quarterly* (1967), XI, 173, 177-79; Zustis, pp. 37-38.

2. *Laws of the State of New York, 1871*, Chapter 12, p. 14. These laws complicated the relations between the Greeks and the Russians because both desired Constantinople. Cf. Michael Cherniavsky, *Tsar and People: A Historical Study of Russian National and Social Myths* (New Haven, 1961), pp. 171, 199, 200; Marriott, pp. 130, 186, 188, 235, 239ff.

3. *Laws of the State of New York*, 1895, Chapter 723, Article III, pp. 468-99.

4. The rank of an archimandrite in the Greek Orthodox Church corresponds to a superior abbot of a monastery or a father provincial of the Roman Church. The title is similar to that of a monsignor in the latter church. The archimandrite ranks below a bishop and chore-bishop and above a priest in the Greek Church.

5. *Greek-American Guide*, *1907*, p. 158; *ibid.*, *1910*, p. 156; *ibid.*, *1912*, pp. 307, 315; Zustis, pp. 56-58.

6. Biblion Baptiseon, Gamon, Kae Kydeion telestheson ti en Nea Iorki artisustato Helleniki Orthodoxon Eccleseia "Hagia Trias" apo tis 1 Ianuariu ton xiliston octakoston ennenkoston deuteron Sutirin etos (1892), *passim*. Hereinafter referred to as the Holy Trinity Book of Sacraments. The manuscript book of the sacraments of baptisms, marriages and funerals included citations in the hand of the Reverends Agathodoros Papageorgopoulos, Zysimus Typaldos and Methodius Kourkoules.

7. *Ibid.*, pp. 3ff.

8. Thomas J. Lacey, *Our Greek Immigrants* (New York, 1918), p. 4.

9. Holy Trinity Book of Sacraments, p. 1.

10. *Ibid.*, p. 51.

11. *Ibid.*, p. 3

12. *Ibid.*, pp. 51, 55. Cf. Maria Sarantopulo-Ekonomidy, *E Hellenes Tis Amerikis Opos Tus Eda* (New York, 1916), pp. 140ff.

13. New York *Atlantis*, October 12, 1895; Holy Trinity Book of Sacraments, p. 28.

14. Holy Trinity Book of Sacraments, p. 55; New York *Atlantis*, September 14, 1895; *New-York Daily Tribune*, August 8, 1895; *New York World*, August 8, 1895; *The New York Times*, August 8, 1895; *New York Herald*, August 8, 1895; New York *The Sun*, August 8, 1895.

15. *Brooklyn Daily Eagle*, August 8, 1895.

16. New York *Atlantis*, September 26, 1896; *The New York Times*, September 26, 1896.

17. Zustis, p. 339; *New-York Daily Tribune*, July 31, 1893; *ibid.*, August 1, 1893.

18. *The New York Times*, August 1, 1893; *ibid.*, August 6, 1893.

19. New York *Atlantis*, April 21, 1899.

20. *Ibid.*, May 12, 1899.

21. Zustis, pp. 60, 61, 62, 63-64.

22. *Ibid.*, pp. 65-68.

23. *Ibid.*, p. 92; New York *Atlantis*, April 5, 1904; *ibid.*, July 5, 1904.

24. *Ibid.*, April 6, 1895; *ibid.*, April 27, 1895.

25. *The New York Times*, November 18, 1895.

26. *Ibid.*, January 6, 1896. The Orthodox Church followed the Julian Calendar until the Hellenic jurisdictions, Ecumenical Patriarchate of Constantinople, Church of Greece and Church of Cyprus accpted the Gregorian Calendar after World War I.

27. Canoutas, p. 166; Lacey, *A Study of Social Heredity As Illustrated by the Greek People*, p. 53; Zustis, pp. 60-61; *Greek-American Guide, 1910*, pp. 154-58; *ibid., 1912*, p. 307.

28. Lacey, *A Study of Social Heredity As Illustrated in the Greek People*, p. 47; Zustis, pp. 72, 81-83; Canoutas, pp. 165-66.

29. Zustis, pp. 72-74.

30. According to Rev. George Mastrantonis the Orthodox Christian believes that "repentance derives from faith in and love of God, and it is accompanied by sorrow and contrition with the sincere decision to correct and better one's spiritual life... Sincere repentance is not a decision derived from fear of punishment... but it is merely an external removal of guilt, it is also a sanctification of the believer," *Confession: A Merciful Privilege and Sacrament* (St. Louis, Mo. n.d.), p. 10.

31. William Miller, *Travels and Politics in the Near East* (London, 1898), pp. 242ff.; *idem, Essays on the Latin Levant* (Cambridge, England, 1921), pp. 359ff.

32. Eusebius Alexander P'Stephanou, *The Orthodox Church Militant* (New York, 1950), pp. 26, 27, 28.

33. Nicolas Zernov, *The Church of the Eastern Christians* (London, 1947), pp. 19-20; Rev. Constantine Callinikos, *The History of the Orthodox Church*, Revised Edition. Translated by Katherine Natzi (Los Angeles, 1957), pp. 104-105; Cherniavsky, pp. 76, 88, 94-95, 117, 121; Sir John Herbert Maynard, *Russia in Flux* (New York, 1948), p. 54; Jesse D. Clarkson, *A History of Russia* (New York, 1962), p. 214.

34. Bernard Pares, *History of Russia* (New York, 1947), pp. 207-208.

35. Basil H. Sumner, *Peter the Great and the Emergence of Russia*. First Collier Brooks Edition (New York, 1969), pp. 125, 126-27; Nicholas V. Riasanovsky, *A History of Russia*. Second Edition (New York, 1969), pp. 257-58.

36. Miller, *Travels and Politics in the Near East*, p. 284.

37. Zernov, p. 53.

38. Very Reverend Michael Contantinides, *The Orthodox Church* (London, 1931), pp. 149ff., 154, 161ff.; Zernov, p. 54; Rev. George Mastrantonis, *The Life of Jesus Christ* (St. Louis, Mo., n.d.) pp. 14-15; Rev. George Mastrantonis, *Main Feast Days of the Eastern Orthodox Church.* Second Edition (St. Louis, Mo., n.d.), pp. 4-5, 12; John, II, 13-15, 23-27. Rev. Mastrantonis' pamphlets are published by OLOGOS, a Greek Orthodox missionary society.

39. New York *Atlantis*, December 4, 1900.

40. *Ibid.*, December 7, 1900. Many early records of the Holy Trinity Church were destroyed in a fire that engulfed the church in the evening of January 11, 1927.

41. *Ibid.*, December 28, 1900.

42. *Ibid.*, January 4, 1901; *ibid.*, January 8, 1901.

43. *Ibid.*, March 26, 1901; *Hemerologion-Thermopylon*, 1904, pp. 129-30.

44. New York *Atlantis*, April 12, 1901.

45. *Ibid.*, April 23, 1901; *ibid.*, April 26, 1901.

46. *Ibid.*, April 30, 1901. The new appointees were Constantine Alexander, John Poulides, George Tragides, Demetrius Polymetis, Constantine Galanopoulos, John Booras, Demetrius Varonis, Peter Minekakes, John Hatzinicholas, Constantine Tseronis, Christos Stavrianopoulos, Nicholas Koumantaras and George Kalamas. The committee contained only prominent provincial immigrants.

47. *Ibid.*, May 3, 1901.

48. *Ibid.*, May 7, 1901.

49. *Ibid.*, May 10, 1901; *ibid.*, May 17, 1901. A supplementary list of new members was also published on May 14, 1901.

50. *Ibid.*, May 21, 1901.

51. *Ibid.*, May 28, 1901.

52. Greek Archdiocese of North and South America, *Regulations and Uniform Parish By-Laws of the Greek Archdiocese of North and South America* (New York, 1955), pp. 7, 10, 12-14, 16-18ff.

53. New York *Atlantis*, June 4, 1901.

54. *Ibid.*, June 28, 1901.

55. *New-York Daily Tribune*, June 6, 1901; New York *The World*, June 6, 1901; New York *The Sun*, June 6, 1901; *The New York Times*, June 6, 1901;

New York *Atlantis*, June 7, 1901; *New York Herald*, June 7, 1901. Reverend M. J. Karidis was 53 years of age at the time of his death. He was born in the region of eastern Rumelia. He was appointed pastor of the Greek church of the Holy Trinity in New Orleans in 1880.

56. New York *Atlantis*, June 11, 1901.

57. *Ibid.*, April 26, 1901; *ibid.*, April 17, 1909; Sarantopulu-Ekonomidy, pp. 151ff.

58. New York *Atlantis*, June 18, 1901.

59. *Laws of the State of New York, 1895*, Chapter 723, Article III, pp. 498-99; Zustis, p. 92; Doumouras, p. 184.

60. Zustis, pp. 91-92.

61. *Laws of the State of New York, 1905*, II, Chapter 749, 2120; Doumouras, p. 185; Zustis, p. 93. Cf. Reverend M. Kourkoules and Leonidas Calvocoressi to Archbishop Meletius Metaxakis, New York, September 25, 1918, cited in Zustis, pp. 58-9.

62. Zustis, p. 74.

63. Athens *Neon Asty*, November 25, 1905; Athens *Patris*, July 14, 1908; Trieste *Nea Hemera*, June 21, 1906; Athens *Oe Kaeroe*, June 20, 1906.

64. Dendia, p. 106.

65. Reverend Joachim Alexopoulos, *Melete Peri Ecclesiastikis Diorganoseos tu en Ameriki Hellenismu* (New York, 1919). Reverend Alexopoulos' study on the proposed ecclesiastical reorganization of the Greek Church was widely received by the immigrants.

66. New York *Atlantis*, December 11, 1900; *ibid.*, May, 1901; *ibid.*, January 27, 1906; *ibid.*, February 10, 1906; *ibid.*, March 22, 1906; *ibid.*, May 17, 1904; Athens *Neon Asty*, November 22, 1905; *ibid.*, November 23, 1905; Trieste *Nea Hemera*, June 10, 1906.

67. Forster, 40, 42ff.; Marriott, pp. 407, 418; New York *Atlantis*, August 25, 1908; *ibid.*, October 1, 1908; *ibid.*, December 9, 1908; *ibid.*, December 16, 1908; *ibid.*, January 7, 1909; *ibid.*, April 24, 1909; Carnegie Endowment for International Peace, *Report of the International Commission to Inquire into the Causes and Conduct of the Balkan Wars* (Washington, 1914), pp. 35ff.; [Anon], "Greek Church Threatened by Young Turks," *Eastern and Western Review*, II (August, 1909), 7-8.

68. New York *Atlantis*, April 19, 1909; Greek Archdiocese of North and South America, *1963 Year Book* (New York, 1963), p. 84.

69. Callinikos, p. 115; Xenides, p. 118; Doumouras, p. 190; Zustis, pp.

149, 153.

70. New York *Atlantis,* April 22, 1908; *ibid.,* April 19, 1909; *ibid.,* April 20, 1909; *ibid.,* April 21, 1909.

71. *Ibid.,* May 1, 1909.

72. *Ibid.,* May 4, 1909.

73. *Ibid.,* May 7, 1909.

74. *Ibid.,* May 8, 1909.

75. *Ibid.,* May 11, 1909; *ibid.,* May 17, 1909; *ibid.,* May 18, 1909; *ibid.,* May 19, 1909; *ibid.,* May 20, 1909; *ibid.,* May 25, 1909.

76. *Ibid.,* April 12, 1908 - May 25, 1909, *passim.*

77. Greek Orthodox Archdiocese of North and South America, *Greek Orthodox Year Book, 1955* (New York, 1955), p. 7; *ibid., 1963,* pp. 78-89; Zustis, pp. 117, 123, 133ff., 400, 401.

78. Malafouris, pp. 184, 185; Saloutos, *The Greeks in the United States,* p. 288.

79. Reverend George Bacopoulos to Michael Contopoulos, New York, September 10, 1964; *Ecclesiasticos Kyrix,* I (September 30, 1921), 75-77; Xenides, p. 119; Doumouras, p. 191. The Certificate of Incorporation of Greek Archdiocese of North and South America is cited in Zustis, pp. 133-35.

Chapter 10

The Immigrant Press

1. New York *Atlantis,* March 3, 1894; Robert Ezra Park, *The Immigrant Press and Its Control* (New York, 1922), p. 252; Canoutas, p. 170; N. W. Ayers & Son, *A Catalogue of American Newspapers,* 1895, p. 537. Hereafter referred to as Ayers. The title of this Philadelphia serial publication varies, such as *Directory of American Newspapers and Periodical.*

2. Park, p. 229.

3. Ayers, 1900, p. 579; *ibid.,* 1904, p. 590.

4. Burgess, p. 67; Fairchild, *Greek Immigration to the United States,* p. 153; Xenides, p. 109; *Greek-American Guide, 1907,* p. 162; *ibid., 1910,* p. 162; Ayers, *1911,* p. 628; Lacey, *A Study of Social Heredity As Illustrated in the Greek People,* p. 51; Efthimiou, pp. 69-70.

5. Canoutas, p. 232; Malafouris, pp. 227-28; Saloutos, *The Greeks in*

the United States, p. 91.

6. New York *Atlantis*, January 5, 1904.

7. Krikou, *E Thesis tu Hellenismu en Ameriki*, p. 53.

8. Burgess, p. 69. The magazine's annual subscription was $2.00.

9. An example of such bitter controversy was the Sarantopulu-Economidy affair in 1908. Cf. New York *Atlantis*, November 27, 1908; *ibid.*, December 2, 1908; *New York Herald*, December 2, 1908; New York *Panhellenius Ephimeris*, December 2, 1908 cited in Fairchild, *Greek Immigration to the United States*, pp. 154-55 n.

10. New York *Atlantis*, March 30, 1895.

11. *Ibid.*, June 1, 1895.

12. Park, p. 69.

13. *Ibid.*, p. 19. The *Atlantis* remained the stalwart defender of the puristic form of the Greek language up to World War II. It should be noted that the literary quality used by the newspaper was highest when the immigrants had the lowest level of formal education in Greece, 1894-1910. The high quality gradually declined after 1945 with the influx of immigrants who had more formal education in their native country.

14. New York *Atlantis*, May 4, 1896; *ibid.*, October 22, 1897; *ibid.*, November 19, 1897; *ibid.*, September 26, 1900; *ibid.*, October 2, 1900; *ibid.*, October 26, 1900.

15. Xenides, p. 110.

16. Cooke, p. 3.

17. Fairchild, *Greek Immigration to the United States*, p. 152.

18. *Ibid.*, p. 209.

19. New York *Atlantis*, August 15, 1896.

20. *Ibid.*, October 17, 1896.

21. *Ibid.*, October 31, 1896.

22. *Ibid.*, November 7, 1896.

23. *Ibid.*, June 23, 1899.

24. *Ibid.*, October 2, 1900; *ibid.*, October 5, 1900; *ibid.*, October 16, 1900; *ibid.*, October 19, 1900; *ibid.*, October 22, 1900. The first article dealt with the silver issue and the following three discussed the emerging American imperialism and colonialism.

25. *Ibid.*, November 8, 1900.

26. *Ibid.*, October 26, 1904, *Supplement*; *ibid.*, October 28, 1904; *ibid.*, November 2, 1904; *ibid.*, November 7, 1904; *ibid.*, November 9, 1904.

27. *Ibid.*, September 26, 1908; *ibid.*, October 23, 1908; *ibid.*, October 24, 1908; *ibid.*, November 2, 1908; *ibid.*, November 3, 1908; *ibid.*, November 4, 1908.

28. *Ibid.*, November 5, 1912; *ibid.*, November 6, 1912.

29. Editorial, *ibid.*, October 8, 1897.

30. *Ibid.*

31. *Ibid.*, October 23, 1897; *ibid.*, October 29, 1897.

32. *Ibid.*, November 5, 1897.

33. Burgess, p. 68; Canoutas, pp. 172, 173, 174; Malafouris, p. 232.

34. Canoutas, pp. 173-4; Lacey, *A Study of Social Heredity As Illustrated in the Greek People*, p. 51; Fairchild, *Greek Immigration to the United States*, p. 153; Burgess, p. 51; Malafouris, p. 7; Saloutos, *The Greeks in the United States*, p. 92.

35. Canoutas, *O Hellenismos en Ameriki*, p. 233.

36. Ayers, *Directory of American Newspapers and Periodicals*, 1911, p. 642.

37. Canoutas, pp. 230-32; Malafouris, pp. 232-33, 240; The back files of the *Thermopylae*, *Simaea*, *Thermopylae-Simaea*, *Panhellenius Ephimeris* and the *Phruros* are not available.

38. Vlasto, pp. 204–06, 260-61, 287-89.

39. New York *Atlantis*, May 16, 1896; *ibid.*, May 23, 1896; *ibid.*, May 25, 1897; *ibid.*, July 2, 1897.

40. *Ibid.*, October 12, 1895; *ibid.*, October 19, 1895; *ibid.*, March 28, 1896; *ibid.*, August 8, 1896; *ibid.*, August 15, 1896; *ibid.*, September 5, 1896; *ibid.*, September 12, 1896; *ibid.*, September 19, 1896.

41. *Ibid.*, July 9, 1897.

42. *Ibid.*, March 3, 1897; *ibid.*, April 16, 1897; *ibid.*, June 18, 1897.

Conclusion

1. Canoutas, pp. 167ff., 172ff., 177, 222; Krikou, *E Thesis tu Hellenismu en Ameriki*, p. 70; Efthimiou, *passim*.

2. Marcus Lee Hansen, *The Immigrant in American History* (Cambridge, 1940), p. 208 n.

Appendices

Appendix 1
I.H. Hill to Christodules Evangelides[1]

My dear Mr. Evangeli,
Athens 8 July 1843

I have this moment heard from Mr. Thos. Scribner, that he is going to Syra on Monday and I avail myself of so good an opportunity to give you a piece of news that I am sure will gratify you very much.

We have just heard from London that Dr. <u>Saml. G. Howe</u> of Boston (so well known in Greece for his philhellenism) is there with his wife and a sister of his wife, on <u>their</u> <u>way to Greece</u> — But who do you think is his wife? She was . . . <u>Julia Ward</u> daughter of your late friend Saml Ward of New York! This news will no doubt surprise and please you—and I hasten to let you know it. We expect Dr. Howe and the ladies in the course of a month or two.

I have only time to add that I shall be happy to hear from you — We are all well. Mr. Scr1bnor has been reading English with me for some time past and has made astonishing progress in our language.

Farewell . . .

truly yours
I H Hill

1. I. H. Hill to Christodules Evangelides, Athens, July 8, 1843, miscellaneous Julia Ward Howe Papers, New-York Historical Society; A.L.S.; No corrections were made; Line 9: words before Julia Howe were illegible; Line 21: part of closing was illegible.

Appendix 2

Christodules Evangelides to Gulian G. Verplanck:[2]

Hon. G. C. Verplanck.

New-York June 19th 1854.

During the Greek Revolution which began in 1821 American philanthropy and charity saved me from the Turks and educated me in America.

As soon as I graduated in Columbia College in 1836 I returned to Greece to do to my countrymen what the sons of Franklin and Washington had done for me.

Seventeen years I have been trying to do my duty, I commenced teaching in private, then opened an infant school, then added a preparatory to it (Syndidaktikon), after that a grammar school (Hellenikon) and after that I opened a college, Gymnasium, also teaching what I was taught, and bringing up the youth that were entrusted to my care in the fear of God and love of country, pointing to them the path of duty and honor as well as I could. More than 400 young Greeks from Macedona, Thessaly, Epirus, Scio, Thrace, Egypt, Asia Minor, Crete and the other parts of the once free and happy country

of my ancestors have been educated by me—I taught them every thing I thought was good, I always held up to them America and her institutions for them to aim at and aspire. I taught to them the Bible. And they translated your speeches and were delighted and instructed by them.

What I have been doing many others have done—The result was, that these people taught the same to others and all with one consent wish to be free.

The people were sore oppressed forced by the Turks to pay taxes for four years in advance and other cruelties being committed against them and wishing to be free they took up arms against the Turks. But the English and the French say that we are paid by Russia. They say that Russian gold and Russian intrigues have made us take up arms. And many of the Americans believe it.

My countrymen have sent me here to defend them, but who am I? And what can I do? To whom shall I go? Who will defend us?

2. Christodules Evangelides to Gulian C. Verplanck, New York, June 19, 1854, Gulian C. Verplanck Papers, File Box 4, E 23, New-York Historical Society; A.L.S.; No corrections were made.

The English and the French and the Turks are fighting against us—and the King of Greece Otho has accepted the offers of the English French and Turks, and ws are left alone. My countrymen are deserted and are persecuted by those who should have assisted, then from Russia we can have no comfort, because all our confidence had been placed on the powers of the West, but the Western powers say that we are paid by Russia, so that we are helpless—All the help that was sent us by the good people of liberated Greece has been captured by French Christians and English Christians that assist the Turks, and thrown overboard.

Thirteen millions of people have sent me here, I call upon you. Examine our cause, if it be just, if it be the cause of freedom, then let us have from you, what <u>freemen</u> ought to give to those who suffer for the cause of freedom.

I tell you sir, the truth. We are <u>innocent</u>, We are true, We do not fight for Russia, We fight for our <u>Liberty</u>—. We wish to be <u>free</u>.

The opportunity, was a good one, but the Europeans who do not wish us to be free always find some thing to say. We took up arms in 1836, in 1840 and in 1843, as we have done now in 1854. but always they find some thing to say.

Sir the present struggle is but the continuation of the one begun in 1821. That struggle has not ended yet, for Macedonia, Thessaly, Epirus, Thrace ... are not yet free— We are true men sir we fight for the exalted rights of human nature, if we are wrong then virtue is wrong, and all that is noble is wrong — We hope in you our only hope on earth is America. If America turn a smiling eye to poor, injured Greece then we shall be happy though we were to perish, Americans have mercy upon us for there is none to help us. We are alone—

Most humbly. yours.

C. Evangelides

Appendix 3

William Cullen Brvant to Moses Grinnell[3]

Office of the Evening Post
1869
New York May 31

Mr. A. C. Evangelides who holds a place in the Custom House by my recommendation and that of several other good republicans~cans has heard that he may perhaps be removed. I earnestly hope that this will not be the case — He came here because his father Mr. Christophorus Evangelides of Syra Greece wished him to be in America and as he is a very clever young man well qualified for any sort of clerkship the post he occupies was procured for him.

His father the 'Greek boy' as he was once called was rescued at Smyrna from Turkish masters when a lad was brought to this country by Mr. P Vandervoort — Mr. S. Ward the elder had him educated at Columbia College — after which he went to Greece and—became a teacher at Syra—and a most useful and valuable citizen of that country..

He is enthusiastically attached to America and both father and son had the right sort of sympathy in the last cruel war—

For the sake of both I sincerely hope that the son will be continued in his present employment.

I am sir
With Great Respect,
Yours very truly —
    W. C. Bryant

Hon. M. Grinnell
    Custom House — N.Y.

3. William Cullen Bryant to Moses Grinnell, New York, May 31, 1869, Unpublished Manuscript, Diary of Alexander C. Evangelides, New-York Historical Society (1864-1869); Copy of letter was in the handwriting of A. C. Evangelides; No corrections were made.

Appendix 4

Letter to the Editor of The New York .Times[4]

Being informed that irresponsible parties have been sending begging letters to persons in this city and out of town, soliciting contributions either for poor Greeks or for a Greek brotherhood called 'Athena,' and also for the support of the Greek Church in this city, I beg to inform the public:

1. That the Greeks in New York are in no need of alms.

2. That there does not exist a Greek brotherhood called Athena, and, finally that the only Greek Church existing is the Church of the Holy Trinity of which I am the pastor, and which is self-supporting, and has no need of outside assistance, and its congregation is fully able to maintain it with dignity and uphold its respectability.

Father Agathodoros, Archimandrite
New York, April 27, 1896

---

4. Letter to the Editor of *The New York Times* published on April 29, 1896; An archimandrite corresponds to a provincial in the Roman Church. Reverend Agathodoros' surname was Papageorgopoulos. He served as the second pastor of the Holy Trinity Church, 1894-1901.

Appendix 5

Letter to the Editor of The Evening Post[5]

TO THE EDITOR OF *THE EVENING POST:*

SIR: The malicious accusations of Mr. Botassi, the Greek Consul at this port, published in your yesterday's issue, are without foundation. I ha~e never instigated any mass-meeting against him; I did not draw the resolutions censuring his unpatriotic conduct recently passed at an indignation meeting of the Greek colony of New York neither did I cable to the King of Greece or anybody else in Athens.

The Greek newspaper <u>Atlantis</u>, when the Cretan trouble began, opened two funds, one for the National League of Greece and another to help the Cretan refugees. These funds, to which almost every Greek in the United States contributed, amount now to nearly forty-three hundred dollars, the money with the name of each contributor being published in the <u>Atlantis</u> weekly. Mr. Botassi thought to start another fund himself, and got up a committee composed of a small corner grocer in Roosevelt Street, one or two small candy-sellers, and a man whom I discharged from my office a couple of weeks ago. This 'committee' was placed under the chairmanship of the Greek priest, and as they were ashamed to give their residences in Mulberry, Baxter, or Roosevelt Street, they put the name of the 'Treasurer,' care of the Union Dime Savings Bank, and they started to collect funds, which they claim that they are sending to the 'King of Greece,' but as the contributors did not see their names in the Greek paper or any acknowledgment in the local press, they called the mass-meeting and denounced the Consul, who at a previous meeting formed without the least authority the committee in question. They also denounced the Consul for having stated that the Greek army is not well equipped and can easily be beaten by the Turks. That the indignation is general is shown from the fact that out of 950 Greeks resident in New York 900 were present at the meeting, and possibly more, a~ can be attested by the reporters of the daily press who were present at the meeting.

Mr. Botassi holds an honorary position. He is not a paid official of the Greek go~government. He only receives some fees for 'vises,' and earns his living as clerk in a commercial house, from

5. Letter to the Editor of New York *The Evening Post*, March 12, 1897

which he draws $12 to $15 weekly. There is no consulate here. He is allowed out of charity a desk-room free of rent at the sample-room of a cotton-house. That such a man should represent Greece hers at the present moment naturally angers the Greeks.

A mass-meeting was held last week at Chickering Hall and reso-lutions passed expressing sympathy with the Greek cause, and letters from Senator Hoar, Dr. Parkhurst, Mayor Strong, Seth Low, and others were read. Mr. Botassi felt angry at this, and he called another mass-meeting for to-night, which in itself is ridicu-lous. A concert was given also by the Greeks, having for patroness-es some of the best-known American women of New York which netted for the refugees nearly $700. Of course Mr. Botassi, again being outwitted, must do something, and he calls upon a teacher of Greek, calling himself of the University of Athens, which is untrue, to give a lecture, and he interests three or four Greek women, the wives of the employees of the house where he has desk-room; and it can be easily understood that these tactics displease and disgust the Greek community. The so-called 'lecturer' was in my employ for some time, nearly two years, and was discharged for reasons unnecessary to mention now.

As to <u>Atlantis</u>, I desire to inform you that the contributors to it are the poet laureate of Greece, who is our regular correspondent from Athens, and whose letters are of immense value from a liter-ary as well as political view; a diplomat of eminent standing, whose letters about the Eastern question often appear in the columns of the <u>Evening</u> <u>Post</u>; Mrs. Lografou, one of the three Greek women who are the best known Greek authoresses, and other writers to whose talent is due the success, the phenomenal success, Or the paper, which from a 'little sheet' became a paper of eight large pages and is now in its fourth year.

As to any business standing, it will be sufficient to inform you that I am an importer of minerals; that I supply most of the paper-manufacturers of the country with nearly a million dollars' worth of sulphur every year; that I am an exporter of petroleum, shipping hundreds of thousands of cases abroad; that I am one of the few importers of Mocha coffee here, and that I have large contracts with Messrs. Carnegie, to whom I supply the manganese used for armorplates. Under these circumstances, I really fail to see what connection I could have with Mr. Botassi, a ten-dollar clerk, travel-ing under the high-sounding title of 'Consul_General.' I have absolutely nothing to do with him. I have not spoken to him for four years, since he returned me a loan made to him, and I certainly ignore the man, and I don't bother my head about politics. I have my own business to attend.

SOLON J. VLASTO

New York, March 12.

Appendix 6

Extract from Report for the Year 1903 on the Trade and Commerce of
the Morea, and Province of Aetolia and Acarnania[6]

When asked why they are so anxious to leave their country they give various reasons. Some say they are tired of living in a land where they see no chance of bettering their position, and this is the characteristic of the Greek; others state that many of those who have emigrated before them are doing extremely well, and that they wish to do likewise; finally, that the taxes weigh too heavily on the peasant classes, and are collected in a harsh and oppressive manner, and that politics, which are the mainspring of the existence of every Greek peasant, constantly lead them into broils, litigation and strife, often ending in fines and imprisonment.t.

The one redeeming feature in this gradual depopulation of the Morea is that the Greek emigrant, unlike his cogener of most other nationalities, has his thoughts turned constantly towards the land and relatives he has left behind.

He is perfectly aware of the risks he runs, he knows he may sink and disappear altogether, but having over whelming confidence in himself, he fully expects to grow rich and prosperous, and then return to his native land and lead a life of ease and comfort amongst his relatives and friends, proud to think that he has carved out his own future.

There are 70,000 Greeks who have emigrated to the United States and remit annually 15,000,000 drachmae . . . representing a saving of £ 6 per head. This is not much when it is borne in mind that the average Greek is extremely abstemious is the matter of drink and very careful and thoughtful in money matters. They earn abroad comparatively high wages of the native workman, but live with greater economy. Establishing themselves in small groups, they occupy together the cheapest tenements, avoid alcoholic beverages almost entirely, and arrange to be supplied from Greece with cheese, olives, dried fish, and other articles of diet, which are not consumed by any other class, and are therefore much cheaper than those which are necessities to the native competitor. They are also not burdened with family cares, as it is quite exceptional for a

6. Report for the Year 1903 on the Trade and Commerce of the Morea, and Province of Aetolia and Acarnania, *D.C.R.*, No. 3156 (1904), pp. 17-18.

Greek to marry outside his own nationality and religion. The Greek peasant could undoubtedly save as much yearly in his own country, were he to devote himself to his work with the same energy and determination and were the conditions of life the same, but the climate of Greece is, of course, warmer and more enervating than that of the United States, the

Orthodox Church also contains enumerable holy days, which are religiously observed by the peasantry in Greece.

But above all to the Greek living in his own country there lacks the stimulus which animates the emigrants who have set out with a settled object in view, when he is determined by all and every means to accomplish.

Appendix 7

Principal Occupations of Alien
Immigrants from Greece: 1875–1890

Year	Laborers	Farmers	Merchants & Dealers	Tot Skilled Workers	Tot Misc.	No Occupation. (incl. Women&Children)
1875	1	0	7	5	10	9
1876	6	0	4	2	9	8
1877	10	0	5	2	16	5
1878	2	0	4	4	6	3
1879	5	0	4	5	10	6
1880	12	0	1	2	13	6
1881	2	0	4	7	7	5
1882	60	31	3	26	95	4
1883	24	0	2	10	27	33
1884	7	3	3	6	15	16
1885	60	0	11	25	96	51
1886	66	0	1	7	67	30
1887	195	4	65	11	265	37
1888	575	39	31	27	647	107
1889	59	18	7	31	89	35
1890	294	26	8	40	352	139
1875–90	1378	121	160	210	1724	494

Explanatory Notes:

1. Twelve weavers emigrated to the United States in 1890.

2. Total miscellaneous category includes professionals.

Sources: Annual Report of the Superintendent of Immigration, 1892, pp. 51ff

Appendix 8
The Number of Parish Organizations of the Greek
Orthodox Church in the United States, New York
State and New York City: 1890–1916

	1890	1906	1916
New York City	0	0	3
Manhattan	0	3	3
Brooklyn	0	0	1
Bronx	0	0	0
Queens	0	0	0
Richmond	0	0	0
New York State	0	30	6
Other States	1	304	81
United States	1	334	87

Note: 1. The *Eleventh* Census listed the Greek Orthodox Church of the Holy
Trinity in New Orleans. The church had a membership of 100 communicants in
1890. It was the first Greek Church in the United States founded by the Benaki
and Botassis families.
Source: Computed on the data found in Zustis, pp. 299-306, 321-339; United
States, Bureau of the Census, *Special Report on Religious Bodies, 1906* (2 pts.
Washington, 1910), I, pp. 29, 240, 340ff.; *ibid., 1916*, I, 450ff.; *Compendium of the
Eleventh Census of the United States, 1890* (2 v. Washington, 1892), I, 475-515,
582, 666.

Appendix 9
The Number of Members or Communicants in the
Greek Orthodox Church in the United States,
New York State and New York City: 1890–1916

Political Divisions	1890	1906	1916
New York City	0	12,575	22,680
Manhattan	0	12,000	21,000
Brooklyn	0	550	1,680
Bronx	0	0	0
Queens	0	25	0
Richmond	0	0	0
New York State	0	15,100	23,030
Other States & Territories	100	75,651	96,841
United States	100	90,751	119,871

Source: Computed on the data found in United States, Bureau of the Census, *Special Report on Religious Bodies, 1906* (2 pts. Washington, 1910), I, 29, 240, 340 ff.; *ibid., 1916*, I, 450 ff.; *Compendium of the Eleventh Census of the United States*, II, *passim*.

Bibliography

Note

There are very few manuscript collections available concerning the Greek immigrant community in New York. The most important sources of social, cultural, religious and economic information are the files of the newspaper, *Atlantis*, and the Book of Sacraments of the Holy Trinity Church. The newspaper represented the policies and sentiments of its influential publisher, Solon J. Vlasto, from 1894 to 1927.

The unpublished letters and diaries of Christodules Evangelides and his son, Alexander, form a general introduction to the origins of the Greek community in the previous century. The manuscripts show the gradual appearance of the Greek cotton merchants, e.g., Ralli, Rodocanachi and Calvocoressi, who became prominent factors after the Civil War. Moreover, Alexander Evangelides participated in the activities of the Holy Trinity Church. Leonidas J. Calvocoressi was also prominent in the affairs of that parish and in the organization of the Greek Archdiocese of North and South America between 1918 and 1921. These manuscripts are deposited in the New-York Historical Society.

The various *Executive* and *Miscellaneous Documents* of the House of Representatives for the several Congresses contain significant reports. To simplify the citation of such publications, the departmental or agency classification has been used. The most fruitful sources were the *Census Reports, Population, 1870-1930* and the *Annual Reports of the Commissioner-General of Immigration.* The British Foreign Office's *Diplomatic and Consular Reports, Annual Series*, provide a wealth of information concerning the economic and social background of the Greek emigration.

The transliteration of titles from Greek to English posed a serious obstacle. The difficulty was created because Greek is an inflected language with declensions of nouns, adjectives, pronouns and the agreement of nouns with objects. The standards of transliteration are different in the New York Public Library and the Gennadius Library of the American School of Classical Studies in Athens. Some contemporary writers, however, established arbitrarily their own standards based on an imperfect form of phonetics. In one instance, the Greek letter *sigma* was transliterated as the sound *sh* instead of the correct *s*.

The accepted translation of surnames was adopted. The name Constantine with the *C* was used and not with a *K* unless the latter was the preference of any author. Another example is the surname Contopoulos. In Greek the surname is written with the letter *kappa* because the letter *C* does not exist in the alphabet. The name may be rendered in English with either the letters *C* or *K*, depending on the personal desires of the writers. The same holds true for the name Demetrius or Demetrios. As much as possible, the diphthongs were transliterated from the Greek to the English as follows: ai=ae, ei=ei, oi=oe, au=au, eu=eu, ui=ui, nu=eu and ou=u.

I. Unpublished Manuscripts, Letters and Diaries

Daniel F. Allen to Christodules Evangelides, Boston, August 21, 1850, Miscellaneous Christodules Evangeles Papers, New-York Historical Society.

Reverend George Bacopoulos to Michael Contopoulos, New York, September 10, 1964. Reverend Bacopoulos is the Chancellor of the Greek Archdiocese of North and South America.

Biblion Baptiseon, Gamon kae Kydeon, telestheson ti an Nea Iorki artis-ustato Helliniki Orthodoxon Eccleseia "Hagia Trias" apo tis 1 Ianuariu ton chilliston octakoston ennenkoston deuterin Sutirin etos (1892) (Holy Trinity Book of Sacraments), Greek Archdiocesan Cathedral of the Holy Trinity of New York.

George M. Colvocoresses to Henry Augustus Wise, Litchfield, Connecticut, January 29, 1867, Henry Augustus Wise Letter Box #13, New-York Historical Society.

E. P. Despotopoulos and C. Anastasopoulos to Michael Contopoulos, Athens, September 24, 1964.

Diary of Christodules Miltiades Evangeles (4v. 1834-39), New-York Historical Society.

Diary of Alexander Evangelides (1864-69), New-York Historical Society.

Christodules Evangelides to Gulian C. Verplanck, New York, June 9, 1854, Gulian C. Verplanck Papers, Box 4, E #23, New-York Historical Society.

I. H. Hill to Christodules Evangelides, Athens, July 8, 1843, Miscellaneous Julia Ward Howe Papers, New-York Historical Society.

L. J. Ralli to Michael Contopoulos, London, September 23, 1964.

II. Newspapers

A. New York (immigrant press)

Atlantis, 1894-1927
Ethnikos Kyrix, 1915-1927

B. New York (general press)

Brooklyn Daily Eagle, 1893-1900
The Evening Post, 1893-1900
The Evening Telegram, 1893-1900
Journal of Commerce, 1887
New-York Daily Tribune, 1893-1900
New York Herald, 1893-1924
New York Herald-Tribune, 1927
The New York Times, 1855-1927
The Sun, 1897-1904
Wall Street Journal, 1889-98

World, 1897-1900

C. Athens

Acropolis, 1900
Asty, 1900
Oe Kaeroe, 1900-02
Neon Asty, 1902-07
Patris, 1906-07
Skrip, 1906-07

D. London

The Times, 1897-1904

E. Trieste

Nea Hemera, 1905-08

III. Government Publications

A. United States

Abstract of the Report on the Greek Padrone System in the United States (Washington, 1911).

Annual Reports of the Commissioner-General of Immigration, 1899-1930.

Annual Reports of the Superintendent of Immigration, 1892-98.

Bureau of Corporations. *Report of the Commissioner of Corporations on the Tobacco Industry* (3v. Washington, 1909-15).

Bureau of Manufacturers. *Commercial Relations of the United States with Other Countries*, 1882-1910.

Bureau of Manufacturers. *Consular Reports, Annual Series*, No. 10, *Greece: 1907*.

———. No. 1, *Turkey: 1907*.

———. No. 30, *Turkey-In-Asia: Trade for the Year of 1907*.

Bureau of Manufacturers. *Daily Consular and Trade Reports*.

Bureau of Manufacturers. *Monthly Consular and Trade Reports*.

Compendium of the Eleventh Census, 1890.

Department of Commerce, Bureau of the Census: *Census Reports, Population*, 1870-1930.

Department of State. *Papers Relating to the Foreign Relations of the United States*, 1873-1910.

Immigration Commission. *Reports of the Immigration Commission* (41v. Washington, 1907-11), III, IV, XV.

Industrial Commission. *Reports of the Industrial Commission* (19v. Washington, 1900-02), XV.

Ninth Census of the United States, 1870, The Statistics at the Ninth Census.
Special Reports, Religious Bodies: 1906.
————: *1916.*
Statistical Abstracts of the United States, 1878-1900.
Statistics of the Population of the United States at the Tenth Census (June 1, 1880).
Treasury Department, *Tables Showing Arrivals of Alien Passengers and Immigrants in the United States, from 1820 to 1888* (Washington, 1889).
Twelfth Census of the United States, 1900, Manufacturers, VII.
Works Progress Administration. *Inventory of Church Archives in New York City. Eastern Orthodox Churches and the Armenian Apostolic Churches. The History Records Survey* (Washington, 1940).

B. Brooklyn

Manual of the Common Council, 1886.
————. *Third Annual Report of the Civil Service Commission of the City of Brooklyn,* 1886.

C. New York State

Laws of the State of New York, 1871.
Laws of the State of New York, 1895.
Laws of the State of New York, 1905, II.
Secretary of State. *Census of the State of New York for 1855.*
————. *1865.*
————. *1875.*

D. Great Britain

Diplomatic and Consular Reports, Annual Series.
Foreign Office. *British and Foreign State Papers.*
Parliament, *Sessional Papers,* XXVI (1923)
Report on Smyrna. Report on the Civil Staff of the Late Hospital (London, 1857).

E. Greece

Bule (Parliament). *E Ekthesis Tis Epitropis Tis Bulis Kae E Schetiki Protasis Nomu* (Athens, 1906).
Hypurgeion Ton Exoterikon (Foreign Affairs Ministry). *Deltion Tu Epi Ton Exoterikon B. Hypurgeion. Meros Deuteron. Meletae Kae Ektheseis.* No. 12. *Ektheseis Peri Tis Hellenikis Metanasteuseos: Kae Peri Tu Emporiu en Taes Henomenaes Politeias Tis Amerikis Kata To Etos 1911* (Athens, 1912).
Hypurgeion Ton Esoterikon (Interior Ministry). *Statistiki Tis Hellados, Plythismos: 1870* (Athens, 1872).

————. *Statistiki Tis Hellados, Plythismos: 1879* (Athens, 1881).

————. *Apographi, April 15,16, 1889* (Athens, 1891).

————. Tmema Demosias Oekonomias. *Statistika Apotelesmata Tis Apographis tu Plythismu 5-6 October 1896* (Athens, 1897).

————. *Apographi tu Plythismu: 27 October 1907* (Athens, 1908).

Les Persécutions antigrecques en Turquie de 1908 à 1921. (Athens, 1921). The report was translated and published by the Press Bureau of the Foreign Ministry on behalf of the Third National Assembly in Athens.

Persecutions of the Greek Population in Turkey (London, 1918).

Repoulis, Emmanuel (Interior Minister). *Meleti Meta Schediu Nomu Peri Metanasteuseos* (Athens, 1912).

IV. Semi-official Collections of Public Documents

Hertslet, Sir Edward, ed. *The Map of Europe by Treaty* (4v. London, 1875-91).

Young, Sir George. *Corps de droit Ottoman* (7v. Oxford, 1905-06).

V. Almanacs, Directories and Guidebooks

Adler's Dictionary (New York, 1940).

N.W. Ayers & Son, *A Catalogue of American Newspapers*, 1895-1911.

The Bankers' Almanac and Year Book, 1960-1961.

Boyd, William H. *New York City Tax Book, Being a List of Persons, Corporations and Co-Partnerships, Residents and Non-Residents Who Were Taxed According to the Assessor's Book,* 1856 and 1857 (New York, 1857).

Burke's Genealogical and Heraldic History of the Peerage and Knighthood, Privy Council and the Order of Precedence. Ninety-seventh edition (2v. London, 1939).

Canoutas, Seraphim G. and N. Helmis, compilers. *Greek-American Guide and Business Directory*, First Edition (New York, 1907).

Dau's New York Blue Book, 1915. (New York, 1915).

Duncan & Co.'s New Orleans Business Directory for 1865. (New Orleans, 1865).

Gardiner's New Orleans Directories, 1860-67.

Heller's New Orleans Business Directory for 1860 and 1861 with Commercial Register of Businessmen of New York City (New York, 1860).

Hemerologion-Thermopylon, 1904 Kae Hellinikos Odigos Tis Amerikis (New York, 1904).

Memphis Cotton Exchange Directories and Books of Reference, 1892-98.

Morton Allan Directory (New York, 1931).

The New York Club. *Club Constitution, By-Laws and Home Rule,* 1867-95.

Rode's New York City Business Directory for 1854-1855 (New York, 1854).

Social Register of New York, 1886-91, 1951.

Trow Business Directory of New York City, 1850-90.
Wilson's Business Directory of New York City, 1850-89.
Xanthakes, Socrates. *O Syntrophos tu Hellinos* (New York, 1903).

VI. Ecclesiastical Publications
A. Ecumenical Patriarchate of Constantinople

————. *The Black Book of the Sufferings of the Greek People in Turkey. From the Armistice to the End of 1920* (Constantinople, 1920).
————. *Persecutions of the Greeks in Turkey, 1914-1918* (Constantinople, 1919).

B. Greek Archdiocese of North and South America

Ecclesiasticon Hemerologion Archiepiscopis Amerikis Boreiu kae Notiu: 1935 (Astoria, 1935).
Year Book: 1955.
1963 Year Book.
Regulations and Uniform By-Laws of the Greek Archdiocese of North and South America, as Adopted and Amended by the Several Biennial Ecclesiastical Congresses of the Archdiocese up to and Including the Twelfth Such Congress (1954) and Ratified by the Ecumenical Patriarchate (New York, 1955).

C. General

Ecclesiasticos Kyrix, 1921-22, New York Edition.

VII. Reports of Commodity Exchanges

New Orleans Cotton Exchange. *Eighteenth Annual Report of the New Orleans Cotton Exchange, 1888.*
New York Cotton Exchange. *Reports of the Managers, Treasurer, Executive Committee, Warehouse and Delivery Committee and the Trustees of the Gratuity Fund, 1870-1915.*
New York Produce Exchange. *Annual Reports of the Board of Managers of the New York Produce Exchange, 1873-90.*
Savannah Cotton Exchange. *Annual Reports of the President and Directors of the Savannah Cotton Exchange, 1878-92.*

VIII. Articles, Books and Pamphlets

Abbott, Grace. *A Study of the Greeks in Chicago* (Chicago, 1909).
Aghnides, Thanassis. *The Ecumenical Patriarchate of Constantinople: In the Light of the Treaty of Lausanne* (New York, 1964).
Alexopoulos, Reverend Joachim. *Melete Peri Ecclseiastikis Diorganoseos tu*

en Ameriki Hellenismu (New York, 1919).

Andreades, Andreas Michael. *E Helliniki Metanasteusis* (Athens, 1917).

———. *Les Effets Économiques et Soçiaux de la Guerre en Grèce, Histoire Économique et Sociale de la Guerre* (Paris, 1929).

———. *Meletae Epi Tis Synchronu Hellenikis Demosias Oeconomias, Erga.* Kyriakos Varvaressos, G.A. Petropoulos, J.D. Pintos, eds. (4v. Athens, 1939).

H.R.H. Andrew, Prince of Greece. *Towards Disaster: The Greek Army in Asia Minor in 1921.* Translated from the Greek by H.R.H. Princess Andrew of Greece (London, 1930). Princess Andrew of Greece was Princess Alice of Battenberg.

Argenti, Philip Pandely. *Chius Vincta: or the Occupation of Chios by the Turks* (1566) *and their Administration of the Island* (1566-1912) (Cambridge, 1941).

———. ed. *Libro d'Oro de la Noblesse de Chio* (2v. London, 1955).

———. *The Expedition of Colonel Fabrier to Chios* (London, 1933).

———. *The Massacre of Chios* (London, 1932).

Argyropoulos, P.A. "Les Grecs au Service de l'empire ottoman," *Le Cinq-Centieme de l'Anniversaire de la Prise de Constantinople, 1453-1953* (Athens, 1953).

Arnakis, G. Georgiades. "The Greek Church of Constantinople and the Ottoman Empire," *Journal of Modern History*, XXIV (September, 1952).

Atlantis, ed. *Historia Tis Hellados* (New York, 1909).

———. ed. *Nea Helleniki Anthologia* (New York, 1913).

Bain, John N. *Cigarettes in Fact and Fancy* (Boston, 1906).

Baker, Ray Stannard. "Seen in Turkey," *The Outlook*, LXXII (October, 1902).

Barker, Sir Ernest. *Social and Political Thought in Byzantium* (Oxford, 1957).

Bickford-Smith, Roander Albert Henry. *Greece under King George* (London, 1893).

Bigham, Clive. *With the Turkish Army in Thessaly* (London, 1897).,

Bikelas, Demetrios. *Seven Essays on Christian Greece.* Translated by the Marquess of Bute (London, 1890).

Blancard, Theodore, *Les Mavroyenni: Essai d'Étude Additionnelle à l'Histoire Moderne de la Grèce, de la Turquie et la Rumanie* (Paris, 1893).

———. *Les Mavroyenni: Histoire d'Orient de 1700 à Nos Jours* (Paris, 1909).

Botassis, Demetrius N. and Sir Charles W. Dilke. "The Uprising of Greece," *North American Review*, CLXIV (April, 1897), 453-61.

Botsaris, Notis. *Visions Balkaniques dans la Préparation de la Révolution Grecque, 1789-1821. Études d'Histoire Économique, Politique et Sociale*, XXXVIII (Geneva, 1962).

Bouras, John A. *Ae Ethnikae Thermopylae* (New York, 1910).

Bratsiotis, Panagiotis. *The Greek Orthodox Church*. Translated by Joseph Blenkinsopp (Notre Dame, Indiana, 1968).

Brown, C.H. *Egyptian Cotton* (London, 1953).

Brown, Carroll N. and Theodore P. Ion. *Persecutions of the Greeks in Turkey Since the Beginning of the European War. American Hellenic Society Publication*, No. 3 (New York, 1918).

Bryant, William Cullen. *Poems* (New York, 1898).

Bryer, Anthony. "The Great Idea," *History Today*, XV (March, 1965).

Burgess, Thomas. *Greeks in America* (Boston, 1913).

Burlemi, Theodore A. *History of Currants and the Currant Vine* (Manchester, 1911).

de Busbecq, Ogier Ghiselin. *The Epistles of A.G. Busbequius* (London, 1694).

———. *The Life and Letters of Ogier Ghiselin de Busbecq*. Translated by Charles Thornton Forster and F.H. Blackburn Daniell (2v. London, 1881).

Byzantios., Scarlatos D. *He Konstantinoupolis He Perigraphi* (3v. Athens, 1862-1890).

Callinikos, Constantine. *The History of the Orthodox Church*. Revised Edition. Translated by Katherine Natzio (Los Angeles, 1931).

Campbell, J. and Philip Sherrard, *Modern Greece* (New York, 1968).

Canoutas, Seraphim G. *O Hellenismos en Ameriki* (New York, 1918).

Cantemir, Prince Demetrius. *The History of the Growth and Decay of the Ottoman Empire*. Translated by N. Tindal (London, 1734).

Carapanayotis, George X. *L'autonomie de la Nation Grecque sous le Protectorat Turc* (Athens, 1912).

Carnegie Endowment for International Peace. *Report of the International Commission to Inquire into the Causes and Conduct of the Balkan Wars* (Washington, 1914).

Cassavetes, Nicholas J. "L'avenir de l'Hellenisme d'Amérique," *Études Franco-Grecque*, III (April, 1920), 86-100.

Castanis, Christophorus Plato. *The Greek Exile or a Narrative of the Captivity and Escape of Christophorus P. Castanis During the Massacre on the Island of Scio by the Turks Together with Various Adventures in Greece and America* (Philadelphia, 1851).

Chalcocondylae, Laonici, Atheniensis. *Historiarum* (Paris, 1650).

Cherniavsky, Michael. *Tsar and People: A Historical Study of Russian National and Social Myths* (New Haven, 1961).

Christophi, C. *Genèse de l'émigration orientale* (Athens, 1916).

Chryssikos, George J. *The Heritage of the Lacedaemonians and American Opportunities* (New York, 1938).

Clarkson, Jesse D. *A History of Russia* (New York, 1962).

Cole, William I. *Immigrant Races in Massachusetts: The Greeks* (Boston,

1919).

Commons, John R. *Races and Immigrants in America* (New York, 1907).

H.R.M. Constantine I, King of Greece. *A King's Private Letters* (London, 1925).

Constantinides, Very Reverend Michael. *The Orthodox Church* (London, 1931). The Very Reverend Michael Constantinides was the primate of the Greek Archdiocese of North and South America, 1949-1958.

Cooke, S.T. "The Greeks in the United States," *Eastern and Western Review*, III (November, 1910).

Cotsakis, Roxane. *The Wing and the Thorn* (Atlanta, 1952).

Couclelis, Alexandre. *Les Régimes Gouvernementaux de la Grèce de 1821 à Nos Jours* (Paris, 1921).

Cox, Reavis. *Competition in the American Tobacco Industry, 1911-1931.* Columbia University *Studies in History, Economics, Public Law*, No. 381 (New York, 1933).

Crankshaw, Edward. *The Fall of the House of Habsburg* (New York, 1963).

Crawley, C.W. "Modern Greece, 1821-1939," *A Short History of Greece from Early Times to 1964* (Cambridge, 1965).

Damiris, Christodoulos I. *Peri Tis ek Zakynthu Metanasteuseos. Phrontistirion tu Kathygitu Tis Demosias Oekonomias*, No. 3 (Athens, 1912).

Daskalakis, Apostolos. *Les Oeuvres Rhegas Velestinlis* (Paris, 1927).

Davison, Roderic H. "Turkish Attitudes Concerning Christian-Muslim Equality in the Nineteenth Century," *American Historical Review*, LIX (July, 1954), 844-64.

Dawkins, Robert M. *Modern Greek in Asia Minor: A Study of the Dialects of Sille, Cappadocia, and Pharasa with Grammar, Texts, Translations and Glossary* (Cambrige, England, 1916).

Dendia, Michael A. *Hellenikae Paroekiae Ana Ton Kosmon* (Athens, 1919).

Diehl, Charles. *L'Histoire de l'empire byzantin* (Paris, 1924).

Dieterich, Karl. *Hellenism in Asia Minor. American-Hellenic Society Publication* No. 4. Translated from the German by Carroll N. Brown (New York, 1918).

Douglas, Paul H. *Real Wages in the United States, 1890-1926* (Chicago, 1930).

Doumouras, Alexander. "Greek Orthodox Communities in America before World War I," *St. Vladimir's Seminary Quarterly*, XI (1967).

Eddy, Charles B. *Greece and the Greek Refugees* (London, 1931).

Efthimiou, Basil. *Skiagraphia Ton Apodemon Hellenon Tis Amerikis Kae Historia tu Kathedriku Neas Iorkes* (New York, 1949).

Elliot, Sir Charles N. *Turkey in Europe* (London, 1908).

Ellissen, A. ed. "Threnes Tis Konstantinoupoleos," *Analekten der Mittel und Neugrieschen Literatur* (Leipzig, 1857).

Eton, William. *A Survey of the Turkish Empire* (London, 1801).

Evangelides, Christos. *Kanonismos tu Helleniku Lykeiu* (Athens, 1877).

Evangelides, Margarites. *Aetia Tis Metanasteuseos Ton en Kaukaso Hellenon tu Pontu* (Athens, 1900).

Fairchild, Henry Pratt. "Causes of Emigration from Greece," *Yale Review* XVIII (August 1904).

———. *Greek Immigration to the United States* (New Haven, 1911).

———. *Immigrant Backgrounds* (New York, 1927).

———. *Immigration (New York, 1925).*

Fermor, Patrick Leigh. *Roumeli: Travels in Northern Greece* (New York, 1962).

Forster, Edward S. *A Short History of Modern Greece, 1821-1945*. Third Edition. Revised and Enlarged by Douglas Dakin (New York, 1958).

Galitzi, Christina Avghi. *A Study of Assimilation Among the Roumanians in the United States*. Columbia University *Studies in History, Economics and Public Law*, No. 315 (New York, 1928).

Geannakoulis, Theodore. "Eisagogi Stin Historia Ton Hellinoamerikanon," New York *Argonautis* (Winter, 1959).

Gergaga, K.N. *E Metanasteusis ek tu Nomu Euboeas: Meleti Statistiki kae Koenoniki* (Chalcis, 1912).

Gkortzi, Nicholas. *Ameriki Kae Amerikanoe* (Athens, 1907).

Gordon, Leland J. *American Relations with Turkey: 1830-1930* (Philadelphia, 1932).

Grant, Madison. *The Passing of the Great Race* (New York, 1916).

"Greek Church Threatened by Young Turks," *Eastern and Western Review*, II (August, 1909).

Hadjimichali, Angeliki. "Aspect de l'Organization Économique des Grecs dans l'Empire Ottoman," *Le Cinq-Centième Anniversaire de la Prise de Constantinople, 1453-1953* (Athens, 1953).

Hall, Prescott Farnsworth. *Immigration: And Its Effects upon the United States* (New York, 1906).

von Hammer-Pugstall. *Histoire de l'empire Ottoman*. French Translation J.J. Hellert (18v. Paris, 1835-43), II.

Handlin, Oscar. *The Uprooted* (New York, 1951).

Hansen, Marcus Lee. *The Immigrant in American History* (Cambridge, Mass. 1940).

Hasluck, F.W. "The Crypto-Christians of Trebizond," *Journal of Hellenic Studies*, XLI (1921), 199-202.

Hayes, Carlton Joseph Huntley. *A Generation of Materialism: 1870-1900. The Rise of Modern Europe*. Edited by William L. Langer (New York, 1941).

———. *Essays on Nationalism* (New York, 1926).

Helm, Elijah. "The British Cotton Industry," *British Industries*, edited by

W.J. Ashley (London, 1907).

Helmreich, Ernest Christian. *The Diplomacy of the Balkan War, 1912-1913* (Cambridge, Mass. 1938).

Hill, Aaron. *The Present State of the Turkish Empire* (London, 1709).

Horton, George. *The Blight of Asia* (Indianapolis, 1920).

Howe, Julia Ward. *Is Polite Society Polite?* (New York, 1895).

——. *Reminiscences, 1819-1899* (New York, 1899).

Howe, Samuel Gridley. *A Historical Sketch of the Greek Revolution* (New York, 1828).

Hughes, Rev. T.S. "An Address to the People of England in the Cause of the Greeks, Occasioned by the Late Inhuman Massacres on the Island of Scio," *The Pamphleteer*, XXX (1822).

Iorga, Nicolae. *Byzance après Byzance* (Bucharest, 1935).

Jones, Maldwyn Allen. *American Immigration* (Chicago, 1960).

Joseph, Samuel. *Jewish Immigration to the United States: From 1881-1910*, Columbia University *Studies in History, Economics and Public Law*, LIX, No. 4 (New York, 1914).

Kaltchas, Nicholas S. *Introduction to the Constitutional History of Modern Greece*. Columbia University *Studies on Research in Social Sciences* (New York, 1940).

Karolides, Paulos. *Historia Tis Hellados* (Athens, 1925).

Kazan, Elia. *America, America* (New York, 1962).

Kerofilas, Constantine. *Une famille patricienne, Les Vlastos* (New York, 1932).

Kolokotrones, Theodore. *The Klepht and the Warrior. Sixty Years of Peril and Daring*. An Autobiography. Translated by Mrs. Edmonds. (London, 1892).

Krikou, Alexander. *E Metanasteusis: Pleonektimata-Meionektimata Synepeiae* (Athens, 1950).

——. *E Thesis tu Hellenismu en Ameriki* (Athens, 1915).

Lacey, Reverend Thomas J. *A Study of Social Heredity: As Illustrated in the Greek People* (New York, 1916).

——. *Our Greek Immigrants* (New York, 1918).

Ladas, Stephen P. *The Exchange of Minorities: Bulgaria, Greece and Turkey* (New York, 1932).

Lampridu, John. *Ae Hellenikae Apoekiae* (Athens, 1895).

Levandis, John A. *The Greek Foreign Debt and the Great Powers: 1821-1898* (New York, 1944).

Levant Trade Review, 1911.

"Life Story of a Pushcart Peddler," *Independent*, LX (February 1, 1906).

Livanos, C.N. *John Sakellaridis and Egyptian Cotton* (Alexandria, 1939).

Lyberer, A.H. "The Ottoman Turks and the Routes of Oriental Trade," *English Historical Review*, CXX (October 1915), 577-88.

Lykoudes, Emmanuel Stylianos. *Oe Metanastae* (Athens, 1903).

Macartney, Charles A. *National States and National Minorities* (London, 1934).

Malafouris, Babes. *Hellenes Tis Amerikis: 1528-1948* (New York, 1948).

Maniakes, Konstantinos D. *America and Greece* (Athens, 1899).

Marriott, Sir John A.R. *The Eastern Question: An Historical Study in European Diplomacy* (London, 1940).

Marshall, Grace E. *Eternal Greece* (Rochester, 1938).

Martin, Percy F. *Greece of the Twentieth Century* (London, 1913).

Mastrantonis, Rev. George. *Main Feast Days of the Eastern Orthodox Church*, Second Edition (St. Louis, Mo., n.d.).

———. *Confession: A Merciful Privilege and Sacrament* (St. Louis, Mo., n.d.).

———. *The Life of Jesus Christ* (St. Louis, Mo., n.d.).

Mavrogordato, John. *Letters from Greece: Concerning the War of the Balkan Allies* (London, 1914).

———. *Modern Greece: A Chronicle and a Survey, 1800-1931* (New York, 1931).

Maynard, Sir John Herbert. *Russia in Flux* (New York, 1948).

Mazarakes-Ainianos, Alexandros. *Historike Melete, 1821-97* (2v. Athens, 1950).

Mears, Elliot Grinnell. *Modern Turkey* (New York, 1924).

Michalopoulos, Phanis. "O Apodimos Hellinismos," Athens *Ethnos* (December 15, 1950), "E Metanasteusi-O Neoteros Apoekismos Stin Ameriki."

Miller, William. *A History of the Greek People, 1821-1921* (London, 1922).

———. *Essays on the Latin Levant* (Cambridge, 1921).

———. "The Genoese in Chios, 1346-1566," *English Historical Review*, CXX (July, 1915).

———. "The Last Athenian Historian: Laonikos Chalkokondylas," *Journal of Hellenic Studies*, XLII (1922), 36-49.

———. *The Ottoman Empire and Its Successors, 1801-1927* (Cambridge, England, 1927).

———. *Travels and Politics in the Near East* (London, 1898).

———. *Trebizond: The Last Greek Empire* (London, 1926).

Morgenthau, Henry. *Ambassador Morgenthau's Story* (New York, 1918).

Munro-Butler-Johnstone, H.A. *The Turks: Their Character, Manners and Institutions as Bearing on the Eastern Question* (London, 1876).

Na'ima. *Annals of the Turkish Empire: 1591-1659*. Translated by Charles Fraser (London, 1832).

Newman, Philip. *A Short History of Greece*. Second Edition (London, 1953).

H.R.H. Nicholas, Prince of Greece. *My Fifty Years* (London, 1926).

Nicol, D.M. "The Fourth Crusade and the Greek and Latin Empires, 1204-61." *The Cambridge Medieval History*, IV, *The Byzantine Empire*, Part I, Second Edition (Cambridge, England, 1966).

Pallis, Alexander A. "Effets de la Guerre en Grèce," *Effets Économique et Sociaux de la Guerre en Grèce* (Athens, 1925).

————. *Greece's Anatolian Venture and After: A Survey of the Diplomatic and Political Aspects of the Greek Expedition to Asia Minor, 1915-1922* (London, 1937).

Pan Hellenic Union. *Katastatikon* (New York, 1910).

Papadopoullos, Theodore. *Studies and Documents Relating to the History of the Greek Church and People under Turkish Domination. Bibliotheca Graeca Aevi Posterioris*, X (Brussels, 1952).

Papadopoulos, Anthimos A. "O Pontus Dia Ton Aeonon" *Archeion Pontu*, I (1928), 7-46.

Paparrigopoulos, Konstantinos. *Historia tu Helleniku Ethnus*. P. Karolides Edition (6v. Athens, 1925), V, VI.

Pares, Bernard. *History of Russia* (New York, 1947).

Park, Robert Ezra. *The Immigrant Press and Its Control* (New York, 1922).

Paspates, Alexander George. *Poliorkia kae Alosis Tis Konstantinoupoleos Ypo ton Othomanon en Etei 1453* (Athens, 1890).

Pears, Sir Edwin. *The Destruction of the Greek Empire* (London, 1903).

The Perkins Institute. *Michael Anagnos: 1837-1906* (Boston, 1906).

Pieropoulos, Nicholas G. *Meleti Peri Tis en Helladi Metanasteuseos Anaphorikos kae ek Tis Eparchias Megalopoleos* (Athens, 1911).

Polyzos, Nicos J. *Éssai sur l'Émigration Grecque, Étude Démographique, Économique et Sociale* (Paris, 1947).

Protestant Episcopal Church in the United States, Domestic and Foreign Missionary Society, Department of New England. *The Peoples of the East: Orthodox Churches* (Springfield, Massachusetts, 1913).

P'Stephanou, Eusebius Alexander. *The Orthodox Church Militant* (New York, 1950).

Ralli, Alexander Pandia. *A Pedigree of the Rallis of Scio 1700 to 1892* (London, 1896).

Rhizos Rhankabes, Alexander. *Greece: Her Progress and Present Position* (New York, 1867).

Rizo-Rangabe, Eugene. *Livre d'or de la Noblesse Ioniènne* (4v. 3 Athens, 1925-27).

————. *Livre d'or de la Noblesse Phanariote et des Familles Princières de Valachie et de Modalvie* (Athens, 1904).

————. *Le Livre d'Or de la Noblesse Phanariote par un Phanariote* (Athens, 1892).

Riasanovsky, Nicholas V. *A History of Russia*. Second Edition (New York, 1969).

Riis, Jacob. *Battle with the Slum* (New York, 1902).
———. *The New Immigration* (New York, 1912).
Rodd, James R. Rennell. *The Customs and Lore of Modern Greece* (London, 1892).
Rose, W. Kinard. *With the Greek Army in Thessaly* (London, 1898).
Ross, Edward A. *The Old World in the New* (New York, 1914).
Runciman, Steven. *The Fall of Constantinople* (Cambridge, England, 1965).
———. *The Great Church in Captivity* (Cambridge, England, 1968).
Rycaut, Sir Paul. *The Present State of the Ottoman Empire* (London, 1668).
Saloutos, Theodore. *The Greeks in America: A Student's Guide to Localized History* (New York, 1967).
———. *The Greeks in the United States* (Cambridge, Mass., 1964).
———. "The Greeks in the United States," *South Atlantic Quarterly*, XLIV (January, 1945), 69-81.
———. *They Remember America: The Story of the Repatriated Greek-Americans* (Berkeley, 1956).
Sarantopulu, Maria Oekonomidu. *Oe Hellenes Tis Amerikis Opos Tus Eida* (New York, 1916).
Schevill, Ferdinand. *The History of the Balkan Peninsula* (New York, 1933).
Searight, Sarah. "The Turkey Merchants: Life in the Levant Company," *History Today*, XVI (June, 1966).
Sergeant, Lewis. *Greece in the Nineteenth Century* (London, 1897).
———. *New Greece* (London, 1878).
Seton-Watson, Robert W. *The Rise of Nationality in the Balkans* (London, 1917).
Sills, Kenneth C.M. "Greek Americans," *The Nation*, XCVII (October, 1913).
Soutsos, Alexander. *Turcomachos Hellas*. Sixth Edition (Constantinople, n.d.).
Soutzo, Prince Nicholas. *Memoires du Prince Nicolas Soutzo, Grand-Logothete de Moldavie, 1798-1871* (Vienna, 1899).
Spatharis, Avrilios. *The Ecumenical Patriarchate: A Many Century Old Institution* (Athens, 1959).
Stavrianos, Leften. *The Balkans Since 1453* (New York, 1958).
Stephanopoli, Jeanne A. "L'École, Facteur du Reveil Nationale," *Le Cinq-Centième Anniversaire de la Prise de Constantinople, 1453-1953* (Athens, 1953).
Still, Bayrd. *Mirror for Gotham* (New York, 1956).
———. *New York City, A Student's Guide to Localized History* (New York, 1965).
Stillman, William. *The Cretan Insurrection, 1866-68* (New York, 1874).
Stoianovic, Traian. "The Conquering Balkan Orthodox Merchant," *Journal of Economic History*, XX (June, 1960).

Straus, Oscar. *Under Four Administrations: From Cleveland to Taft* (Boston, 1922).

Sturdza, Alexander A.C. *L'Europe Orientale et le Role Historique des Mavrocordato, 1660-1830* (Paris, 1913).

──. *Regne de Michael Sturdza, Prince Regnant de Moldavie, 1834-1849* (Paris, 1907).

Sumner, Basil H. *Peter the Great and the Emergence of Russia*. First Collier Brooks Edition (New York, 1969).

Svolos, Alexandre. "L'Influence des Idées de la Révolution Française sur les Constitutions Helleniques de la Guerre d'Indépendance," *Révolution Française*, N.S. No. 4 (1935).

Svoronas, Nicolas G. *Le Commerce de Salonique au XVIIIe Siècle* (Paris, 1956).

Ta Patria, 1902-03.

Tennant, Richard B. *The American Cigarette Industry*. *Yale Studies in Economics*, No. 1 (New Haven, 1950).

Theodorides, Aristomenos. *Peri Tis Eis Amerikin Metanasteuseos: Kae Ton Aetion Autis* (Athens, 1907).

Thompson, Maurice S. "Notes on Economic and Social Conditions in Greece," *Sociological Review*, VI (July, 1913), 213-21.

Toynbee, Arnold Joseph. *Nationality and the War* (London, 1915).

──. *Turkey: A Past and a Future* (London, 1917).

Trevelyan, George M. *History of England*. Third Edition (London, 1945).

──. *English Social History* (London, 1942).

Triantaphyllides, M. A. *Hellenes Tis Amerikis* (Athens, 1952).

Trikoupes, Spyridon. *Historia Tis Hellenikis Epanastaseos* (4v. London, 1860-72).

Turlington, Edgar. "The Settlement of Lausanne," *American Journal of International Law*, XVIII (October, 1924), 696-706.

U.S. Tobacco Journal, 1900-02.

Vardoulakis, Mary. *Gold in the Streets* (New York, 1945).

Venizelos, Eleutherios K. *The Vindication of Greek National Policy, 1912-1917* (London, 1918).

──. *La Politique de la Grèce* (Paris, 1916).

Villeman, M. Lascaris, *Les Grecs du Quinzième Siècle* (Paris, 1825).

Visvisis, J. "L'Administration Commerciale des Grecs Pendant la Domination Turque," *Le Cinq-Centième Anniversaire de la Prise de Constantinople, 1453-1953* (Athens, 1953).

Vlachos, N. "Le rélation des Grecs Asservis avec l'État Musselman Souverain," *Le Cinq-Centième Anniversaire de la Prise de Constantinople, 1453-1953* (Athens, 1953).

Vlasto, Alexander M. *Chiaka* (2v. Hermoupolis, 1840).

Vlasto, Solon J. *Historia Ton Henomenon Politeion Tis Amerikis*. Revised

Edition (New York, 1919).

Voyatzidis, J. "La Grande Idée," *Le Cinq-Centième Anniversaire de la Prise de Constantinople, 1453-1953* (Athens, 1953).

Welles, F.R. "American Hellenes," *The Nation*, XCIX (July 23, 1914).

Williams, Charles. "The Thessalian War of 1897," *Fortnightly Review*, XLVII (June 1897), 959-71.

Wood, Alfred C. *A History of the Levant Company* (Oxford, 1935).

Woodhouse, C.M. *et al. A Short History of Greece from Early Times to 1964* (Cambridge, England, 1965).

———. *The Greek War of Independence* (London, 1952).

———. *The Story of Modern Greece* (London, 1968).

Xenides, J.P. *The Greeks in America* (New York, 1922).

Young, William W. *The Story of the Cigarette* (New York, 1916).

Zakythinos, D.A. *Byzantion: Kratos Kae Koenonia Historiki Episcopisci* (Athens, 1951).

———. *E Alosis Tes Konstantinoupoleos kai e Turkokratia* (Athens, 1954).

Zernov, Nicholas. *The Church of the Eastern Christians* (London, 1947).

Zioga, Elias K. *O Hellenismos Tis Amerikis: Autos O Agnostos* (Athens, 1958).

Zoras, George T. *Ae Pro Kae Meta Tin Alosin Diamorphotheisae Ideologikae Kae Politikae Kateuthynseis. Spoudastirion Byzantinis Kae Neohellenikis Philologias*, University of Athens (Athens, 1953).

———. *E Xeniteia En Ti Helleniki Poiesei* (Athens, 1953).

———. *Peri Tin Alosin Tis Konstantinoupoleos* (Athens, 1959).

Zustis, Basil. *O En Ameriki Hellenismos Kae E Drasis Autu* (New York, 1954).

IX. Miscellaneous Reference Works.

Cutsumbis, M.N. *Selective Bibliography for the Sociological Study of Greek-Americans* (Lancaster, 1967).

Dictionary of American Biography (22v. New York, 1937-58).

Index